Pioneer and Priest

Pioneer and Priest

Jesus Christ in the Epistle to the Hebrews

R. J. McKelvey

PICKWICK *Publications* · Eugene, Oregon

PIONEER AND PRIEST
Jesus Christ in the Epistle to the Hebrews

Pickwick Publications
An Imprint of Wipf and Stock Publishers
199 W. 8th Ave., Suite 3
Eugene, OR 97401

www.wipfandstock.com

ISBN 13: 978-1-61097-861-3

Cataloging-in-Publication data:

McKelvey, R. J.

Pioneer and priest : Jesus Christ in the Epistle to the Hebrews / R. J. McKelvey

xxiv + 250 p. ; 23 cm. Includes bibliographical references and indexes.

ISBN 13: 978-1-61097-861-3

1. Bible. N.T. Hebrews—Criticism, interpretation, etc. I. Title.

BS2775.52 M55 2013

Manufactured in the U.S.A.

Previous Publications

The New Temple: The Church in the New Testament, Oxford University Press, 1969.
The Millennium and the Book of Revelation, Lutterworth Press, 1999.

for John Paul McKelvey

Preface

I was made intensely aware of the relevance of Hebrews to today's world when I taught ordinands in South Africa. It was during the apartheid regime when the churches were under pressure to play safe and domesticate their message. I had a somewhat similar experience when I returned to the United Kingdom and found churches often preoccupied with maintenance, pushed out of public debate and intimidated by an aggressive secular or anti-Christian rhetoric. But it is not only Christian communities that are challenged by this part of the New Testament. Individuals find their cherished traditions and comfortable cultural or theological enclaves questioned as they are urged to leave these behind and follow Jesus Christ in new and uncertain ways. Whether it is the community or the individual, the message is the same: follow Christ "outside the camp." This is demanding discipleship but with the demand is the gift. Coupled with the pioneer is the priest who is ready to help those who undertake the journey of faith. The relationship of these disparate images and the part they play in Hebrews is the subject of this study.

The pioneer and priest motifs are integral to the author's very practical aim of helping a community that was experiencing a crisis. It was caused by societal pressures and an imperfect understanding of Jesus Christ and consequently a less than whole-hearted commitment to him. Their problem was by no means unique. It also affected communities of St. Paul's time. It affects Christian communities today. What Hebrews does to help those addressed is therefore of contemporary relevance.

In addressing the situation before him the author of Hebrews shows that however much religio-socio-political influences impinge upon those who hear the message, inhibiting or encouraging the response that he believes they have to make, it is God's word that is of paramount importance and it is this that must command attention. Fundamental to everything the author has to say is Jesus Christ, the Son through whom God still speaks. It is the word that God is speaking through his Son and in the Scriptures that offers the church hope and direction. It is a challenging message, but it is accompanied by great pastoral sensitivity, care, and encouragement throughout.

From the different images Hebrews employs to describe Christ and renew the recipients' commitment to him, I have chosen pioneer and priest because of the light these images and especially their conjoined use have to throw on the message. I am well aware that singling out particular images that are part of a veritable web of ideas is a difficult, not to say, dangerous business. Consequently I have attempted to pay attention to the whole to which the images belong.

Anyone who is at all familiar with Hebrews knows that it has much material that the modern reader finds strange and not easily accessible. The extended treatment of the Levitical priesthood, the tabernacle and the use of Hellenistic philosophy soon make the reader aware of the different world of the writer and those he sought to help. But having said that, one wishes to emphasize that Hebrews contains very valuable insights that are not found anywhere else in the New Testament and those who make the effort to enter this world and familiarize themselves with it are amply rewarded. The more one gets into the document the more one appreciates the effort taken by the author to deal with the problems affecting the community and the lengths to which he goes in order to help them. Here is theology related to life, produced not for its own sake but to meet a pressing practical problem. It is my hope that this study will play some part in demonstrating that studying Hebrews is well worth the effort and essential for us today.

Many good commentaries are available to those interested in studying Hebrews. In my second chapter I survey a number of these. This attempts to put my subject in the wider context of Hebrews and note what the writers have to say or fail to say on the subject.

Quotations from the Bible and the Apocrypha are from the New Revised Standard Version of the Bible (Anglicized Edition) and the Revised Standard Version, except where I provide my own translation. For writings from Second Temple Judaism I quoted from James H. Charlesworth, *The Old Testament Pseudepigrapha*. I used Danby's translation of the Mishnah and the Soncino edition of the Babylonian Talmud. Quotations from Philo, Josephus, and the classical authors are from the Loeb edition.

For the Qumran material I have used Florentino García Martínez, *The Dead Sea Scrolls Translated: The Qumran Texts in English*.

This is the place to acknowledge what I owe to others. I had numerous helpful and enjoyable discussions with my friends and former colleagues Dr. Stanley Russell and the Revd. Roger Tomes. The latter deserves a special word of thanks for the time he spent on the manuscript and the numerous helpful comments he made. Professor George Brooke was ever ready to help when I needed guidance on the Qumran scrolls. The members of the Ehrhardt Seminar in the University of Manchester had useful comments to offer on material I presented to them on a number of occasions. I owe my thanks to Dr. Paul Ellingworth, professors David Charles and Philip Davies, and to the Revd. F. Gerald Downing and Dr. Peter Oakes for their assistance at particular stages of my work. My ever-helpful wife Myrtle very patiently and graciously undertook a lot of the work on the computer, while our son David used the computer to good effect in bringing the manuscript into conformity with the publisher's house rules.

I am grateful to the publishers for producing my book so promptly and efficiently. It was a pleasure to work with Chris Spinks, Christian Amondson, Matthew Stock, Ian Creeger, and Raydeen Cuffe.

R. J. McKelvey
Manchester

Acknowledgments

The Division of Christian Education of the National Council of Churches of Christ in the United States of America for the use of the Revised Standard Version of the Bible and the New Revised Standard Version (Anglicized edition); the Oxford University Press and the Cambridge University Press for the use of the New English Bible and the Revised English Bible; J. H. Charlesworth (ed.), *The Old Testament Pseudipgrapha*, 2 vols. (New York: Doubleday, 1983, 1985); Loeb Classical Library (Cambridge, MA: Harvard University Press). For the Qumran material I have used Florentino García Martínez, *The Dead Sea Scrolls Translated: The Qumran Texts in English*, translated by W. G. E. Watson, 2nd ed. (Grand Rapids: Eerdmans, 1996).

Abbreviations

Bible Texts, Versions, Reference Works, Journals

AB   Anchor Bible

ABD   Anchor Bible Dictionary. 6 vols. David Noel Freedman, edi-
          tor. New York: Doubleday, 1992

ANTC   Abingdon New Testament Commentary

AV   Authorized Version = King James Version

AUSS   Andrews University Seminary Studies

BDAG   Walter Bauer, Frederick W.Danker, William F.Arndt, and
          F.William Gingrich, editors. *A Greek—English Lexicon of the
          New Testament and Other Early Christian Literature.* 3rd ed.
          Chicago: University of Chicago Press, 2000

BDF   Friedrich Blass and Albert Debrunner, editors. *A Greek
          Grammar of the New Testament* and *Other Early Christian
          Literature.* Translated and revised by Robert W.Funk. Chi-
          cago: University of Chicago Press, 1961

BI   *Biblical Interpretation*

Bib   *Biblica*

BibSac   *Bibliotheca Sacra*

BIS   Biblical Interpretation Series

BJRL   *Bulletin of the John Rylands University Library of Manchester*

BNT   Black's New Testament Commentaries

BTB   *Biblical Theology Bulletin*

BU   *Biblische Untersuchungen*

BZ	*Biblische Zeitschrift*
BZAW	*Beihefte zur Zeitschrift für die Alttestamentliche Wissenschaft*
CBQ	*Catholic Biblical Quarterly*
CJT	*Canadian Journal of Theology*
DJD	Discoveries in the Judean Desert
DSD	Dead Sea Discoveries
ESV	English Standard Version
EvQ	*Evangelical Quarterly*
EVT	*Evangelische Theologie*
ExpTim	*Expository Times*
GNB	Good News Version of the Bible
GTJ	*Grace Theological Journal*
HeyJ	*Heythrop Journal*
HKNT	Handkommentar zum Neuen Testament
HNT	Handbuch zum Neuen Testament
HTR	*Harvard Theological Review*
IBS	*Irish Biblical Studies*
ICC	International Critical Commentary
Int	*Interpretation*
JB	Jerusalem Bible
JBL	*Journal of Biblical Literature*
JEH	*Journal of Ecclesiastical History*
JETS	*Journal of the Evangelical Theological Society*
JJS	*Journal of Jewish Studies*
JQR	*Jewish Quarterly Review*
JSNTSS	Journal for the Study of the New Testament —Supplement Series
JSOTSS	Journal for the Study of the Old Testament —Supplement Series
JSJ	*Journal for the Study of Judaism in the Persian, Hellenistic and Roman Periods*
JSNT	*Journal for the Study of the New Testament*
JSP	*Journal for the Study of the Pseudepigrapha*
JSQ	*Jewish Studies Quarterly*
JTS	*Journal of Theological Studies*
JSS	*Journal of Jewish Studies*
KEK	Kritisch-exegetischer Kommentar über das Neue Testament
KJV	King James Version

LSJ	Henry George Liddell, Robert Scott and Henry Stuart Jones, *A Greek-English Lexicon*. 9th ed. Oxford: The Clarendon Press, 1996
LSTS	Library of Second Temple Series
LXX	Septuagint MeyerK H.A.W.Meyer, (ed.), Kritisch-exegetischer Kommentar über das Neue Testament
MM	James Hope Moulton and George Milligan, *The Vocabulary of the Greek New Testament: Illustrated from the Papyri and Other Non-Literary Sources*. 1930. Reprinted, Peabody, MA: Hendrickson, 1997
MT	Masoretic Text
NB	New Blackfriers
NCBC	New Century Bible Commentary
NEB	New English Bible
NKJV	New King James Version
Neot	*Neotestamentica*
NESTR	*Near East School of Theology Theological Review*
NICNT	New International Commentary of the New Testament
NIGTC	New International Greek Testament Commentary
NIV	New International Version
NJB	New Jerusalem Bible
NKZ	*Neue kirchliche Zeitschrift*
NovT	*Novum Testamentum*
NovTSup	Novum Testamentum Supplements
NRT	*La nouvelle revue théologique*
NTS	*New Testament Studies*
NRSV	New Revised Standard Version
parr.	parallels
PCNT	*Paideia* Commentary on the New Testament
PNTC	The Pillar New Testament Commentary
PTMS	Princeton Theological Monograph Series
RB	*Revue Biblique*
REB	Revised English Bible
RevExp	*Review Expositor*
RevQ	*Revue de Qumran*
RomCiv	*Roman Civilization*
RSR	*Recherches de science religieuse*
RSV	Revised Standard Version
RV	Revised Version

SBL	Society of Biblical Literature
SBLDS	Society of Biblical Literature Dissertation Series
SBLMS	Society of Biblical Literature Monograph Series
SHR	*Studies in the History of Religion*
Sem	*Semeia*
SJSJ	Supplements *to the Study of Judaism*
SJT	*Scottish Journal of Theology*
SNTS MS	Society for New Testament Studies Monograph Series
SPhA	*Studia Philonica Annual*
ST	*Studia theological*
STDJ	Studies on the Texts of the Desert of Judah Str-B Hermann L. Strack and Paul Billerbeck, *Kommentarzum Neuen Testament aus Talmud und Midrasch. 6 vols.* Munich. 1922–61
StudNeot	*Studia neotestamentica*
SUNT	Studien zur Umwelt des Neuen Testaments
TDNT	*Theological Dictionary of the New Testament.* 10 vols. Edited Gerhard Kittel and Gerhard Friedrich (eds.), *Theological Dictionary of the New Testament.* Translated by Geoffrey W.Bromíley. Grand Rapids: Eerdmans, 1964–76
THE	*Theologische Existenz Heute*
ThRev	*Theological Review*
TLNT	*Theological Lexicon of the New Testament*
TNIV	Today's New International Version
TS	*Theological Studies*
TLZ	*Theologische Literaturzeitung*
TZ	*Theologische Zeitschrift*
TynBul	*Tyndale Bulletin*
Vg	Vulgate
VoxEv	*Vox Evangelica*
VT	*Vetus Testamentum*
VTSup	Vetus Testamentum Supplements
VGT	See Moulton and Milligan
WBC	Word Biblical Commentary
WMANT	Wissenschaftliche Monographien zum Alten und Neuen Testament
WUNT	Wissenschaftliche Untersuchungen zum Neuen Testament
ZNW	*Zeitschrift für die neutestamentliche Wissenschaft*

THE BIBLE

Abbreviations of the books of the Bible follow standard practice

THE APOCRYPHA

Bar	Baruch
Esd	Esdras
Jdt	Judith
Macc	Maccabees
Sir	Sirach
Tob	Tobit

PSEUDEPIGRAPHA

Apoc Ab	Apocalypse of Abraham
Asc Isa	Ascension of Isaiah
Bar	Baruch
En	Enoch
Jub	Jubilees
Pss Sol	Psalms of Solomon
Sib Or	Sibylline Oracle
T	Testament
T Abr	Testament of Abraham
Test	Testament of Dan, Judah, Levi, etc.= Testaments of the 12 Patriarchs

DEAD SEA SCROLLS

CD	Damascus Document
1QS	Manuel of Discipline
1QSa	Appendix A to 1QS
1Q28b	Appendix B to 1QS
1QH	Hymns of Thanksgiving
1QHpHab	Habakkuk Commentary
1QM	War Scroll
4QFlor	Floregium
4Q400/3/5	Songs of the Sabbath Sacrifice

4Q491	Self-Glorification Hymn
4QMMT	Songs of the Sabbath Sacrifice
11Q17	Songs of the Sabbath Sacrifice
11QMelch	Melchizedek

RABBINIC WRITINGS

Mishnah

Mid	Middoth
Par	Parah
Shek	Shekalim
Sot	Sotah

Talmud: Babylonian

Ber	Berakhoth
Git	Gittin
Hag	Hagigah
Meg	Megillah
Men	Menahoth
Ned	Nedarim
Sot	Sotah
Ta'an	Taanith
Yom	Yoma
Zeb	Zebahim

Further Rabbinic Sources

Bet ha Midr	Bet ha Midrash
Gen R	Genesis Rabbah
Hekh	Hekhalot
Targ Ps-Jon	Targum Pseudo Jonathan

PHILO

| *Abr* | Abraham |
| *Agric* | Agriculture |

Cher	Cherubim
Conf Ling	Confusion of Languages
Decal	Decalogue
Deus	Unchangeableness of God
Ebr	Drunkeness
Flacc	Flaccus
Fug	Flight and Finding
Gig	Giants
Her	Who is Heir
Migr Ab	Migration of Abraham
Mos	Moses
Mut	Change of Names
Opif	Creation
Plant	Noah as a Planter
Post	Posterity and Exile of Cain
Prelim S	Preliminary Studies
QG	Questions and Answers on Genesis
QE	Questions and Answers on Exodus
Sacr	Sacrifices of Cain and Abel
Sobr	Sobriety
Somn	Dreams
Spec Leg	Special Laws
Virt	Virtues

JOSEPHUS

Ant	Antiquities
Ap	Apion
J. W.	Jewish War

GRECO-ROMAN WRITINGS

Antig	Antigone
Ap	Apion
Crat	Cratylus
Disc	Discourses
Ench	Enchiridion
Epit	Epitome

Fin	Finibus
Fur	Furens
Her Oet	Hercules Oetaeus
Hist	Histories
Inst	Institutes
Meta	Metaphysica
Onom	Onomasticon
Or	Orationes
Pro Rab	Pro Rabiro
Rep	Republic
Rhet	Rhetorica
Tim	Timaeus
Tim Loc	Timaeus Locreus
Tro	Troades
Verr	Verren

EARLY CHRISTIAN WRITINGS

Adv Marc	Against Marcion
Adv Prax	Against Praxean
Apos Const	Apostolic Constitutions
Barn	Barnabas
Dial	Dialogue
Ign	Ignatius
Paed	Pedagogue
Pan	Panarion
Phil	Philippians
Phld	Philadelphians
Sim	Similtudes
Smyrn	Smyrians

Introduction

A good case can be made for regarding Hebrews as the most prag-matic book of the New Testament. It is directly addressed to the needs of those who apparently sought the help of the writer. What it says is an enduring message of hope for Christians of any age who are prone to discouragement and opposition, or who find themselves beset by uncertainties and insecurities. The writer deals with the situation in a systematic and carefully argued way. Fundamental to all he says is Jesus Christ—who he is and what he has done and continues to do for his followers.

Many of the titles used for Christ in Hebrews belong to the early Christian tradition: Son, Christ, Lord, firstborn.[1] Others are unique to it and mark a ground-breaking development in Christology, in particular the concepts of pioneer (*archēgos*) and high priest (*archiereus*). Both im-ages belong to topics that form virtually the entire content of Hebrews, the pioneer (along with the forerunner, *prodromos*) being part of the pil-grimage motif, while the high priest is integral to the Day of Atonement analogy and the heavenly sanctuary. The two motifs appear throughout Hebrews even though, as is the case in regard to pioneer, the actual terms are not always used. The way in which the motifs interact and converge is particularly important. Jesus is not only pioneer, but priest as well, and he is not priest without also being pioneer. I attempt to show that the double analogy is fundamental to our understanding of Hebrews.

In 4:14 the figure who travels through the heavens (so reminiscent of travelers to the heavenly sanctuary in Jewish writings), who is referred to as high priest, is very obviously a pioneer figure. Similarly, the closely

---

1. Son (1:2, 5, 8; 3:6; 4:14; 5:5, 8; 6:6; 7:3, 28; 10:29); Christ (3:6, 14; 5:5; 6:1; 9:11, 14, 24, 28; 10:10; 11:26; 13:8, 21); Lord (2:3; 7:14; 13:20); firstborn (1:6).

related figure of the forerunner (*prodromos*) in 6:20 is actually called high priest. In both 9:11–12 and 10:19–20, where the context has to do with Christ's priestly work in the heavenly sanctuary, it is the pioneer who opens the way into the sanctuary. And in 12:18–24, which depicts the pioneer and his followers assembled on the heavenly Mount Zion, the language used makes Christ appear as high priest, his blood being more effective than that of the old order (12:24). How such antithetical concepts came to be linked together is a puzzle. One deploys the language of the athletic track, pilgrimage, or battlefield, the other the language of the sanctuary. Their binary character commands attention. Hebrews, it is true, likes to mingle concepts,[2] and some scholars believe the epistle revolves around the "Son" and the "high priest."[3] No one would dispute the importance of the latter, but also oscillating in the thought world of Hebrews is the pioneer-priest (high priest) duo. This dual Christology contributes to its essential message and makes Hebrews the very important part of the New Testament that it is.

Much has been written on Christ the high priest, but, notwithstanding the fact that Käsemann showed that the pioneer as part of the pilgrimage motif is an essential clue to Hebrews,[4] little attention is paid to this daring interpretation of Christ and nothing that I know of on the close connection of the two concepts. Roman Catholic exegetes have tended to devote their attention to what the epistle says about priesthood and cultus, while Protestants, influenced by Käsemann's interpretation of Hebrews in terms of pilgrimage, have concentrated on exhortation. I attempt to show that pioneer and priest must be taken together. Otherwise what they stand for will be in danger of veering off in separate directions, thus denying the Christian gospel.

The appendices contain background material on the key concepts. They contribute to our understanding of the interaction of the two concepts.

I offer this study in the belief that it is a way of looking at Hebrews that aids our understanding of both its innovative Christology and its intensely practical aim.

---

2. On the mingling of other motifs in Hebrews see 3:1; 5:5–6; Schrenk, "Archiereus," 3:276–79; Lane, *Hebrews 1–8*, cxxxix.

3. Loader, *Sohn und Hoherpriester*; Ellingworth, *Hebrews*, 69–73; Lane, *Hebrews 1–8*, cxliii; Mackie, *Eschatology and Exhortation*, 174; cf. 227, 230.

4. Käsemann, *Wandering People*. For bibliographical information see Johnsson, "Issues," 169–87; Johnsson, "Cultus," 104–8.

1

Why Hebrews?

The aim of the homily, like its authorship and provenance, addressees, and date, is a challenge and a subject of continuing debate among scholars.[1] It is best that we learn from Hebrews by interpreting it on its own terms. This means attempting to relate the author's description of the letter as a "word of exhortation (*parakleseōs*)" (13:22) to what precedes it. The systematic way in which theological exposition is followed by practical instruction, and itself contains practical admonitions, shows very clearly that the author of Hebrews wrote very specifically with the aim of helping the troubled community. His work is a good example of how theology and pastoralia interact. For our purpose it is instructive to find that the author's response to pastoral life situation is directly related to his deployment of the titles and functions of "pioneer" and "priest."

The author begins by praising and encouraging the addressees.[2] He recalls the help they gave to others in trouble (6:9–11; 10:34) and recalls how they had stood a severe test as Christians, "sometimes being publicly exposed to abuse and persecution and sometimes being partners with those so treated" (10:33). He remembers how they had risked getting into trouble by befriending those in prison (10:34). Their property had been plundered. In spite of everything the wonderful thing was that their joy had not been spoilt (10:34).

---

1. For Rome as the probable location for the letter see Brown and Meier, *Antioch and Rome*, 140–57; Lane, *Hebrews 1–8*, lviii–lx; Ellingworth, *Hebrews* (1993), 28–29; Koester, *Hebrews*, 51–52. For a critique of this view see, e.g., DeSilva, *Perseverance*, 1, 21.

2. That the author was male may be deduced from the use of the masculine participle at Heb 11:32.

But the author moves quickly to the problems affecting the congregation. Some of its members were tempted to drift away and neglect their Christian confession (2:1; 3:12; 6:4–6; 10:35, 39). They lacked a firm hope (3:6; 6:11; 10:23), and they were in danger of losing their confidence (3:14; 10:35). They were failing to make progress in their understanding of the Christian faith (5:11–6:2) and they had become disenchanted and lethargic (5:11; 6:12). Tragically, some were no longer worshipping with the rest of the community (10:25).Worse still, apostasy was a real threat (6:6; cf. 3:12; 9:14). Lax moral standards were harming the life of the church (13:4–5). Concern over the delay of the return of Jesus Christ also was a problem (9:27–28; 10:25).

Clues to the aim of the author are to be found in the numerous contrasts drawn between Christ and the people and institutions of the old covenant (angels [1:5–14]; Moses [3:1–6]; the high priest [5:1–10; 7:1–28]; Christ in the heavenly sanctuary [8:1–5,6–9]; the old covenant and the new [8:8–9:22]; Christ's offering [10:1–14]; God's pilgrim people [11:39–40]; Sinai and Mount Zion [12:18–24]; outside the city gate [13:10–12]).These contrasts reveal that the recipients needed to have a much clearer understanding of Jesus Christ and make a greater commitment to him.

The traditional view that the recipients were in danger of lapsing back into Judaism has come in for reappraisal, not only because there is nothing in the writing that supports this but because Hebrews was written well before Christianity broke apart from Judaism to go its own way.[3]

More credible is the suggestion that the recipients had some connection with members of the local synagogue, possibly operating as a house church within its precincts, and were having difficulty in fully appreciating their Christian identity and maintaining their Christian confession *vis a vis* Judaism. This is attributed to a failure to understand the uniqueness of Christ and the new faith or a fear of persecution.[4] Persecution of some sort had been experienced (10:32–33; cf. 12:3–11), and this may have resulted in reluctance to venture "outside the camp" and suffer abuse for Christ (13:13). Much is to be said for the view that the author

3. See, e.g., Dunn, *Parting of the Ways*, 86–91. Cf. Salevao, *Legitimation*, 109–14; Becker and Reed, *Ways That Never Parted*. On the difficulty of determining the identities of Jews and Christians at the beginning of the Christian era, see Lieu, "The Parting of the Ways," 101–19.

4. For example, Manson, *Hebrews*, 1–24; Bruce, *Hebrews*, 266–70; cf. Lane, *Hebrews 1–8*, lxvi, 301; Koester, *Hebrews*, 67–71; Lindars, *Theology*, 4–15.

is urging the recipients not so much as to fall back into Judaism but to make progress in their understanding of Christ and devotion to him and to become independent of the synagogue.[5]

Odd as it has seemed to many readers of Hebrews it is suggested that the recipients were Gentile Christians.[6] This is based on the assumption that appeals not to fall away from the living God (3:12), avoid "dead works" (9:14) and "strange teaching" (13:9) could only apply to Gentiles. But care is needed here. Jews in the Greco-Roman world not infrequently absorbed influences from their cultural context.[7] The "strange teachings" referred to in 13:9, in a context which reflects an incontestably Jewish background, suggests this possibility. On the other hand, it should not be automatically assumed that what the author says about Levitical cultus is addressed exclusively to Jewish Christians. Gentiles who were God-fearers could very well have been members of the church. As converts to Judaism they would have been expected to accept the Scriptures as the record of the divine revelation and may have attempted to demonstrate their sincerity by developing a conservative stance.[8] We note that the author of Hebrews tells us that the recipients had been taught the Jewish Scriptures (5:12).[9]

What is beyond conjecture is the fact that those to whom Hebrews is addressed had made a Christian profession.[10] For them Jesus was "the

---

5. So, for example, Manson, *Hebrews*, 15–16; Hooker, "Christ, the 'End' of the Cult," 207.

6. For a recent presentation of the view that Hebrews was sent to a predominantly Gentile community see Schenck, *Understanding Hebrews*, 85–105; Schenck, *Cosmology and Eschatology*, 193–94.

7. Cf. Hengel, *Judaism and Hellenism*, 283, 308. On the censures of the Jews in Rev 2:9 and 3:9 see McKelvey, "Jews in the Book of Revelation," 175–94. For the complex nature of Jewish identity in the Greco-Roman world see Trebilco, *Jewish Communities*, 173–85; Barclay, *Jews*, 259–81. Cf. Ellingworth, *Hebrews* (1993), 24–25.

8. On the question how one may square Gal 5:3 with Acts 15:28, see the commentaries. The latter passage is evidence that Gentile converts to Judaism could be exempted from circumcision on condition of obeying food laws. More often than not obeying the Noachian laws, which were believed to be enjoined on all peoples (Gen 9:1–17), was all that was required of Gentile converts to Judaism. See McEleney, "Conversion," 316–41, who concludes "First-century Judaism seems to have been much more open on this question than it has previously been given credit for" (332). Cf. Moore, *Judaism*, 1:323–53; Tomes, "Educating Gentiles," 208–17.

9. Ellingworth's view that the author's argument from the Levitical cultus "would probably have left gentile readers cold" (*Hebrews* (1993), 25) does not seem warranted.

10. The attempt of Kosmala to argue that the recipients were unconverted Essenes

---

3

Lord" (2:3), "the Son of God" (4:14), and they had made their confession of faith (3:1; 4:14; 10:23).

The congregation was very likely ethnically mixed,[11] and probably predominantly Jewish. Since we are dealing with the period before Christians and Jews went their separate ways we should assume that these believers had some connection with their local synagogue. According to the Book of Acts, the early Christians frequented the temple (2:46; 3:1; 21:26). We do not know whether Hebrews was intended for the whole community or a part of it, though the latter may be inferred from 10:25. From 13:17 we get the impression that the author is addressing a dissident group (cf. 13:1). What is not in any doubt is the serious view the author took of the entire situation (6:1–9).

The other introductory matter that has produced different views is how one should account for the numerous different problems mentioned throughout the writing. These problems, in the opinion of a number of scholars, are not in themselves the primary issues but are symptoms of an underlying problem.

Charles Moule focuses on the emphatic "we *have* a high priest" (8:1), "we *have* an altar" (13:10), and believes that the letter was sent to Christians who were missing the temple of Jerusalem.[12] Somewhat similar is the view of Lindars, who suggests that the community's problems stemmed from its doubting whether Christ's death adequately dealt with sin and guilt.[13]

Mathis Rissi thinks Hebrews was addressed to a group that held a realized eschatology, which did not look beyond the immediacy of Christian experience (2:9; 6:4).[14] James Thompson, similarly, believes that the recipients were troubled by the apparent contradiction between the glory promised to God's people and the reality of their experience of suffering in the world (2:8c).[15] Noting the promise of the second coming (9:27–28; 10:25), George MacRae thinks Hebrews was an attempt to bolster the

(*Hebräer, Essener, Christen*) has not been accepted.

11. Ellingworth, *Hebrews* (1993), 21–27; Eisenbaum, *Jewish Heroes*, 7–11; De Silva, *Perseverance*, 3–5. Cf. Koester, *Hebrews*, 46–48.

12. Moule, "Sanctuary and Sacrifice," 37–38.

13. Lindars, *Theology*, 10–15.

14. Rissi, *Theologie*, 15–16, 21–25. Cf. Scholer, *Proleptic Priests*, 206; Ellingworth, "Jesus and the Universe," 337–50.

15. Thompson, *Hebrews*, 20.

flagging eschatological hopes of the community with a Philonic (Middle Platonic) view of Christian faith.[16]

Many scholars, impressed by the sustained attention paid to Jesus Christ, conclude that it is in the area of Christology that we can find the author's primary motivation.[17]

DeSilva offers a different explanation. Basing his approach on sociological and cultural approaches to the New Testament that have put great store on the place of honor and shame in the social, political, and economic world of the time, this argues that Hebrews was sent to people who had suffered from the dishonor associated with worshipping a leader who had been executed as a criminal and died the disgraceful death of crucifixion (12:2).[18]

Given the number of problems that the writer finds in the church it might appear hazardous to look for a single underlying cause. However, I share the view that the considerable attention paid to Jesus Christ throughout the presentation indicates that Christology is the key to the problems generally. The author could see that Christology and ecclesiology were intimately related and had an immediate bearing on the questions of Christian identity and the church's position in relation to Judaism and its mission in the world.

At the outset, in the exordium (1:1–4), Christ's uniqueness and significance are deliberately and very obviously introduced. Its implications are worked out throughout what follows. Jesus is presented as the one who identified himself with humankind "in the days of his flesh" (5:7) and who effectively represents them before God and helps them "in time of need" (4:16). The images selected are directly related to the needs of the community. The pioneer challenges the members to leave where they are and make a definite decision to follow Christ to their divinely-appointed destination, whatever the cost (2:10; 6:20; 9:24; 10:19–20; 12:1–2; 13:13). The high priest, in the heavenly sanctuary, provides all the help they need to respond to the challenge (2:17–18; 4:14–15; 5:7–10; 7:23–25; 8:1–2).

16. MacRae, "Heavenly Temple," 179–99.

17. For example, Eisenbaum, "Locating Hebrews," 222. So also Hooker, who refines this as follows, "(the recipients) had not yet understood the implications of their confession of the crucified and risen Jesus as the Son of God" ("Christ, the 'End' of the Cult," 207).

18. DeSilva, *Despising Shame*. Similarly, Salevao believes that the problems being experienced by the recipients were connected with their self-understanding in relation to their local Jewish synagogue (*Legitimation*, 213–24).

Who Jesus Christ is, what he did on the cross, what he continues to do for his people, and what he invites them to be is the substance and message of Hebrews. In support of this the author shows the recipients that Jesus Christ fulfills the promises of the Jewish covenant and makes good its deficiencies. He has positive things to say about the old order (9:13) and he holds up its representatives as examples to be copied by the recipients (11:1–40), but he does not hesitate to say that the law (and thus everything under it) is "weak and useless" (7:18) and the Levitical system ineffective and superseded (9:8–10; cf. 10:1–4, 9). In fact, he goes so far as to say that "the way into the sanctuary has not yet been disclosed as long as the first tent is still standing" (9:8). Trenchant criticism of the sacrificial system and priesthood was not of course unknown in the Jewish tradition, though it was not absolute. But should we say that the supersessionism of Hebrews implies the anti-Jewish stance that some scholars find in it?[19] In a document which aims to legitimate Christianity a polemical element is to be expected, but this is not to say that Hebrews is a direct attack on Judaism. The author's use of the rhetorical device of comparison for purposes of evaluation (*synkrisis*)[20] is aimed not at denigrating Israel's ancient institutions but demonstrating the object of its comparison, the greatness of Jesus Christ.[21]

Hebrews was produced within and not apart from Judaism: both author and to a great extent the congregation were themselves Jews. Whilst discontinuity with the ancestral faith is evident throughout, continuity is maintained. There is all the difference in the world between the critique of Judaism in Hebrews and the anti-Jewish invective read into Hebrews by later generations who approached it from an entirely different thought-world. We have to be careful not to censure the author for his treatment of an urgent topic of his day because of the use made of

19. So Gager, *Origins of Anti-Semitism*, 183; Wilson, *Related Strangers*, 110–27; Koosed "Double Bind," 89–101; Williamson, "Anti-Judaism in Hebrews?" 266–79. Kim argues for a qualified supersessionism in which the Levitical priesthood, the Mosaic covenant and the Levitical sacrifices have been superseded by Jesus' priesthood, the new covenant and his once-for-all sacrifice. In other words, it is Jewish institutions that are replaced, not the Jewish nation (Kim, *Polemic in the Book of Hebrews?*). On the subject of supersessionism see the balanced treatment by Gordon, *Hebrews*, 36–53.

20. On the classical use of comparison, not for polemical aims, but to demonstrate the greatness of the subject under discussion, see Aristotle (*Rhet* 1.9.39). Cf. Lane, *Hebrews 1–8*, cxxiv–cxxx; Thompson, *Hebrews*, 36.

21. For a robust presentation of Hebrews as an anti-Judaic polemic see Salevao, *Legitimation*, 213–24.

it by others of a later time. The baseline of the judgment that the author passes on the Levitical sacrificial system and its priesthood is his christological/eschatological position. There is a direct line from the one to the other. Recognition of this reasoning explains why in the first instance the recipients of Hebrews had converted to Christianity and the Gentile members became Christians rather than proselytes.[22]

Our subject is bound up with the eschatological orientation of the entire work.[23] Christ's saving action has taken place at the "end of the age" (9:26) and his people are living in the "last days" (1:2), before Christ comes a "second time" (9:28). God will yet bring his faithful people to their promised inheritance (10:37–38). Christian life is consistently portrayed as forward-looking. It is a journey or pilgrimage to the heavenly "rest" (4:11) or the heavenly city (11:16; 13:14). Even images and verbs convey movement and anticipation.[24] But simultaneously the futurist hope is finely balanced by the realized eschatology of the sermon and the help this gives to pilgrims here and now (4:3–7, 16; 7:19, 25; 10:19–22; 12:2).

The pioneer motif is intimately connected with the theme of pilgrimage. Käsemann demonstrated the importance of this subject.[25] It is integral not only to the appeal to the readers to join the journey to the "rest" promised to God's people in the earlier part of the writing (3:7–4:11), but is sustained right through to the concluding challenge to follow Christ "outside the camp" (13:13). It thus provides coherence and emphasis to the central message. Käsemann used the word *wanderschaft* for the pilgrimage rather than the more specific term *pilgerschaft*, which had for some of his readers the unfortunate connotation of an unfocused wandering, not a purposeful, goal-directed journey. The criticism is not quite fair. Käsemann speaks of "wandering orientated to a goal" and "wandering toward the city of God."[26] He emphasizes what he calls the "verbs

---

22. Lincoln, *Hebrews*, 118.

23. On the eschatology of Hebrews see the landmark study of Barrett, "Eschatology," 366, 373.

24. Attridge, "Paraenesis," 221–22.

25. Käsemann, *Wandering People*. See also Johnsson, "Pilgrimage Motif," 242–43. Johnsson compares the pilgrimage motif with the phenomenology of religious pilgrimages. Common features are separation from one place and journey to a destination that has religious connotations, difficulties and dangers on the way, with incorporation rites on arrival (244–47).

26. Käsemann, *Wandering People*, 22, 23.

of motion": "approach" (*proserchomai*) (10:22; 11:6; 12:18, 22), "enter" (*eiserchomai* (4:1, 11; 6:19, 20; 9:12, 24; 10:5), as conveying a clear picture of movement towards a clearly-defined objective (11:8–28).[27] Barrett has very good reason for building upon Käsemann's interpretation and making pilgrimage the key to the futuristic eschatology of Hebrews.

But while acknowledging the important role that Käsemann shows the pioneer to have in the pilgrimage theme, I aim to show that the pioneer motif should not be taken on its own but seen in relation to the priestly motif; they belong together and together they are directly related to the needs of the community. I want to emphasize that their conjunction is in fact at one and the same time the clue to the nature of those needs as well as their solution.

The writer calls his work a "word of exhortation" (13:22), using a phrase which appears in Acts 13:15 for a synagogue address. Like other ancient writings of its kind, Hebrews was very likely intended for oral delivery. It very likely had homiletic form.[28] The author could not be present to deliver his work (13:19), but the literary devices he uses doubtless produced the rhetorical effect he obviously intended.[29]

One should think of the recipients as hearers or listeners. What they received in request for help is remarkable for the way in which doctrine is related to their pastoral needs and the very sensitive way in which this is done. Each exegetical section is followed by exhortation (2:1–4; 3:7—4:13; 5:11—6.12; 10:19–39; 12:1–3, 4–17, 25–29; 13:1–17). In his effort to develop rapport with the congregation, the writer employs a deliberately personal touch. In an endearing way he calls them "brothers" (3:1; 10:19) and "partners" (3:1, 14). He consistently includes himself in the warnings and exhortations by the frequent use of the word "we" (2:1, 3; 4:11, 16; 6:1–3; 7:19; 10:19–25; 12:1; 13:13). Very movingly, he asks them to pray for him (13:18).

Recognition of the oral character of Hebrews has led scholars to study the use of the rhetorical devices employed by orators of the times to convey their argument and persuade their hearers to accept it. The results

---

27. Käsemann, *Wandering People*, 22–23; Attridge, "Paranesis," 221–22.

28. Wills, "Form of the Sermon," 277–99.

29. Lane says the author of Hebrews "stresses the actions of speaking and listening, which are appropriate to persons in conversation, and he identifies himself with his audience in a direct way (2:5; 5:11; 6:9; 8:1; 9:5; 11:32)," (*Hebrews 1–8*, lxxiv). Cf. Lane, "Standing Before the Moral Claim of God," 203.

have identified numerous parallels in Hebrews.[30] The sermon has a message or plot (the superiority of Jesus Christ), characters (the community, Christ, angels, Moses, Melchizedek, heroes and heroines of faith), setting (earthly and heavenly sanctuaries, "outside the camp").[31] The whole work is carefully arranged to convey the message, and although evidence of an identifiable rhetorical structure, like agreement over the author's use of deliberative and epideictic forms, remains somewhat uncertain,[32] we shall find very obviously demarcated units and the use within them of particular devices that help one with the interpretation of the message.[33] The finished work is a masterpiece of audience-orientated literary rhetoric aimed at eliciting a response.

Who the highly accomplished author of this book was remains an enigma. We can say that he was a Hellenistic Jew who on becoming a Christian had acquired a quite remarkable understanding of the new faith and was able to interpret it in terms both of Judaism and Hellenistic philosophy. His knowledge of the Septuagint, his grasp of the christological core of the Christian faith along with his rhetorical skills and the artfully crafted structure of his work, all go to make the finished product one of the most impressive books of the New Testament.

Where and when the sermon was composed is a mystery. The author probably wrote from Rome (13:24). I believe that the date was very likely in the period between the expulsion of Christians under Claudius around 49 CE and the persecutions by Nero in the 60s. That means I have no difficulty over the absence of any reference to the destruction of the temple of Jerusalem in 70 CE. Considering the effort the author expends on describing the shortcomings of the Levitical system, I find it hard to believe that if the temple had been destroyed by the time of writing he would have omitted any mention of what would have been his best argument, although I recognize that this might not have suited his strategy. I

30. Spicq, *Hébreux* 2, 351–78; Swetnam, "Form and Content in Hebrews 1–6," 368–85; "Form and Content in Hebrews 7–13," 333–48; Cosby, *Rhetorical Composition and Function*; Vanhoye, *Structure and Message*; Lane, *Hebrews 1–8*, lxxii–lxxx; De Silva, *Perseverance*, 35–64.

31. Following Schenck, who defines the rhetorical structure of the speech or writing as a complex of persons, settings and events (*Cosmology and Eschatology*, 25). There is a comprehensive list of the rhetorical devices used in Hebrews in Attridge, *Hebrews*, 20–21.

32. Lane, *Hebrews 1–8*, lxxix–lxxx; Koester, *Hebrews*, 82; Thompson, *Hebrews*, 16.

33. On discourse analysis see Übelacker, *Hebräerbrief als Appell*, 214–29; Guthrie, *Structure*; O'Brien, *Hebrews*, 22–34.

believe that although the author keeps speaking about the tabernacle it is the temple that is the real point of reference.

Summary

Those to whom Hebrews is addressed were very likely a house church in the diaspora, possibly in Rome. They were ethnically mixed, but predominantly of Jewish origins. It is likely that they had their meeting place within or close to a synagogue. The author's chief aim in what is best understood as a sermon is to help the community define its Christ-centered identity and ethos in relation to Judaism. With great rhetorical skill, he conveys Christ's significance and paramount importance. Integral to the argument is the deployment of the titles and functions of the pioneer and priest and their interconnectedness.

The author's understanding of the Christian faith, knowledge of the Septuagint and Hellenistic philosophy and his ability to communicate his message mark him out as a person of considerable ability.

2

Hebrews Today

Hebrews continues to fascinate students of the New Testament, notwithstanding the challenges it presents. Recent years have witnessed the publication of a number of important commentaries. I draw attention to some of these in order to put my study in the context of present-day scholarship and alert readers to key features they can expect to encounter in what follows. Selecting some works and not others and drawing attention to only some of the subjects treated in these works is necessarily an invidious business. The bibliography will show that I am indebted to many other authors. By focusing on commentaries in order to give as wide a coverage of Hebrews as possible, I have not commented here on scholars who have produced works on particular aspects of Hebrews, especially Paul-Gerhard Müller's study on the pioneer (*archēgos*). My indebtedness to such studies will be found in the text.

Before we look at the books that deal with the theology of Hebrews I draw attention to the important work on the structure of the epistle undertaken by George H. Guthrie (*The Structure of Hebrews: A Text-Linguistic Analysis*, 1994). Guthrie is a widely acknowledged representative of literary or discourse analysis. The fundamental importance of studying texts in their contexts has long been recognized, but the task is not straightforward in the case of Hebrews. How, for example, does one explain its perplexing tendency to introduce a subject only to drop it and return to it later? Or what is the striking resemblance of 4:14–16 and 10:19–23 meant to convey? Building on the work of Albert Vanhoye,[1] Guthrie pays particular attention to units (in many cases paragraphs) often using an *inclusio* (so-called "book ends"), 4:14–16 and 10:19–23

1. Vanhoye, *La structure littéraire*, 37–52, 274–303.

being the most striking example.[2] Credit is also to be given to Guthrie for the attention he pays to the crucial place exhortation occupies in Hebrews.

Harold Attridge's much-acclaimed volume (*The Epistle to the Hebrews*, 1989) excels in bringing out the theological meaning of Hebrews. It begins by showing that Hebrews cannot be interpreted correctly unless the preacher's rhetorical aims are recognized. As a specialist in Greco-Roman philosophy, Hellenistic Judaism, and Gnosticism, Attridge is well-equipped to draw upon relevant ancient literature to good effect. If I needed confirmation of the important function that the pioneer has in Hebrews, I found it in Attridge. Commenting on the crucial statement in Heb 10:19–20 ("We have confidence to enter the sanctuary by the blood of Jesus, by the new and living way that he opened for us"), this scholar says, "here the full significance of Christ's evocative titles *archēgos* and *prodromos* becomes apparent."[3] Attridge quotes the striking parallel for the pioneer in Lucius Annaeus Florus. This describes Decius Mus as hurling himself into the thick of the battle that "he might open a new path to victory along the path of his own lifeblood" (1.9.14).[4] At the same time, Attridge devotes extensive treatment to the high priestly motif. However, I have to say that I have not found any suggestion that the pioneer and high priestly motifs work together.

On the subject of Melchizedek it is strange that, although Attridge is convinced that one must allow for some extrabiblical influence from contemporary Judaism, he does not emphasize its contribution to our understanding of Melchizedek as the eschatological priest. But this apart, the commentary is enhanced by fourteen excurses on leading features of Hebrews. The extent to which the commentary is quoted or referred to since its publication is evidence of its great importance.

In his commentary Craig Koester challenges the widely held view that priesthood is the central theme of Hebrews (*Hebrews: A New Translation with Introduction and Commentary*, 2001). He believes that the main theme is introduced in the *propositio* in 2:5–9, viz. that humanity's God-given destiny is fulfilled in Jesus Christ, who took human nature

2. Guthrie, *Structure*, 76–89. Other examples are 1:3, 13 (right hand of God); 1:5—4:13 (pay attention to God's word); 3:12, 19 (unfaithfulness); 4:14; 5:10 (high priest); 8:7–13; 10:16–17 (new covenant). On the use of "hook words" and the various transitional techniques used in Hebrews see Guthrie, *Structure*, 94–111.

3. Attridge, *Hebrews*, 285.

4. Attridge, *Hebrews*, 285.

upon himself so that by means of his saving work he might lead his many "sons" to their great destiny. Koester sees this developed in three arguments, connected by the *narratio* (2:10—6.20; 7:1—10:39; 11:1—12:27). Jesus is the pioneer who leads his followers to glory (2:10): pioneer and perfecting belong together. Those who follow him enter the presence of God, persevering all the while through suffering, till they, like their pioneer, are made perfect/complete (10:1—12:27). The idea of completion, the meaning of the verb *teleioun* (from *telos*), thus frames the arguments of Hebrews. Having begun by declaring that God made Jesus perfect/complete in order to lead others to their divinely appointed destiny, the sermon culminates in the vision of his followers made perfect/complete in the heavenly Jerusalem (12:23). For our purpose the connection Koester very rightly emphasizes between the pioneer and the dominant perfecting/completing theme is of particular interest.

Paul Ellingworth's thorough and balanced commentary (*The Epistle to the Hebrews: A Commentary on the Greek Text*, 1993) maintains that Hebrews revolves around the two poles represented by the Son and the high priest. He observes that these major titles are expertly linked to one another in 5:5-6 and asks if it is possible to define their relationship precisely. Quoting Michel—"Son he was and high priest he becomes"[5]—Ellingworth proceeds to show that this is in fact the way the author of Hebrews develops the message of his sermon. Ellingworth does not ignore the pioneer motif but he concentrates on the high priest theme. In giving his attention to the significance of Melchizedek's endless life, Ellingworth takes issue with those scholars who think that here Hebrews does not go beyond the biblical sources (Gen 14 and Ps 110).[6] The superiority of Christ results from his self-offering and his never-ending life. The recipients can rest assured that they have Christ's assistance as they brace themselves for the trials ahead of them. The way is thus prepared for Christ's ministry in the heavenly sanctuary, which Ellingworth, for very good reason, connects with the author's pastoral intention. In line with his christological exposition, Ellingworth takes the vision of Jesus in the heavenly city at 12:24 as the climax not only of 12:18–24 but of the entire work.[7] It is a daring statement, but it is Hebrews and not Ellingworth that makes Jesus rather than God center stage: Hebrews is a rhetorical work.

5. Michel, *Hebräer,* 164, cited by Ellingworth, *Hebrews* (1993), 70.

6. Ellingworth, *Hebrews* (1993), 49.

7. Ellingworth, *Hebrews* (1993), 681.

The massive two-volume commentary by William L. Lane (*Hebrews 1–8, Hebrews 9–13* (1991) is a meticulous and detailed work of scholarship. His very extensive bibliographical lists for every unit are an invaluable help. The work starts with a helpful analysis of the literary structure of Hebrews and its use of the Old Testament. This prepares the reader for the numerous references to the author's literary techniques, which illuminate the text. The introduction also orients readers by its extended treatment of Christology. It makes an essential point by observing that the titles given to Jesus often flow into one another and the merging is integral to the meaning. Lane sees the importance of the pioneer motif and argues energetically that it draws on the divine hero figure of Hellenistic mythology. *Archēgos*, he maintains, should be translated as "champion." While Hebrews 2:14 may point in this direction, as far as 2:10 is concerned, this nuance does not suit 12:2. There the word can only mean "initiator."

Lane's treatment of the high priestly theme in 5:1—10:18 elucidates the introduction of Christ as a "merciful and faithful high priest" in 2:17. The distraught and suffering community should draw comfort from the fact that, unlike the Levitical priests, Christ's is an endless priesthood. Lane shows how crucial Melchizedek is to the argument. The acknowledgment that Jesus is a priest "like Melchizedek" means that he is a priest by virtue of his resurrection (7:16c). The goal of direct access to God has been completed (perfected) by Jesus through his sacrificial death and exaltation, and this has opened the way to the same goal for those who approach God through his good offices (4:14–16; 10:19–22). Lane helps us understand the enigmatic "we have an altar" (13:10) by showing the implied chiasm in the sentence: "we have" and "they do not have."[8] In other words, it is a further example of the author's argument for the superiority of Christianity over the Levitical system. Correspondingly, Jesus' death "outside the gate" (13:11) is followed by the injunction to go to him "outside the camp" (13:13).

David A. DeSilva's book, *Perseverance in Gratitude: A Socio-Rhetorical Commentary on the "Epistle to the Hebrews"* (2000) systematically uses the resources of interdisciplinary studies and socio-rhetorical analysis for the study of Hebrews. This author takes as his starting point the fact that the culture of the Mediterranean world was a complex matrix of divergent and different groups and Christians were as much a part of this

---

8. Lane, *Hebrews 9–13*, 537–46.

culture as of the Judeo-Christian culture. Specifically, DeSilva argues that Hebrews makes extensive use of the social code of reciprocity, with its well-defined mutual expectations and obligations of patrons and clients.[9]

The somewhat unusual title of DeSilva's book is explained by the fact that he sees "perseverance" as the aim of the rhetoric of the sermon. Nurturing and maintaining "gratitude" is one of the ways by which the preacher attempts to achieve his aim. In so many ways the sermon emphasizes what Jesus has done to bring human beings into contact with God as a patron (4:14—5:10; 7:1—10:18). "The crowning of Jesus with glory and honor thus becomes the public recognition of a benefaction."[10]

The pioneer and the high priest are pressed into the service of DeSilva's presentation, but it is the latter that is of special interest to DeSilva. He writes of the high priest, He is the broker or mediator (*mesitēs*, 8:6; 9:15; 12:24) who secures favor from God on behalf of those who have committed themselves to him as client dependents, who "approach God through him" (7:25).[11] By extolling the benefits Christ has won for his followers the preacher seeks to engender in his listeners the confidence and motivation they need to undertake the changes they must make (e.g., 13:13). The significance of both the pioneer and high priestly concepts is highlighted by DeSilva though he does not acknowledge their conjoined use. This winsomely delivered presentation and its reflections at the end of each section make this particular commentary a valuable resource for those seeking to understand what Hebrews might have to say to them today, though some reviewers are not sure that the patron-client relationship is the most appropriate one for interpreting this book of the New Testament.

Scott D. Mackie's book, *Eschatology and Exhortation* (2007), brings together two foundational subjects in Hebrews. The first part examines the two-age eschatology so fundamental to Jewish and Christian apocalyptic thought and proceeds to show how Hebrews sees the new age inaugurated in Jesus Christ. Much of this section traces how the two-age theme is employed throughout the sermon. It is eschatology that drives the urgency of the exhortations. The second part of the book is devoted to the heavenly sanctuary, located in the highest heaven (9:24). Quite

---

9. DeSilva, *Perseverance,* 59–64 and *passim.* "'Grace' is a relationship with mutual obligations and expectations into which we are welcomed. Accepting God's gifts means accepting an obligation to the giver" (*Perseverance,* 77).

10. DeSilva, *Perseverance,* 111.

11. DeSilva, *Perseverance,* 284.

properly, Mackie thinks that the fact suppliants are presently able to gain access to its inner sanctum (4:14–16; 7:19; 10:19–25; 12:22–24) indicates that what Hebrews says about the heavenly sanctuary is an example of the inaugurated eschatology of the New Testament.[12] Mackie finds ample evidence of Middle Platonism in Hebrews, and shows how this is subordinated to the Jewish apocalyptic linear understanding of history which in turn is reconfigured in terms of Christian eschatology. Hence the terms "copy" (8:5; 9:23), "true" (8:2), and "shadow" (10:1) need to be handled circumspectly.

Mackie emphasizes the intimate connection of the Son and high priest in Hebrews, but says it is the high priest who is the focus of attention in the heavenly sanctuary. However, it is curious to find Mackie saying that Jesus the high priest steps offstage and the enthroned Son takes his place. The opposite in fact is the case. We do not hear of the Son in the central part of the sermon. But that said, this is a well-written, closely argued and frequently insightful account of the way in which eschatology influences Hebrews.

James W. Thompson believes Hebrews was sent to Christians who experienced a chasm between their confession of the exalted Christ and the reality of the testing situation in which they found themselves (*Hebrews*, 2008). They did not see everything in subjection to their Lord (2:8). To make his case, the author affirms the Christian confession but reminds his recipients that the glorified Christ began precisely where they are, experiencing suffering before he was crowned with glory (2:9). He in fact is alongside his followers, divinely appointed to be their pioneer to lead them to glory (2:10). Hence Thompson rightly shows that Jesus' solidarity with Christians is an essential feature of the sermon. The assertion of Christ's superiority over Jewish institutions is to be understood not as a polemic attack on Judaism (and therefore taken as anti-Semitism) but as a didactic device using comparison for the purpose of demonstrating the greatness of Jesus Christ. Thompson is representative of much contemporary scholarship by acknowledging Platonic (Middle Platonic) influence in Hebrews. As an expert in this field Thompson makes a persuasive case for thinking that the assumptions of Middle Platonism provided Hebrews with a convenient way of developing its argument, pointing its discouraged hearers to the reality that lies beyond what they see. "Those who possess the eternal invisible reality can have the courage

12. Mackie, *Eschatology and Exhortation*, 157.

to withstand the visible and temporary time of wandering through the wilderness."[13] The pioneer motif is kept in mind throughout the sermon, culminating in 12:18–24. "The community has approached this heavenly world because Christ, the forerunner, opened up the way for his people to enter the heavenly sanctuary (6:20; 10:19)."[14]

Ernst Käsemann's book on the theme of pilgrimage in Hebrews (*The Wandering People of God: An Investigation of the Letter to the Hebrews*, 1984) influenced much subsequent work on Hebrews. It was a belated influence because the book had the misfortune of being published in 1939 shortly before the outbreak World War II and has never been revised. Its impact was also marred to some extent by the gnostic background Käsemann gave to his treatment of Hebrews. He develops his argument from Hebrews 3:7—4:11 and 11:10, 14, 16; 13:13 and in the process shows that integral to the pilgrimage theme is the pioneer. The pilgrims follow their pioneer (2:10—12:2) and forerunner (6:2) until their destination in the heavenly city is reached (12:23–24).[15]

Käsemann's interpretation held good, despite its having cast the pioneer in the guise of the gnostic redeemer. Subsequent interpreters of Hebrews have acknowledged the pilgrimage motif as intrinsic to Hebrews. Its relevance to the German nation which Käsemann saw so clearly is noteworthy. "By describing the church as the new people of God on its wandering through the wilderness, following the Pioneer and Perfecter of faith, I of course had in mind the radical Confessing Church which resisted the tyranny in Germany, and which had to be summoned to patience so that it could continue its way through the endless wastes."[16] It is clear to many today that the challenge Käsemann issued to Christians who cooperated with the policies of the Third Reich has its parallel today in those who are controlled by the prevailing culture.

Kenneth L. Schenck's book (*Cosmology and Eschatology: The Settings of the Sacrifice* (2007), brings together two subjects that have a crucial place in Hebrews. In the case of cosmology the "setting" is space; in the case of eschatology it is time (present and future). This helps us understand the basic dualism underlying Hebrews. Cosmologically, it embraces heaven and earth; eschatologically, it is now and not yet. The eschatological is the

---

13. Thompson, *Hebrews*, 26.

14. Thompson *Hebrews*, 267.

15. See Käsemann, *Wandering People*, 48–55.

16. Käsemann, *Wandering People*, 13.

predominating theme: its two ages correspond to the two covenants and the two sanctuaries. Like Thompson and others, Schenck believes that Hebrews 1–2 sets the scene. Begun on earth, the work of Jesus corrects what humanity failed to achieve (its earthly setting), and is perfected or completed (heavenly setting). The one represents the once-for-all event of Jesus' ministry, the other the abiding reality of heaven where Christ ministers as high priest in the true sanctuary. The heavenly sanctuary is the unshakeable realm—"heaven itself" (Heb 9:24). This is the goal of the Christian pilgrimage. Schenck's recourse to Josephus (*Ant.* 3.180–81) to explain his cosmologically conceived tabernacle of Hebrews[17] is justified since Hebrews, as we shall see, like Hellenistic Judaism, thought of the cosmos as a vast temple. Concerning the end of all things, that follows the *parousia*, Schenck acknowledges that Hebrews is not very clear about its specifics, but having made a distinction between the shakable realm (creation) and the unshakeable (heaven) he ventures to suggest that 12:25–29 has in mind the destruction of the created realm.[18] As a postscript I might add that Schenck suggests that the superiority of Christ over Jewish institutions is not polemical but intended to offer consolation to those mourning the loss of the temple of Jerusalem.

Peter T. O'Brien's commentary (*The Letter to the Hebrews* (2010), in many ways a companion to Ellingworth's commentary, garners recent scholarship on Hebrews and offers many fresh insightful comments. The introduction has a helpful description of the different analyses suggested for the structure offered by scholars. O'Brien uses discourse analysis to good effect, generously acknowledging his debt to George Guthrie. He shows the light which the analysis of structure can throw on units of Hebrews and the connections between units. The high points of the interrelated passages at 4:14–16 and 10:19–25 are expounded with care and insight. The same is true of his treatment of the central section of the sermon where the controlling thought of Christ's single, efficacious and enduring sacrifice is skillfully expounded. O'Brien emphasizes the Son of God and high priest Christologies and their "inseparable connection," but unfortunately has little to say about the pioneer/forerunner Christology and nothing on its relation to the high priest Christology. The practical aim with which the author of Hebrews writes is consistently kept in mind and is properly emphasized by O'Brien in his description of the

17. Schenck, *Cosmology and Eschatology*, 144–81, especially 151–52.
18. Schenck, *Cosmology and Eschatology*, 125–32,

preacher's appeal to go to Christ outside the camp (13:13) as "a stunning exhortatory conclusion."[19]

Summary

All of the books commented upon very properly emphasize the great importance Christology plays in Hebrews and the central role of the high priest, but not all of them devote a great deal of attention to Christ as pioneer. What DeSilva says is one of the exceptions. He writes, "The author capitalizes on the fact that Jesus is not merely priest but 'forerunner for us.'"[20] Käsemann's work on pilgrimage in Hebrews still receives attention from scholars, though it is regrettable that the same cannot be said about the emphasis he gave to the pioneer. Attridge has done much to correct this, showing how the pioneer concept plays a significant role throughout Hebrews. Importantly, Lane and Thompson balance the emphasis on pioneer and high priest. The significance that the pioneer theme acquires from its close association with the perfecting theme of the homily comes across from what Koester and others have shown is the essentially dynamic character of perfecting (completing) (2:10). On a broader front, Lane's observation that the way in which motifs flow together in the Christology of Hebrews is important for our appreciation of the message of the sermon, though he, like Mackie and others, find the interweaving of motifs only in the Son and high priest duo. There is nothing in these writers of the very obvious interweaving of the pioneer and priestly concepts in Heb 4:14; 6:20; 9:11–12 and 10:19–20. The light which the latter throws upon the message of the sermon is thereby missing. It is my hope that what I have to offer will help rectify this.

19. O'Brien, *Hebrews*, 523.
20. DeSilva, *Perseverance*, 70.

3

Pioneer and Priest in Hebrews

Studying the usage of particular words is a hazardous business. It requires one to pay attention not simply to multiple meanings before attempting to discern what is the sense or senses in a particular text, but to be aware of the way in which meanings, motifs, and images flow into one another, all the while paying careful attention to how meanings are affected by context. Etymologies may be significant, although they do not always have a bearing on usage. The author of Hebrews expected his hearers to be familiar with the semantic fields in which key terms appear. Moderns are not in such a fortunate position. I refer my readers to the appendix on "Words, Contexts and Meanings."

Basic to what Hebrews says about Christ the pioneer (*archēgos*) is the concept of God as the leader of his people (Exod 3:8, 17; 6:6–7; 7:4–5; etc.; Pss 77:20; 78:52–54; 80:1; etc.).[1] They are a people uniquely led by God. We find a particularly strong and often vividly portrayed sense of God as the one who accompanies and guides his people. The destination is the land of promise. God leads in different ways. Frequently he employs an angel (Exod 14:19; 23:20, 23; 32:34; 33:2). At other times he uses a cloud by day and fire by night (Exod 13:21–22; 40:34–38; Deut 31:15; etc.), or the ark of the covenant (Josh 3:3; Num 10:35; 1 Sam 4:5–7). All these representations of the divine presence bear witness to the one fundamental fact: God leads his people "at each stage of their journey" (Exod 40:36). For the author of Hebrews the typological significance of God's

---

1. Müller, *ΧΡΙΣΤΟΣ ΑΡΧΗΓΟΣ*, 141–48. Cf. appendix B.

leading his people is plain for all to see (3:7—4:10).[2] Jesus is the new leader of God's people.[3]

The key word *archēgos* conveys, above all, the meaning of leadership. However, as will be seen in appendix A, the word has other nuances, especially "founder" or "initiator." The latter sense is clearly in mind in 12:2, whereas the meaning in 2:10 is different. In the latter it is leadership that is the predominant meaning, as we see from the use of the participle "leading" (*agagonta*). However, we should be open to the possibility that the mention in the context of what Christ undertook for others (2:9d; 2:10d, 14c) may mean that in 2:10 *archēgos* has echoes of "founder." (This sense is in mind at 5:9 in the statement that Christ became "the source (*aitios*) of eternal salvation.")[4] But having acknowledged this, there is no disputing the fact that leadership is the overriding meaning in 2:10. In this respect *archēgos* resembles *prodromos*.[5] Although the word *archēgos* actually occurs on only two occasions in Hebrews (2:10; 12:2) the underlying idea runs throughout the entire narrative. It is present in the pilgrimage sections (3:7—4.10 and 11:1–40) and also in the texts depicting Christ entering into the heavenly sanctuary (9:11–12, 24; 10:20).

Where the title "high priest" is concerned we find it used throughout Hebrews (2:17; 3:1; 4:14; 5:10; 6:20; 8:1; 9:11). "Priest" is found when Psalm 110 is quoted (5:6; 7:11, 15, 17, 21, 24); except at 5:10 and 6:20. On the high priest and the eschatological and the angelic high priest see appendix C.

The presentation of Christ in the highly rhetorical exordium (1:3b) sets the scene for what is to follow. It functions as the *narratio* for the rest of the homily. "He sustains all things by his powerful word. When he made purification for sins, he sat down at the right hand of the Majesty on high." This strikingly succinct statement, in which the writer moves from Christ's cosmic role to his redeeming work, alerts us to what we shall find is a characteristic feature of great importance, viz. the juxtaposition of Christ's death and his exaltation. Similarly, the comparison of the superiority of Christ to everything on earth (*kreittōn*, "greater than," 1:4) is amplified in what follows (1:5–13; 3:1–6) and heralds the crucial role of comparison (*synkrisis*) in the main body of the sermon (chapters

---

2. Kurianal, *Jesus Our High Priest*, 157; O'Brien, *Hebrews*, 104–5.

3. Peterson, *Hebrews and Perfection*, 58; O'Brien, *Hebrews*, 106.

4. O'Brien, *Hebrews*, 106.

5. See appendix B.

8–10). Next to the exordium is the introductory *narratio* (1:5—4:13), which naturally brings on the pioneer and high priest (2:10, 17).

The unit in which the pioneer and the high priest appear (2:5–18) serves to address possible questions that the triumphant Christology of the preceding verses may have raised in the minds of the troubled hearers. Markedly, the pioneer and the high priest are bracketed together in the unit, with verse 17 used to throw light on verse 10, thus providing "book ends" for the unit. Literary analysis of the unit and the wider context shows how 2:10–18, in turn, prepares the way for the reappearance of the high priest in 5:1–10.[6]

The Pioneer of Their Salvation

The introduction of Jesus as the pioneer (2:10) appears in a passage which contains themes of great importance for the argument of the sermon (2:5–18).[7] Notwithstanding the densely theological nature of the passage its paraenetic intention is clear.

> It was fitting that God (*lit*. he), for whom and through whom all things exist, in bringing many children (*huios,* sons) to glory, should make the pioneer (*archēgon*) of their salvation perfect through sufferings (*dia pathēmatōn teleiōsai*). For the one who sanctifies and those who are sanctified all have one Father (*lit*. are all of one). For this reason Jesus is not ashamed to call them brothers and sisters (*adelphous*) (2:10–11).

First to be noted is the striking expression of the solidarity of the "Son" and the "sons." The familial language of 2:11–18 is remarkable. All are "one family" (2:11). Whatever their shortcomings, "Jesus is not ashamed to call them brothers and sisters" (2:11). The solidarity of Christ and his followers, conveyed in 2:10 under the pioneer concept, becomes particularly strong in use of the forerunner (*prodromos*) concept in 6:20. The solidarity Christians share with their exalted leader provides them with assurance that they can depend upon his help in leading them out of their perilous situation.

---

6. Guthrie, *Structure*, 97–98.

7. On the importance of 2:5–18 for the christological emphases of Hebrews see Mackie, *Eschatology and Exhortation*, 47–48; Gäbel, *Kulttheologie*, 214. For a close analysis of the literary structure of 2:5–18 see Westfall, *Discourse Analysis*, 100–104.

Integral to 2:10–11 is the way in which Christ's role as leader is set in the closest possible proximity to his suffering and exaltation.[8] These themes, already introduced in the exordium (1:3) are now taken up. Christ is "crowned with glory and honor because of the suffering of death"(2:9). The way is thus prepared for the exposition on the subject of the pioneer who through suffering is made high priest.

God's purpose in making Jesus pioneer is to bring many "sons" to glory. In other words, God has delegated leadership of his people to his Son. The tense of the participle "bringing" (*agagonta*) in 2:10 is best explained as an ingressive aorist, indicating the starting point of God's action.[9] God perfects Christ who leads his "sons and daughters" to the heavenly world (2:10; cf. 4:14–16; 9:24–25; 10:19–22). Müller comments, "God who leads appoints his Son as the leader . . . Those who have trusted God's leadership now recognize the exalted Jesus as the eschatological leader."[10] The thought of the leader accompanied by his people contrasts with the stories of the lone travelers to the heavenly world that one finds in the apocalyptic and mystical texts.[11]

The closest parallel to Hebrews' pioneer is Philo's leader who acts as a forerunner (*proēgoumenos*) for the souls bound for heaven (*Mos.* 1.166). What our author says about the pioneer leading his followers to glory connects directly with what he has just said about Christ being "crowned with glory and honor" in 2:7. The glory Christ had in eternity (1:3), with which he was crowned at his exaltation, will be shared with his followers and that necessarily means suffering. His trajectory is theirs. Like him, they will experience sufferings *en route*, but they are encouraged to look beyond their trials to their great destiny (12:2, 22–24). The connection made in 2:10 between the pioneer, his perfecting and leading his followers to their goal influences much of what follows in the sermon.

The thought of 2:10 belongs to the overarching theme of pilgrimage and anticipates chapters 4 and 11. It bears such close similarity to 12:2 that this text should be interpreted in the light of 2:10 and seen as its development. The solidarity of the leader and his followers and their

8. Klappert, *Eschatologie*, 34; Schenck, *Understanding Hebrews*, 14–15. On the subject of Christ's exaltation in Hebrews 1:3, 13 see Michel, *Hebräer*, 116–17.

9. On the crux that is created for exegetes by the participle see Hughes, *Hebrews*, 101–2; Attridge, *Hebrews*, 82; Koester, *Hebrews*, 227; O'Brien, *Hebrews*, 104. *Agagonta* and *archēgon* agree in case, gender and number.

10. Müller, *ΧΡΙΣΤΟΣ ΑΡΧΗΓΟΣ*, 289.

11. Appendix B.

journey together to the heavenly sanctuary, which the leader opens up for his followers, becomes, as we are to see, a theme of great importance in the central section of the letter.

Jesus is both *arch-ēgos* ("chief leader") and *arch-iereus* ("chief priest") (2:10, 17). This juxtaposition of words is a favorite rhetorical device of the writer. Bengel observes, "*archēgos* is compounded of *archē* and *agō*; and *archē* looks forward in the text to *teleiōsai* (cf. 12:2), but *agō* looks back to *agagonta*."[12] The fact that, as we shall see, there is a strong case for believing that in 2:10 *teleioun* has a cultic nuance, does not mean that it is emptied of its primary meaning of bringing something to a goal.[13] A similar juxtaposing of terms is also present in 3:14 (*tēn archēn . . . mechri telous*, "beginning . . . to end") and in 7:3 (*archēn . . . telos*, "beginning of days . . . end of life"). Similarly, in 12:2 we find *archēgos . . . teleiōtēs*, "beginner and completer."

The eschatological thrust of 2:10 is anticipated in the previous verse. "Jesus . . . now crowned with glory and honor because of the suffering of death" (2:9). Integral to 2:5–9 is the remarkable interpretation of "man" (*anthrōpos*) and "son of man" (*hē huios anthrōpou*) of Psalm 8:4–6 (LXX),[14] although its significance is lost in translations which, in the interests of inclusive language, speak of "human beings" and "mortals" (2:6, NRSV, TNIV).[15] The RSV reads as follows:

> What is man that thou art mindful of him, or the son of man, that thou carest for him? Thou didst make him for a little while lower than the angels; thou hast crowned him with glory and honor, putting everything in subjection under his feet (2:6–8).

Scholars debate the question whether the writer in his exegesis of the Psalm 8 takes the words about "man" (*anthrōpos*) and "son of man" (*huios anthrōpos*) to refer to Christ or to human beings as well.[16] The

---

12. Bengel, *Gnomon of the New Testament*, III.359–60. Quoted by Hughes, *Hebrews*, 101.

13. Ellingworth, *Hebrews* (1993), 162–63. See further below.

14. For detailed work on the use of Ps 8 in Heb 2 see Ellingworth, *Hebrews* (1993), 148–57; Schenck, *Cosmology and Eschatology*, 54–59.

15. Hooker, "Christ the 'End' of the Law," 199.

16. In favor of the view that the text has humans in mind see Kögel, *Der Sohn und die Söhne*; Caird, "Exegetical Method," 49; Hurst, "Christology," 151–64; DeSilva, *Perseverance*, 110–12; Schenck, "Celebration of the Enthroned Son," 472–73; Schenck, *Understanding Hebrews*, 26–28; Schenck, *Cosmology and Eschatology*, 56–59; Blomberg, "But 'We See Jesus,'" 88–99. The following scholars contest the view that Ps 8 in

Psalm as originally delivered refers specifically to humans, and the fact that Hebrews makes a point of stressing the humanity of Jesus makes it highly likely that the author is interpreting the Psalm anthropologically as he develops his Christology. The same conclusion is strongly suggested by the emphasis on the solidarity of Christ and his people (2:11). Indeed, it is only as a human being that Christ can be said to fulfill the words of the Psalm; he fulfills it as the true representative of the human race. Because Christ shared flesh and blood and experienced death for everyone he is its representative. It was to help humanity realize its perfected or completed state that he set it free from sin (2:15, 17). The fact that he is already crowned with glory and honor is thus the sign that what Psalm 8 promised will eventually be fulfilled. Thus he pioneers the way of salvation and acts effectively as high priest (cf. 6:20).[17]

Ellingworth brings out the double sense in which the author is speaking about "man" in the Psalm and its link with what he proceeds to say about Christ leading his people to glory in 2:10. "The text is not about humanity as it is; it is about Jesus. Yet in another sense it is about humanity too: humanity as it can become now that Jesus has taken hold of it to lead it back to God."[18]

What this part of the sermon would have meant to the dispirited church is expressed well by Lincoln.

> In 2.5–18 the writer employs LXX Psalm 8, read in the light of the new situation in Christ, as a word of exhortation that addresses the tension the readers are experiencing between the inauguration of the world to come and their continuing suffering, dishonor and persecution. His point is that all things are meant to be subject to humanity, as the psalm asserts, but if humanity is understood in the light of *the* man, Jesus, light is shed on how to live with the tension of this not yet being the case.[19]

The members of the church are given a preview of their great destiny. They may not "see" the realization of God's promises in the here and now (2:8c), but they should "see" in Jesus' exaltation the assurance that

---

Heb 2:6–8 refers to humans: Käsemann, *Wandering People*, 122–28; Michel, *Hebräer*, 138–39; Attridge, *Hebrews*, 70–75; Guthrie, *Hebrews*, 96.

17. Bruce, *Hebrews*, 74; Schenck, *Understanding Hebrews*, 27; DeSilva, *Perseverance*, 110.

18. Ellingworth, *Hebrews* (1991), 17.

19. Lincoln, *Hebrews*, 61.

they will share his glory at his return from heaven (9:28).[20] In following the same route as their pioneer they can expect suffering since he was perfected through suffering.[21] In both 2:9 and 2:10 it is emphasized that it was precisely because Jesus suffered death that he was crowned with glory, and, as we shall see very clearly in 12:2, his exaltation is the direct consequence of his suffering and humiliating death. The thought of the sermon at this point is thus very close to Philippians 2:9, except that Hebrews goes farther by binding Christ's destiny with that of humankind. God's purpose in his Son's death has the astounding result of "bringing many sons and daughters to glory" (2:10a). How close Hebrews is to the thought of Paul elsewhere is not always clear. The sermon's use of Psalm 8:6 for Christ's eschatological authority is also paralleled in 1 Corinthians 15:27,[22] but, surprising as it may seem,[23] Hebrews 2:5–9 does not appear to make reference to the Adam-Christ typology (cf. Rom 5:12–17).

Christ's identification with the human race is total (2:17; 4:15; cf. 5:7–8). The consequences this has for the author become clear as the sermon proceeds. This is of great importance for our understanding of the pioneer/high priestly Christology and indeed the meaning of Hebrews at large. Thus Christ's humanity helps us understand faith in Hebrews as faithfulness (10:38 with reference to Hab 2:4) and the bold assertion that Christ is the one who lives by faith and is simultaneously the perfecter of faith (12:2). Moreover, the humanity of Christ has an important bearing on the pastoral orientation of the letter. It is a great encouragement to the hearers of the sermon to be assured that they have a high priest who is like them "in every respect" (2:17) and they may "draw near" to him in prayer, assured that they have his help on their earthly journey.

The familial character of the passage is exceptional. The pioneer appears not on his own but with his many siblings in his train (2:10). The same is true of the high priest; he is surrounded by suppliants (4:14–16). Introduced in 2:10–11, the solidarity of Christ and his followers becomes a recurring theme of great importance in the homily (2:13, 14, 17; 3:1, 14; 4:15; 5:1–3; 12:1).[24] "For a consecrating priest and those whom he

---

20. Koester, "Hebrews, Rhetoric," 23.

21. Lincoln, Hebrews, 62.

22. Dunn, Christology, 110–13.

23. Contra Dunn, Christology, 109–11; Blomberg, "'But we see Jesus,'" 88–99.

24. Schrenk, "Archiereus," 276–79; Grogan, "Christ and His People," 68–69; Attridge, Hebrews, 88, 178, 285. On the bond between the Son and the "many sons" God gives to Jesus see Lane, Hebrews 1–8, 55.

consecrates are all of one stock" (2:11, NEB).[25] Hence we see how Jesus being perfected is able to perfect his people (cf. 10:14 where the terms "make perfect" and "consecrate" appear together). "The common element of the two consecrations is that each brings about the possibility of access to God. As high priest, Jesus has entered into the holy of holies (9:12), into heaven itself, there to appear before God on our behalf (9:24); the believers are able confidently to make their entrance after him and draw near to God (7:19)."[26] The question whether Christians are thought of as priests in 4:16; 6:19; 10:14, 22 will be considered at a later stage.

Made Perfect through Suffering (2:10)

The suffering and vindication/exaltation theme begun in 2:9 is here developed in this crucially important verse. This is done with specific reference to the "glory" to which Jesus' perfecting is leading and by words taken from Ps 22:22 (21:23 LXX) in 2:12. But what perfecting through suffering entails is not explained. For that we have to wait until 5:7–9.

If Jesus was "the reflection of God's glory and the exact imprint of God's very being" (1:3) one naturally wants to ask what Hebrews means when it says that he has been made perfect (2:10; 5:9; 7:28). In what sense was Jesus perfected? [27] The question is important: perfection, as we shall see, is fundamental to all that follows.

We begin by noting that while perfection has some moral content in Hebrews (12:10, 14) it has other meanings which predominate and should not be taken simply as moral goodness. The writer could not be more forthright: Jesus, though "holy, blameless, undefiled and separated

---

25. The Greek of 2:11 is ambiguous. It is not clear whether "one" (*henos*) is masculine and refers to God or neuter and refers to a common bloodline (cf. Acts 17:26). The latter is suggested by 2:14, but most commentators think the reference is to God (e.g. Koester, *Hebrews*, 29–30).

26. Bourke, "Hebrews," 925.

27. On this question and the uses of *teleioun* and *teleiōsis* in Hebrews see Westcott, *Hebrews*, 63–67; Windisch, *Hebräerbrief*, 44–46; Delling, "Teleioun," 79–87; Spicq, *Hébreux* 2, 214–25; Du Plessis, *ΤΕΛΕΙΟΣ*, 206–33; Wikgren, "Patterns of Perfection," 159–67; Michel, *Hebräer*, 137–38; Attridge, *Hebrews*, 83–87; Peterson, *Hebrews and Perfection*, 21–48, 66–73; Silva, "Perfection and Eschatology," 60–71; Lindars, *Theology*, 42–47; Carlston, "Vocabulary of Perfection," 133–60; Attridge, *Hebrews*, 83–87; Ellingworth, *Hebrews* (1993), 161–63; Vanhoye, "La 'teleiosis' du Christ," 321–38; Scholer, *Proleptic Priests*, 183–200; Koester, *Hebrews*, 122–25; Schenck, *Cosmology and Eschatology*, 64–73; O'Brien, *Hebrews*, 108.

from sinners" (7:26; cf. 4:15), still needed perfecting (2:10; 5:7–9; 7:28). Moreover, Hebrews speaks not only of Jesus being perfected but connects this directly with the perfecting of Christians.[28]

Intrinsic to the meaning of the verb *teleioun* is the root *telos* "end" or "goal." The verb has a strong sense of completing something or achieving its intended goal. Aristotle says that a thing is perfect (*teleios*) when it "in respect of goodness or excellence cannot be surpassed in its kind." He adds that a physician or musician is perfect when they do not lack anything in regard to the form of their peculiar excellence (*Meta.* V.16). This understanding of *teleios* is universal. The LXX uses the verb for the completion of the work on the temple of Jerusalem (1 Kgs 7:22; 14:10; 2 Chron 8:16; 2 Macc 2:9), or martyrdom as the sealing of a life of fidelity to the law (4 Macc 7:15). In Philo and Josephus it refers to the fulfilling of one's personal plans or tasks (*Agric.* 159, 160; *Ant* 10:58). The New Testament uses it similarly (Luke 13:32; John 17:4; Acts 20:24). This sense of perfecting as completion is clearly evident in Hebrews, though there are other shades of meaning.

Jesus' perfecting leads to the perfecting of his followers. "By a single offering he has perfected (*teteleiōken*) for all time those who are sanctified" (10:14). The writer moves easily from the one to the other, but there is this difference: Jesus is perfected through suffering (2:10; 5:5–9); his followers, although they suffer, are perfected not by this, but by Christ himself (2:11; 10:14; 12:2a). They run their race with perseverance, following their leader (12:1–2), and in the life to come they are "made perfect (*teteleiōmenōn*)" or complete (12:23). Notably, this forward-looking meaning of perfecting is present in 11:39–40.

Consonant with *teleioun* as completion is the eschatological perspective of the entire discourse.[29] This is expressed in the themes of pilgrimage and entering into God's rest and also in the repeated use of dynamically charged words and metaphors. To Silva belongs the credit for showing that eschatology is the key to our understanding perfection. He demonstrates that Jesus' perfecting leads to his glorifying and points to God's declared intention of having the pioneer lead his people to their appointed goal. Always the language of perfection is celestially oriented (2:10; 5:8–9; 7:26–28; cf. 10:12; 12:2).[30]

28. Wikgren, "Patterns of Perfection," 159–67.

29. Barrett, "Eschatology," 363–93; Silva, "Perfection and Eschatology," 60–71.

30. The connection between perfecting and exaltation or glorification is emphasized by Riggenbach, "Der Begriff der *teleiōsis*," 184–95; Käsemann, *Wandering*

The eschatological thrust of perfection language in Hebrews is illustrated and confirmed by the link the author makes between perfection and the new covenant (7:11, 19).[31] The perfection that was not attainable in the Levitical dispensation is now achievable in the new covenant (cf. 9:9; 10:1). Silva says, "The writer of Hebrews is unwilling to call the Mosaic economy *perfect*, not because there was anything intrinsically wrong with it, but because in the divine arrangement it was designed as a shadow, anticipating the substance. The substance, therefore, far from opposing the shadow, is its *fulfillment*—this is *perfection*."[32]

However, while perfecting in the sense of completion or fulfillment features prominently in Hebrews this does not exhaust the meaning of the verb *teleioun*. The statement in 2:10 that Jesus was perfected by means of his sufferings suggests that in this text perfecting, like his learning obedience through his sufferings in 5:8, also has the sense of vocational preparedness.[33] This takes the preposition *dia* in 2:10 in its instrumental sense: suffering is the means *through which* Jesus' perfecting takes place. This view does not suggest that Jesus was previously ill-prepared for ministry or was incompetent, but through experience he perfected his potential and acquired additional preparedness for new tasks. As Schenck says, "These experiences qualify Christ for his high priesthood, both in terms of the ability he gains to sympathize with our weaknesses and in that he undergoes this suffering without sinning (4:15), rather learning obedience (5:8)."[34] Similarly, in 12:4–11 the sufferings experienced by Christians prepare them for what God has in store for them.

The statement in 5:7–9 that Christ learned obedience through his hardships suggests that his perfecting also includes a moral component.[35]

People, 139–40; Cody, *Heavenly Sanctuary*, 99–103; Attridge, *Hebrews*, 87. Silva shows the idea that perfecting means glorifying goes back a very long time ("Perfection and Eschatology," 65).

31 Sowers, *Hermeneutics*, 113; Silva, "Perfection and Eschatology," 68.

32. Silva, "Perfection and Eschatology," 68. The italics are the author's.

33. Moffatt, *Hebrews*, 32; Manson, *Hebrews*, 110; Peterson, *Hebrews and Perfection*, 66–70; Attridge, *Hebrews*, 86; Lane, *Hebrews 1–8*, 57–58. But while understanding Jesus' vocational preparation to refer to his suffering as equipping him to help those similarly tested we should not limit it to this but give it a wider interpretation (cf. Peterson, *Hebrews and Perfection*, 67).

34. Schenck, *Cosmology and Eschatology*, 68.

35. Westcott, *Hebrews*, 49; Manson, *Hebrews*, 101; Delling, "Teleioun," 83; Cullmann, *Christology*, 92–97. For critiques of this view see Käsemann, *Wandering People*, 139–40; Peterson, *Hebrews and Perfection*, 98; Koester, *Hebrews*, 124.

This is not to say that Jesus' learning obedience necessarily implies a prior disobedience. The thought rather is of obedience of a fuller degree.[36] Cullmann reasons that since Jesus was a fully human being and had experienced temptation and fear of suffering he must be understood as having developed morally, notwithstanding the fact that he did not sin (4:15; cf. 9:14). He says "This (being made perfect) happens in a really human life—in Jesus, the High Priest, who is made perfect; and in the brothers, the sanctified, who are made perfect by him (Heb. 2:11)."[37] But one would be hard-pressed to find in Hebrews evidence that the writer is interested in Jesus' moral development.[38] However, if we follow Ellingworth and take the perfecting of Jesus, not in the negative sense of the removal of moral imperfection (9:9; 10:1–2), but positively for successfully enduring the sufferings that tested his vocation and repelling sinful onslaughts, we can attribute an ethical dimension to his perfecting. Thus Christ qualified to be appointed high priest (*prosagoreuein*) (5:10).[39] His perfecting is his integrity when confronted by every kind of assault, thus contributing to his integrity.[40, 41]

Not very different from the foregoing interpretation of 5:7–10 is the view that takes the perfecting of Jesus to be his personal growth and developing maturity.[42] In so far as Jesus was truly human he experienced human growth and development. The experiences mentioned in 5:7–8 are taken as evidence of his learning process. Spicq says that Jesus acquired "an enriching psychological experience, a practical comprehen-

36. Wikgren, "Patterns of Perfection," 165.

37. Cullmann, *Christology*, 93.

38. Scholer, *Proleptic Priests*, 188; Attridge, *Hebrews*, 87.

39. Ellingworth, *Hebrews (1993)*, 163. Delling, in support of his argument for believing that the perfecting of Jesus has an ethical meaning, writes, "As the one who has shown Himself completely innocent by doing God's will (10:7), He is qualified for actual discharge of the high-priestly office" ("Teleioun," 83).

40. Hughes, *Hebrews*, 187–88.

41. Since the Qumran scrolls take holiness as synonymous with perfection one naturally asks whether the moral nuance some scholars see in Heb 5:7–9 bears any relation to what we find in the scrolls. The members of the community are repeatedly exhorted to "walk in perfection" (1 QS 2:2; 3:9–10; 8:1; 9:2; 1QH 1:16; 4:31–32; 1 QM 14:7; etc.). However, the basic orientation of the idea of perfection at Qumran rules this out. It means walking according to the law. In Hebrews it is Jesus Christ who perfects his followers; "the law made nothing perfect" (7:19).

42. On theories of personal growth see Rengstorf, "Manthanein," 411; Motyer, *Discovering Hebrews*, 71. See criticism of this view by Peterson, *Hebrews and Perfection*, 93–96; Scholer, *Proleptic Priests*, 187–88.

sion and an appreciation of suffering which was indispensable for him to sympathize as priest with those who are his brothers."[43] But it cannot be said that there is anything in Hebrews that suggests Jesus' psychological development was of interest to the author. In any case, the verbs used for Jesus' perfecting are passives, with God as the implied active subject.[44]

A cultic nuance in Jesus' perfecting may also be present in 2:10–11. The LXX uses *teleioun* for the consecrating of a priest (Exod 29:9, 29, 33, 35; Lev 4:5; 8:33; 16:32; 21:10; Num 3:3).[45] The sacrifice of the ram at the time when Aaron and his sons began their priestly office is called "the flesh for the ordination" (*tēs teleiōseōs*) (Exod 29:34), and the ram itself is referred to as the "ram of ordination" (*teleiōseōs*)" (Exod 29:27) or simply "perfection" (*teleiōsis*) (29:22; cf. 29:26, 27, 31; Lev 8:22, 28, 29, 31). The Semitic idiom means "to fill the hands" (*teleioun tas cheiras*). Occasionally this idiomatic expression is dropped, as in Lev 21:10,[46] and in Exod 29:33 the underlying meaning is clarified by the verb "sanctify" (*hagiazein*), "to consecrate or qualify for priestly service."

The use of *teleioun* for priestly consecration in Hebrews 2:10 is seen by a number of scholars.[47] This is an attractive suggestion. It resonates well with the emphasis on Christ as high priest and the parallel between Christ and Aaron. It has its critics who argue we do not have the evidence that *teleioun* was used uniformly in a cultic sense.[48] However, there is no gainsaying the fact that in certain texts it had this meaning (Exod 29:9; cf. Lev 21:10). The fact that the accounts of the consecration of priests involved moral cleansing (Exod 29:10–21; Lev 8:14–24) may be considered to be a problem for this interpretation: Jesus was without sin (4:15).

---

43. Spicq, *Hébreux* 2, 117.

44. Cf. e.g., Kurianal, *Jesus Our High Priest*, 230–33.

45. For example, Delling, "Teleioun," 80–83; Loader, *Sohn und Hoherpriester*, 40, 47–48; Cullmann, *Christology*, 92; Lane, *Hebrews 1–8*, 57–58; Scholer, *Proleptic Priests*, 188–94.

46. On which see Delling, "Teleioun," 82; Du Plessis, *ΤΕΛΕΙΟΣ*, 213; Ellingworth, *Hebrews* (1993), 162.

47. Du Plessis, *ΤΕΛΕΙΟΣ*, 94–103, 121, 213–15; Delling, "Teleioun," 82–84; Bourke, "Hebrews," 925; Lane, *Hebrews 1–8*, 57.

48. Peterson questions whether *teleioun* translates a Hebrew expression for the consecration or ordination of a priest (*Hebrews and Perfection*, 27, 47). See also Attridge, *Hebrews*, 85; Scholer, *Proleptic Priests*, 188–94; Isaacs, *Sacred Space*, 101. Cf. Vanhoye, *Old Testament Priests and the New Priest*, 165–66.

However, as Silva points out, authors are free in their use of analogies and metaphors to use or ignore whatever aspects they wish.[49]

A deciding factor is the use of "the one who sanctifies" (*ho hagiazōn*) in 2:11a. In Israel's cult worshippers were sanctified or consecrated to God in order to be admitted to his presence.[50] God is the one "who sanctifies you" (Exod 19:10–25; 31:13; Lev 20:8; 21:15; etc.; 1 Sam 16:5). What we have in 2:11 is a subtle transposition of imagery. The pioneer image morphs into the image of the high priest: Jesus is the one whom God made perfect through suffering in order that he in turn might consecrate his people (10:14; cf. 13:12), who might then draw near to him in prayer (4:16; 7:19, 25; 10:22) and finally enter his presence (12:22–24). However, we should not take the expression "the one who sanctifies and those who are sanctified" necessarily to mean that Christians share Christ's priesthood. The reference is rather to their solidarity with him.[51]

From the foregoing we can conclude that while completion or fulfillment is very clearly the predominant meaning of perfecting in Hebrews other meanings are evident, though as often as not these have some connection with the major theme. Thus the nouns *teleios* and *teleiōtēs* translated "mature" and "maturity" in 5:14 and 6:1 have the sense of a fuller or more complete understanding of salvation. The same is true of the concept of vocational preparedness in 5:8–9: it is goal-oriented. The use of *teleioteras* in 9:11 looks like an exception since it means little more than "better" or "superior" (the heavenly sanctuary is better than the earthly one). But this particular use of perfecting may well be ancillary to the author's main intention: motivating the recipients to keep pressing forward towards the true sanctuary. The use of perfection in 10:14 is obviously related to the all-time sacrifice of Christ, but underlying it very likely is perfection as completion. This is supported by the fact that 10:14 looks back to the juxtaposition of these ideas in 10:1.[52] It implies that Christ by his unique offering accomplished all that the Levitical priesthood never succeeded in achieving, thereby signifying the fulfillment of

---

49. Silva, "Perfection and Eschatology," 62.

50. Procksch, "Hagios," 89–97.

51. Lane, *Hebrews 1–8*, 58. On the question whether Hebrews thinks of the priesthood of Christians see below.

52. "The author has framed 10:14 specifically as the answer to 10:1" (DeSilva, *Perseverance*, 324).

the Christian goal, viz. access to God.[53] In 12:2 the artful play on the *arch*-and *tel*-stems (3:6; 7:3) conveys perfecting as completion: "Jesus on whom faith depends from start to finish" (NEB). The exaltation of Jesus (1:3) and his entry into "honor and glory" (2:9), followed by his taking his place of great eminence at God's right hand (8:1; 10:12; 12:2) and his installation as high priest (2:17; 5:9–10; 7:28), all signify the consummation of his perfecting.

The same core meaning of perfecting as completion or fulfillment is present in the parallel idea of the perfecting of believers. The writer urges his listeners not to stop with their elementary understanding of faith (5:11–14), but to "go on towards perfection" (6:1). This exhortation follows 5:7–9 in which the writer says Jesus became the "source of salvation" through suffering and it foresees the attention paid to the community's suffering in 12:4–11, also described as a learning experience. What the author is implying would not be lost on the congregation. By connecting their life situation to that of their leader he is providing them with material for reflection.[54] As Christ learned through obedience, so they too have to pay attention to the confession of faith. Included in their perfecting is "the discipline of the Lord" (*paideia*, "education") (12:5).

Specifically, it is through the death of Christ that Christians are perfected. "He has perfected (*teteleiōken*) for all time (*eis to diēnekes*) those who are consecrated (*hagiazomenous*)"(10:14). The perfect tense followed by the present is considered significant by some commentators.[55] Riggenbach takes the present tense as a timeless present and believes it means that Christ has eternally consecrated his people.[56] This may be reading too much into the use of the present tense: the perfect is used in 10:10. Michael probably goes as far as one can safely go when he says, "That which is a once for all event (*teteleiōken*) takes place as an ongoing process (*hagiazomenous*)."[57]

53. The use of the perfect (*teteleiōken*) in 10:14 might appear to oppose the futuristic thrust of *teleioun* but the present participle (*hagiazomenous*) denotes a continuous process. Cf. Peterson, *Hebrews and Perfection*, 149–53, 167; Isaacs, *Sacred Space*, 103; Lane, *Hebrews 9–13*, 256.

54. Thompson, *Hebrews*, 116–18.

55. Riggenbach, *Hebräer*, 307–8; Michel, *Hebräer*, 314; Bruce, *Hebrews*, 247.

56. Riggenbach, *Hebräer*, 307. So also Bruce, *Hebrews*, 247.

57. Michel, *Hebräer*, quoted by Peterson (*Hebrews and Perfection*, 150). Spicq similarly refers to the use of the present tense in 10:10 as "an incessant and progressive application of the merits of the offering of Christ" (*Hébreux 2*, 310). The phrase "for all time" (*eis to diēnekes*) simply strengthens the emphasis on the continuing benefits of

The perfection of the followers of the pioneer takes place when they, like him, finish the race (12:1–2) and enter heaven to become "the spirits of the righteous made perfect (*dikaiōn teteleiōmenōn*)" (12:23). Although the writer moves easily from the perfecting of Christ to the perfecting of believers there is an essential difference: God perfects Christ through suffering (2:10; 5:5–9); Christ's followers, although they suffer (10:32–34), are perfected not by their sufferings but by Christ's atoning work (2:11; 9:28; 10:14; 12:2a). As in the case of their Lord, believers have their perfection consummated in heaven when they join "the spirits of the righteous made perfect"(12:23c).

Having introduced the pioneer the author gets ready to bring on his complementary motif of high priest. He does this by drawing out the implications of the common humanity Jesus shares with his siblings which he introduced in 2:10. By his death Jesus broke the power of the devil (2:14) and set humans free from the fear of death (2:15). The preacher recapitulates before moving on: "therefore (*hothen*, lit. "it was for this reason")[58] he had to become like his brothers and sisters in every respect" (2:17). The hearers are now prepared for the historic statement in 2:17.

A Merciful and Faithful High Priest

Therefore he had to become like his brothers and sisters in every respect, so that he might be a merciful and faithful high priest in the service of God, to make a sacrifice of atonement for the sins of the people (2:17).[59]

Christ's sacrifice. There is support for this in the use of the present participle in 2:11. The present tense in 10:14 may in fact have been used to preclude the possible conclusion that Christians have already reached their destination.

58. See also the use of *hothen* in 3:1; 7:25; 8:3; 11:19. Cf. BDF 451 (6); O'Brien, *Hebrews*, 118.

59. The connection of the high priest with "the confession (*homologia*)" in 3:1 underscores its importance. For very good reason Ellingworth calls 2:17 the "nerve centre" of Hebrews (*Hebrews* (1993), 179). On Christ as a merciful and faithful high priest see, e.g., O'Brien, *Hebrews*, 119–22.

The introduction of Jesus as high priest in this verse is not as abrupt as some scholars have thought.[60] The subject is introduced at 1:3c, d.[61] But as is the custom of the preacher to alert the congregation to what to expect (1:3c, d; 4:14; 5:6; etc.), the subject is no more than announced. Its explication would follow (4:14–16; 5:5–10; 7:1–28).[62] It will have our attention in later chapters. What is to be registered at this point is the humanity of Jesus (2:9, 14, 17)[63] and his solidarity with his followers (2:10–14, 17). These pivotal features reappear when the merciful nature of Christ's high priesthood is dealt with (4:15; 5:1–3).

Integral to the author's creative writing on the subject of Jesus as high priest is his analogy of the Levitical high priest on the Day of Atonement (Lev 16). Deftly introduced at 1:3 ("He [the Son] made purification (*katharismos*) for sins"), it makes a literary allusion to Exodus 30:10, thereby alerting the congregation to all that is to come on the new Day of Atonement. Somewhat more is added in 2:17 and a good deal more will follow, with a significant dimension added when the priesthood of Melchizedek is introduced in 5:1–10. Before we consider Melchizedek in chapter 5 we remind ourselves that the author's comparison of Christ's priesthood with the Levitical priesthood, like his use of comparison (*synkrisis*) elsewhere, is used to exalt Christ and not to denigrate his counterpart.

When specifically Christ became high priest is much debated.[64] The question is not whether the death of Christ was an atoning sacrifice but

60. On the possible antecedents of the high priestly figure and on the subject generally see appendix C.

61. For the strong cultic associations of "purification" (*katharismos*) in the LXX and the New Testament see Attridge, *Hebrews*, 46. Surprisingly, Attridge does not indicate that the use of *katharismos* in 1:3c prepares for all the central part of the sermon has to say about Christ the high priest.

62. On 2:17 and the links between 2:17 and 4:14–16 see Gäbel, *Kulttheologie*, 214–18.

63. See especially Lincoln, *Hebrews*, 88–89.

64. Peterson, *Hebrews and Perfection*, 191–95; Lincoln, *Hebrews*, 87–88. Heb 4:14 is understood by some exegetes to represent Christ as high priest before entering his sanctuary, i.e., having made his offering on the cross he proceeds "into the Holy Place . . . with his own blood" (9:12). Those who argue for a high priesthood which began with Christ's exaltation include Windisch, *Hebäerbrief*, 42; Luck, "Himmlisches und irdisches," 205. For the view that Christ's priesthood began at the incarnation see Cody, *Heavenly Sanctuary*, 97; Spicq, *Hébreux 2*, 111; Scholer, *Proleptic Priests*, 85–89. Scholer says, "Time and again, the author connects his statements about the perfected, 'after the order of Melchizedek' high priest with the life, sacrifice and death of Jesus

how this relates to his heavenly ministry. In favor of the view that it was at his exaltation at God's right hand he became high priest is both the close connection between priesthood and exaltation and the emphasis on Christ's heavenly status and ministry. Alternatively, the view that his priesthood commenced on earth, at the moment of his death, is supported by the fact that his death is portrayed as an offering (9:14, 25–26; 10:5–10). The two possibilities are not as discrete as might appear when we view them in relation to Christ's perfecting (5:9; 7:16). The solution to the dilemma that many see here is to be found in the author's typological use of the Day of Atonement imagery in what we have seen is the cosmological context of the universe as a sanctuary. Just as the high priest on Yom Kippur sacrificed his offering outside the holy of holies and straightaway carried the blood inside the holy of holies to complete his priestly work, so by analogy, what Jesus did on earth and what he did on entering the heavenly sanctuary are, similarly, a single indivisible priestly action. His offering in heaven is not thought of as separate from or subsequent to his offering on the cross. What we have here are two ways of referring to one and the same act. The complex imagery that Hebrews uses for the heavenly sanctuary still has to be considered but, without anticipating the outcome, I believe we have in the Day of Atonement imagery the solution to the quandary over the question when Christ became high priest. What Christ did on the cross and what he does now in heaven are his Day of Atonement, which our author makes the definitive Day of Atonement by virtue of his unique offering.[65]

Christ in his death is sacrifice and priest—a remarkable paradox that is fundamental to all the author says about Christ's becoming high priest. The offering he makes is the means by which the pioneer priest is able to proceed on his way to the heavenly sanctuary. Israelite practice helps us understand Hebrews. The death of the victim was not the whole of the sacrificial action but the prelude to the priest's bringing the blood before God by applying it to the mercy seat, the incense altar and the

---

(1:3; 2.9–10; 4:14–16; 5:7–10; 7:26–28; 8:1–10.18; 10:19–20; 12:2), thereby illustrating the indivisibility of the earthly and the heavenly high priesthood of Christ" (*Proleptic Priests*, 88). Still other scholars think that the author of Hebrews does not give a clear indication as to the question when Jesus became high priest (Braun, *Hebräer*, 71–74); Attridge, *Hebrews*, 147; Koester, *Hebrews*, 109–10; cf. Peterson, *Hebrews and Perfection*, 191–95. Laub is very likely correct in thinking that Hebrews is interested not in the question when Christ became high priest but how (*Bekenntnis und Auslegung*, 59).

65. On Melchizedek functioning on the special Day of Atonement in 11Q Melch see chapter 5 and appendix C.

main altar (Lev 16:14–19): "it is the blood, which is the life, that makes expiation" (Lev 17:11, REB; cf. Heb 9:22).[66] Accordingly, Hebrews, with the high priest's action on the Day of Atonement very definitely in mind, depicts Christ, as presenting his blood in the heavenly holy of holies (9:12), declaring that "without the shedding of blood there is no forgiveness of sins" (9:22). What Christ did on the cross and what he does in heaven are one continuous action.

The foregoing interpretation is confirmed by the spatial imagery underlying the discourse. Since heaven and earth are conceived of as one great temple, the place where the cross stands is sacred space, corresponding to the outer part or court of the tabernacle (the *skēnē . . . protē*, 9:2; cf. 9:6–7).[67] The outer part is not merely a vestibule or foyer to the holy of holies, but as the place where the altar stands is the designated place for the sacrifice to be offered.[68] In other words, earth and heaven are all of a piece. One recalls how Hellenistic Judaism thought of heaven and earth forming a vast temple, with the earth as the outer court and heaven as the inner sanctuary (Josephus, *Ant.* 3:123,181; Philo, *Spec.* 1:66; *Mos.* 2:88).[69] In terms of the Yom Kippur analogy what Hebrews is saying is that just as the service of the high priest at the altar and in the holy of holies is a single action so the action of Christ on the cross (the outer part of the sanctuary) and in heaven (the holy of holies) is one action, which implies that we should understand Heb 9:11–14 to mean that Christ offers his blood (metaphorically) through the eternal spirit in the heavenly sanctuary (9:14). There is simultaneity in Christ's offering on earth and in heaven.[70] This is in marked contrast to apocalyptic thought that makes

66. Cf. Nelson, *Raising up a Faithful Priest,* 79–80.

67. "The syntax of *vv* 11–12 demands that a distinction be made between the *skēnē*, 'front compartment' through which Christ passed, and *ta hagia*, 'the sanctuary,' into which he entered" (Lane, *Hebrews 9–13*, 238).

68. Westcott, *Hebrews*, 256.

69. On the cosmic temple see further in chapter 6. For the idea of the temple-structured universe in Hellenistic Judaism see Cody, *Heavenly Sanctuary and Liturgy*, 26–36; MacRae, "Heavenly Temple and Eschatology," 184–87; cf. Luck, "Himmlisches und irdisches Geschehen," 207–8; Schenck, *Understanding Hebrews*, 85. For the view that the "first tent" of Heb 9:8 refers to the earth and the "second tent" of 9:7 a symbol of heaven see Peterson, *Hebrews and Perfection*, 249 n 28. On this subject see further in chapters 6 and 7.

70. Spicq, *Hébreux 1*, 287; Cody, *Heavenly Sanctuary*, 170–72; Smith, *A Priest Forever*, 111; Attridge, *Hebrews*, 248; Thompson, *Hebrews*, 203, 205, 283. Käsemann writes, "*Hebrews no longer regards Golgotha as an essentially earthly fact, but as the beginning of Jesus' ascension. For this reason alone the sacrificial death is already a*

the consecration to the heavenly priesthood take place only in heaven (*T Levi* 4:2; 18:6–7). As Himmelfarb says, commenting on the ascent of Levi to heaven, "The purpose of the ascent is God's appointment of Levi as priest, and the consecration is thus the fulfillment of the ascent."[71] In other words, only heaven is here thought of as sacred space.

Very importantly, we are told what precisely it is that makes Christ high priest. Introduced pointedly in 1:3b, the theme begins in 2:9–10 and is précised in 2:17.[72] In the clearest possible terms the incarnation is made the *sine qua non* of the atonement: Jesus had to be made like his brothers and sisters in order to become a merciful and faithful high priest and make atonement for the sins of people (2:17). This is similar to 2:14–15: Jesus assumes human nature and by means of his death destroys the one who has the power of death. The importance of Jesus' having become a human being for his priesthood is further elaborated, with increased emphasis, in 4:15–16 and 5:7–8. But Christ has another very important qualification for being high priest. It is his offering. "For every high priest is appointed to offer gifts and sacrifices; hence it is necessary for this priest also to have something to offer" (8:3). What this offering is has been stated in 7:27 ("he offered himself") and will be elaborated upon in 9:12–14, 23–26, and 10:5–10, where its nature and efficacy are spelt out.

Before the author embarks on his exposition of the high priest and Melchizedek he pauses to deal with the situation in the congregation. What follows (3:1—6:11) is one of the panels of practical application that follows theological presentation. It is widely taken as evidence that the sermon was prepared for a group of Jewish converts to Christianity who were having difficulty in appreciating the Christian faith in relation to Judaism. Other warnings of the dangers they faced are mentioned elsewhere (2:1; 4:11; 5:11—6:12; 10:32–39; 12:3–17; 13:9). The writer begins by declaring that Jesus is "worthy of more glory than Moses" (3:2), for although Moses was faithful as a servant, Jesus was faithful as a son (3:5–6). Citing the case of the Israelites who failed to trust God and follow Joshua to their destination, the writer cautions his readers of the peril of unbelief

component of the heavenly high priesthood" (*Wandering People*, 231, the author's italics). What Hebrews does is to retroject Christ's high priestly life back into his earthly life. See below on 5:7–10.

71. Himmelfarb, *Ascent to Heaven*, 37.

72. On the links between 2:17 and 2:9–10 see Gäbel, *Kulttheologie*, 215–16. At 5:5 the writer is careful to say that Christ did not arrogate high priesthood to himself, but was divinely appointed.

(3:12, 19). The faith they need involves a determination to reach their God-appointed destination, the "rest" he promised.

Summary

Basic to everything the preacher does to help the dispirited and lethargic community are the twin concepts of pioneer and high priest. Each image is distinctly recognizable and plays a vital part in the whole, and their merging together (4:14; 6:20; 9:11–12; 10:19–20) is mutually illuminating, thus providing an indispensible key to the author's understanding of Christian discipleship. Without the help of the pioneering leader the community cannot hope to get out of its enclave. Equally, without the help of the high priest it will not be able to follow the pioneer out into an uncertain and risky world. Significant among the features that make the Hebrews stand out as a presentation of New Testament Christology is the prominence given to the solidarity of Christ and his followers. It has particular relevance to Christ's priestly ministry and the dual pursuit of perfection by Christ and by his followers. Perfecting in Hebrews expresses the teleological argument of the sermon, depicting salvation as moving towards its fulfillment or completion in the heavenly world. *Teleioun* has several meanings, but completing or fulfilling is the main sense. Its consummation is in heaven. Christ is already there as humanity's true representative. The question when Christ became high priest is best answered in the light of the author's use of the Day of Atonement analogy. By making his high priestly offering on the cross Christ has made Golgotha consecrated ground. It has, so to speak, become the forecourt of the cosmic sanctuary.

4

To the Heavenly Sanctuary

It is time for the author to develop his pilgrimage theme. Already he has introduced Jesus as the pioneer who leads his people to their appointed destination (2:10). Now he introduces the accompanying pilgrimage motif under the subject of the "rest" God planned for his people (3:7—4:11). It is one of the images used by the author to depict the goal set before them. The "rest" is carefully defined as "my rest" (*tēn katapausin mou*, 4:3, 5). As Brooke Foss Westcott says, it was not simply a case of entering into rest, but *"into the rest"* of which the Psalmist spoke, "into the rest of God."[1] The ease with which the author can move from speaking about the pilgrimage image of the entry into the "rest" to the sacerdotal figure going into the holy of holies (illustrated by his use of the verb "enter" (*eiserchomai*) in 4:1; 3:10–11 and in 6:19, 20; 9:24, 25 is noteworthy. It masks what the author is about. Images are mixed, the pioneer turns into the high priest, and, astonishingly, the high priest enters the holy of holies not on his own but in the company of others.

The parallel which the preacher draws in 3:7—4:11 between the wilderness generation of Israelites and the pilgrimage on which his listeners are engaged could not be clearer or the rhetorical power stronger.[2] Basing his sermon on Psalm 95, he attributes the failure of the Exodus generation to enter Canaan to the fact that they did not trust God's word and encourages them to see themselves as those who are figuratively in the wilderness. He issues the strongest possible warning to his congregation to avoid a fate similar to their forerunners. Like them, they had made a

1. Westcott, *Hebrews*, 95.

2. The unit 3:7—4:13 is well defined and occupies a vital position in the developing narrative (Ellingworth, *Hebrews* (1993), 212–17).

start. They had "tasted the goodness of the word of God and the powers of the age to come, and then had fallen away" (6:5–6). They should learn a lesson from their ancestors, who allowed the hostility and might of the Canaanites to undermine their trust in God. The opposition of unbelievers (10:32–33) must not cause them to distrust God. Instead, they should listen to God's word.

> Take care, brothers and sisters, that none of you may have an evil, unbelieving heart that turns away from the living God. But exhort one another every day, as long as it is called "today" . . . As it is said, "Today, if you hear his voice, do not harden your hearts as in the rebellion . . . let us therefore make every effort to enter that rest, so that no one may fall through such disobedience as theirs" (3:12–13, 15; 4:11).

The author points his listeners to Jesus. "For we have become partners (*metochoi*) of Christ" (3:14; cf. 3:1).[3] This connects with the emphasis on the solidarity of Christ and his followers which we saw is an important emphasis in 2:10–14. The writer is referring to the blessings that await those who stick with the pioneer. Much the same point is made in the wordplay in 4:8. The name Joshua in Greek is *Iēsous*, Jesus (cf. Acts 7:45).[4] The KJV translates 4:8 as "Jesus." The wordplay was favored by the early fathers (*Barn.* 12:8; Justin, *Dial.* 24:2; 75:14; Origen, *Hom. On Ex* 11:5). Joshua who led the tribes of Israel foreshadows Jesus who leads his followers to their heavenly destination.[5] An event marked by failure and ignominy is reconfigured around the new leader God has provided and used to challenge the congregation to embrace the opportunity now being given to them.

3. The Pauline concept of participation "in" Christ is not what is meant here. Manson writes, "There is in Hebrews nothing of the faith-mysticism of St. Paul which comes to expression in the doctrine of Christ 'in us' or us 'in Christ.' The eyes are outwardly and objectively directed towards Christ as the Pioneer, the Forerunner, and the Perfecter of our faith (xii.1–2), and we are 'partakers with Christ' in the sense of being loyal to, and following Him into the life of the World to Come" (*Hebrews*, 57).

4. Synge, *Hebrews and the Scriptures*, 19; Hanson, *Jesus Christ*, 61; Bruce, *Hebrews*, 108–9; Ellingworth, *Hebrews* (1993), 252–53.

5. Attridge sees "a typological comparison between one *achēgos* of the old covenant and that of the new" (*Hebrews*, 130). So also Thompson, *Hebrews*, 96. Cf. Windisch, *Hebräerbrief,* 97; Loader, *Sohn und Hoherpriester*, 122; Bruce, *Hebrews*, 109.

The Promise of Entering God's Rest (4:1)

What exactly the author means by the "rest" (*katapausis*) God has planned for his people (4:1, 9) and when they enter it is not explicit.[6] The exposition is based on the Pentateuch, where the "rest" refers to the Israelites settling in the land of Canaan (Deut 12:9–10, LXX). This was reinterpreted by later writers. Apocalyptists, rabbis, Philo, and the gnostics all understood the "rest" with reference generally to heaven.[7] Hofius' exhaustive study produced what many regard as a convincing case for believing that the background is to be found in Jewish apocalyptic where heaven is portrayed as the resting place of God and the righteous (4 *Ezra* 7:95; 8:52; 1 *En* 45:3; 2 *En* 42:3 (J); 2 *Bar* 85:11–12; *T.Levi* 18:9; *T.Dan* 5:12). The idea of the temple of Jerusalem as God's resting place is developed (Ps 132:8, 13–14; cf. 1 Kgs 8:54–56). A connection between the "rest" and the Messiah is made in 2 Baruch 73:1. Hofius concluded that the "rest" in Hebrews refers primarily to the entry of Christ's follow-ers into the heavenly sanctuary.[8] Spicq also takes the "rest" to mean the heavenly world.[9] "Resting place" (in heaven) for these scholars is thus essentially the meaning the phrase is believed to have in Hebrews.

By contrast, some others believe that the "rest" refers to life on a renewed earth.[10] This view, which goes back to the early church (*Barn.* 15:4–5, 8), connects the "rest" with the *parousia* (9:26–28; 10:25) and the subjection of Christ's enemies to him (2:8), and it interprets this as the millennial kingdom.[11] This suits the strongly futuristic slant of Hebrews

---

6. Hofius, *Katapausis*, 137–43; Lincoln, "Sabbath, Rest, and Eschatology," 197–220; Laansma, "*I Will Give You Rest*"; Wray, *Rest as a Theological Metaphor*; Mackie, *Escha-tology and Exhortation*, 48–54; Schenck, *Cosmology and Eschatology*, 60–64; Thomp-son, *Hebrews*, 84–86. The superscription of Ps 94 (95) bears David's name. Since David lived centuries later than Joshua the "rest" must refer to a time much later than Joshua and the wilderness generation (cf. 4:7).

7. Attridge, *Hebrews*, 127–28. For the gnostic conception of the "rest" see Käse-mann, *Wandering People*, 72–75.

8. Hofius, *Katapausis*, 53–54, 58. Cf. Attridge, *Hebrews*, 128.

9. Spicq, *Hébreux* 2, 64–65; Isaacs, *Sacred Space*, 207; Son, *Zion Symbolism*, 100, 136–37 and *passim*. For the association of "rest" with the temple of Jerusalem see 1 Kgs 8:54–56; Attridge, *Hebrews*, 126; Son, *Zion Symbolism*, 138. Cf. Ps 132:8, 13–14. *Eiserchomai* in 3:11 ("they shall never enter my rest"); 3:18, 19; 4:1, *passim*, is used repeatedly for entry into the heavenly sanctuary (6:19–20; 9:12, 24, 25; 12:22).

10. Scholer, *Proleptic Priests*, 203–4. The "rest" is equated with Jewish national sov-ereignty by Buchanan, *To the Hebrews*, 64–65, 72–73.

11. Kaiser, "The Promise Theme and the Theology of Rest," 135–50; Toussaint,

(9:15; 10:36; 11:9, 13, 17, 39–40) and with Hofius' conclusion that the background to the "rest" is to be found in Jewish apocalyptic,[12] but a number of things make it a doubtful interpretation. The eschatology of Hebrews contains nothing that would lend support to the idea of a ter-restrial kingdom. The *parousia* is expected, but this and the subjection of all things to Christ, does not in any way imply an earthly reign of Christ. The "rest" and the second coming stand unrelated in Hebrews and should not be forced together by the influence of the Book of Revelation.[13] Some commentators as a matter of fact see in Hebrews 12:26–29 not the renew-al of the earthly realm but its destruction.[14] The nearest the writer gets to saying anything about the ultimate destiny of God's people is 12:23c ("the spirits of the righteous made perfect"). His interests are more immediate. They have to do with discipleship in this world, to which he returns once he has given his friends a glimpse of their great destiny (12:22–24).

We shall find the underlying idea of entering "God's rest" is devel-oped in the images of entering "the inner shrine" (6:20), "drawing near" to God (10:22), reaching a "better, heavenly country" (11:16), and "look-ing for the city that is to come" (13:14). It is, in short, the rest that Jesus entered as pioneer and forerunner (2:10; 6:19–20).

Entering the Rest (4:11)

Assuming that the "rest" is located in the heavenly world one naturally thinks of the pilgrims making their entry when they complete their pil-grimage. However, commentators frequently draw attention to the use of the present tense in 4:3. "We who have believed enter (*eiserchometha*) that rest." This is taken as an actual present and understood to mean that the entrance to the "rest" is a possibility now.[15] Today the "rest" is

---

"Eschatology of the Warning Passages," 67–80.

12. For the hope of a renewed earth in apocalyptic see 2 *Ezra* 7:25–44; 10:27; 1 *En* 45:4; cf. Rev 21:1–8.

13. For a critique of the traditional interpretation of Rev 19:11–21 as the return of Christ to earth to establish the millennium kingdom see McKelvey, *Millennium*, 77–80.

14. Attridge, *Hebrews*, 381. See Ellingworth, *Hebrews* (1993), 688; Schenck, *Cosmology and Eschatology*, 124–28.

15. So Moffatt, *Hebrews*, 51, Michel, *Hebräer*, 194; Lincoln, "Sabbath Rest and Eschatology," 212; Lane, *Hebrews 1–8*, 99. See the full discussion in DeSilva, *Perseverance*, 153–56.

accessible. Faith makes the future hope a proleptic reality.[16] Support for realized eschatology is also found in the exhortations to "draw near" to the throne of grace (4:16; 10:19–22). Divine help is an experience now, in the present life. Hebrews is thus seen to share with other New Testament writers the belief that believers now enjoy a foretaste of the future blessings of God (Rom 8:23; 2 Cor 1:22).

The alternative view relates the entry into the "rest" to the end time. This maintains that the very obvious parallel drawn between the situation of the recipients of the letter and the wilderness generation (3:7—4:11) suggests that the writer is indicating that the "rest" lay in the future.[17] The verb *eiserchometha* ("enter") in 4:3 is taken as a present continuous tense and the sense as futuristic. Moffatt, who believes that *eiserchometha* is emphatic, translates as follows, "we do (we are sure to) enter," the futuristic present (*ingrediemur*, vg)."[18] Scholars who interpret the text in this way correctly challenge the use of the word "today"(4:7) and "another day" (4:8) as support for entry into the "rest" as a present experience on the grounds that the new "today" should be interpreted in terms of its use in 3:13 ("as long as it is called 'today'").[19] This interpretation agrees with the forward–looking genre of the sermon. Christians cannot be said to be at rest from their labors as God is at rest (4:10; Gen 2:2). But whilst doing justice to the futuristic character of Hebrews this reading of the text fails to acknowledge salvation as a present reality, i.e., the "already" of the "already–not yet" paradox of the sermon. The author's hearers have even now tasted the powers of the age to come (6:5). The encouragement to enter the "rest" *now* thus prepares the way for the author's sustained appeal to his listeners to "draw near" to the heavenly sanctuary while still *en route* (4:16; 7:25; 10:19, 22).

The synthesis offered by Barrett is attractive. He says, "The 'rest,' precisely because it is God's, is both present and future; men enter it, and must strive to enter it. This is paradoxical, but it is a paradox which Hebrews shares with all early Christian eschatology."[20] I have to say, however, that, while taking due account of the heavily accentuated fact that

16. Lane, *Hebrews 1–8*, 99.

17. Laansma, *"I Will Give You Rest,"* 264.

18. Moffatt, *Hebrews*, quoted by Barrett, "Eschatology," 372.

19. DeSilva, *Perseverance*, 154, who quotes Lane, "The prophetic announcement of another day in which the *promise* of entering God's rest would be renewed" [DeSilva's emphasis] (*Hebrews 1–8*, 104).

20. Barrett, "Eschatology," 372.

the high priest is in the heavenly sanctuary and is receiving those who approach him, I think what Barrett says is rather too finely balanced. Hebrews tilts the emphasis towards the future.

We sum up this discussion by noting that the position of the section on the "rest" within the larger context of Hebrews is significant. The "rest" is the goal of the Christian pilgrimage. It has at its core the pioneer motif. The introduction of Christ as the pioneer who leads his followers to glory (2:10) is joined with the pilgrimage of God's people in chapters 3–4 and is now about to be focused on the journey of the pioneer through the heavens (4:14–16). Attridge puts this well. "The Christians' 'entry into rest' parallels Christ's entry into the divine presence and in fact their entry is made possible by his."[21] With Christ on the throne of grace there is help for pilgrims at any point of the journey, "today," or any day. It is puzzling therefore that Mackie finds the "entry" and the pilgrimage incompatible ideas.[22] Hebrews sees them as complementary. The pilgrim way is punctuated by moments when the pilgrims enter the presence of God and find help.

The writer having for the moment finished what he wants to say about the pilgrimage of the faithful to their heavenly destination now returns to their leader.

> Since, then, we have a great high priest who has passed through the heavens (*dielēluthota tous ouranous*), Jesus, the Son of God, let us hold fast to our confession. For we do not have a high priest who is unable to sympathize with our weaknesses, but we have one who in every respect has been tested as we are, yet without sin. Let us therefore approach the throne of grace with boldness, so that we may receive mercy and find grace to help in time of need (4:14–16).

These verses form a transition which concludes the passage on the wilderness journey and, by recapitulating the references to Christ's high priesthood in 2:17 and 3:1, serve as the *propositio* to introduce the main argument in the long central section on the high priest and his heavenly ministry (7:1—10:25). The author, in telling the members of the community that they have "a high priest who has passed through the heavens" and has taken up his position in the sanctuary in heaven, is preparing the way for the contrast he will draw between their high priest and his

---

21. Attridge, *Hebrews*, 128. Cf. Son, *Zion Symbolism*, 140.
22. Mackie, *Eschatology and Exhortation*, 208–11.

(true) sanctuary and that of the Levitical priesthood which is earth-bound (7:11–28; 8:12; 9:11–12; 10:19–20). The movement of Jesus into the heavenly sanctuary although not explicitly mentioned until now was already implied in the references of Christ's exaltation at 1:3, 13; 2:9–10.[23] Presently it will be portrayed in terms of the Day of Atonement symbolism where the high priest makes his ceremonial entry into the holy of holies (6:19–20; 10:19–21).

The language and imagery of 4:14–16 are so similar to 10:19–22 that the two passages are widely regarded as forming a major *inclusio*, marking the beginning and the ending of the central section of the homily.[24] The journey of Jesus to the sanctuary in heaven introduced in 4:14 is what is elsewhere his exaltation, and, as 10:20 shows, is his entry into the sanctuary in heaven. We shall return to the linkage of the two passages in chapter 9.

The captivating picture of the pioneer-priest who has passed through the heavens [25] is usually taken to refer to Christ's ascension.[26] That is permissible so long as we acknowledge that the author, unlike other New Testament writers who distinguish Christ's death, resurrection, ascension, and session at God's right hand, telescopes them into a single happening. The result, as we shall see, is an impressive metaphor modeled on the Day of Atonement, in which Christ's offering, like that of the high priest, is one continuous and uninterrupted action, though, unlike it, expressed in terms of a single entry into the holy of holies. This single, defining event is already in mind in the earlier references to Christ's exaltation (1:3, 13; cf. 7:26). In the text before us, Christ's passage through the heavens is metaphorically conceived of as his entry into the innermost part of the sanctuary, heaven itself (9:24).

The thought of Christ passing through the heavens raises questions about the cosmology which we shall consider in chapter 8. Here

23. Attridge, *Hebrews*, 139; O'Brien, *Hebrews*, 181.

24. As the *inclusio* of 4:14–16 (cf. 10:19–25) indicates, the core theme is holding on to the confession (4:14, cf. 6:19; 10:23). On the similarity of the language and imagery of 4:14–16 and 10:19–25 see Vanhoye, *Structure littéraire*, 173–81; Mackie, *Eschatology and Exhortation*, 139, and the authorities cited there.

25. The perfect tense suggests Christ has already made the journey and in terms of 9:24 is now to be found in the highest heaven (Gäbel, *Kulttheologie*, 215). On the multiple heavens see Bietenhard, *HimmlischeWelt*, 53–56; Peterson, *Hebrews and Perfection*, 143; Ellingworth, *Hebrews* (1993), 446; Lincoln, *Hebrews*, 93, 99; and see further below.

26. For example, Farrow, *Ascension and Ecclesia*, 33–35. Cf. Rissi, *Theologie*, 39.

we compare the ascent of Christ in 4:14 with the ascents of apocalyptic and mystical travelers. Such a comparison cannot but impress upon us the restraint with which our author writes. Levi in the *Testament of Levi* undertakes the journey for his consecration as priest in the temple in heaven. In his vision he travels from the lower heavens, in which are the angels charged with punishing sinners and the angelic armies prepared to attack the demonic powers, till he reaches the highest heaven of all where God dwells in the company of archangels who offer bloodless propitiatory sacrifices (3:4–5). Similarly, Isaiah in the *Ascension of Isaiah* sees the wonders of the seven heavens (7–9) as he goes to the place "above all the heavens" (7:22). Hebrews has little to say about Christ's journey through the heavens. It follows biblical custom and speaks of heaven in the plural (1:10; 4:14; 7:26; 8:1; 12:23, 25), and thus thinks of heaven as multitiered, but fascinatingly it refers specifically to heaven in the singular and emphasizes this: Christ "entered heaven itself" (*eisēlthen. . . eis ton auton ouranon*) (9:24).[27] The latter very likely is referring to the highest heaven. We shall return to this subject in chapter 7, but here note the fact that there is a justifiable case for believing that while Hebrews does not number the heavens its use of the singular at 9:24 permits us to think of the topmost one as the place where God has his temple and Christ exercises his ministry.[28]

If 4:14 implies that Christ travelled through successive celestial spheres on his ascent it is noteworthy that no mention is made of the obstacles that Jewish writers never fail to tell us the mystics encounter on their way to the heavenly temple. Still less is there any suggestion that, as Käsemann believed, Christ bursts through the barrier that the gnostics believed separated heaven and earth.[29]

Spatial imagery of the vertical kind common in apocalyptic is used by the writer, but it is simply intended as a backdrop to the epigrammatic statement at the outset of the sermon: "when he had made purification for sins, he sat down at the right hand of the Majesty on high"(1:3). The journey Christ made is for the purpose of taking him to the place where he can undertake his ministry (4:15–16), occupying the position

27. Cf. Heb 7:26c ("exalted above the heavens," i.e., the heaven above all heavens). Cf. Traub, "Ouranos," 528. On the heavens in Hebrews see Ellingworth, *Hebrews* (1993), 476; Lincoln, *Hebrews*, 93–94, 99; Mackie, *Eschatology and Exhortation*, 157–64; Schenck, *Cosmology and Eschatology*, 173–75.

28. So Hofius, *Vorhang*, 70–71; Lane, *Hebrews 9–13*, 248.

29. On the rending of the veil in 10:19–20 see chapter 9.

of highest honor (7:26). Cosmology is not the primary interest of the writer and to expect consistency in the different references to the heavens may ultimately be futile, but if one may attempt to tease out what is said one may say that in his ascension/exaltation Jesus passed through the "heavens"[30] that represent the upper part of outer court of the sanctuary to enter and "heaven itself," the holy of holies.

Like Philo and Josephus, our author visualizes the cosmos as a temple and the uppermost part as the holy of holies.[31] Cosmological associations are apparent, but they are much less important to the writer than those connected with the cult. The journey of Christ through the heavens is modeled on the movement of the high priest into the holy of holies on the Day of Atonement,[32] and it is the idea of movement inherent in the use of this analogy, more than the stories of the journeys of apocalyptic travelers and Jewish mystics, that governs the imagery. This is clear not simply from the author's naming the pioneer high priest, but from the language of the passage. As Ellingworth points out, the syntax of 4:14 (*dierchomai* followed by the accusative) denotes movement through an area and beyond it (Acts 14:24; 15:3, 41; 16:6; 19:1, 21; 20:2; 1 Cor 16:5) and this is confirmed by the spatial imagery in Hebrews 7:26 ("above the heavens").[33] Attridge's comment is apt. "This passage (through the heavens) will later be described in terms of movement through the temple and Christ will be depicted as entering 'through the veil' into the true heavenly sanctuary (cf. 6:19–20; 8:1–2; 9:11, 24; 10:20)."[34]

The presentation of the exaltation or ascension of Christ to heaven and his entry into the holy of holies in terms of the high priest processing into the holy of holies on the Day of Atonement forms the basis of

30. DeSilva, *Perseverance*, 70. One must question Rissi when he says that in Heb 4:14, "the movement of the high priest is not 'vertical,' but 'horizontal'" (*Theologie*, 39). Although this accords with the movement of the high priest into the holy of holies it ignores the very obvious vertical imagery of the companion text, 7:26, not to speak of the vertical imagery implied in the passages on Jesus' exaltation (1:3; 7:26; 8:1; 12:2). Cf. Traub, "Ouranos," 527–28; Cody, *Heavenly Sanctuary*, 78–84; Mackie, *Eschatology and Exhortation*, 157–64.

31. See chapter 6. Helmut Koester interprets the "tent," i.e., the outer part, as "a symbol for the heavenly regions through which Christ was to pass to enter the sanctuary itself" ("Outside the Camp," 309).

32. Moffatt, *Hebrews*, 120; Schrenk, "Archiereus," 281; Spicq, *Hébreux* 2, 256; Attridge, *Hebrews*, 139; Isaacs, *Sacred Space*, 210–11; Koester, *Dwelling of God*, 160.

33. Ellingworth, *Hebrews* (1993), 267.

34. Attridge, *Hebrews*, 139.

everything that follows in the main body of the sermon. In the course of his exposition the author will stress the definitive nature of Christ's single entry into his sanctuary, contrasting it with the repetitive entries of the Levitical high priests into the holy of holies (9:12; *mYoma* 5). The use of both the adverbs "repeatedly" (*pollakis*) and "once" (*hapax*) conveys the absolute nature of Christ's entry and offering (9:12, 26; 10:10). Yet for all the importance of Christ's entry into the heavenly sanctuary has for the author it is not followed by a display of the embellishments one finds in accounts of the heavenly temple in Jewish writings. The impressive architectural features of the sanctuary that fascinated the author of the *Songs of the Sabbath Sacrifice* obviously held no interest for this writer. The angels who crowd around the triumphant Melchizedek in 11 QMelch.ii.10 do not wait on this high priest. We hear nothing like the *Songs*. What our author wants his friends to know about the sanctuary in heaven, more than anything else, is that it is occupied by Jesus Christ and has been opened up to receive all (10:20; cf. 6:19).

With Christ installed in the heavenly sanctuary the great invitation is issued: "Let us therefore approach the throne of grace" (4:16). This appeal will be repeated more than once.[35] The author is obviously anxious that his congregation should know that Christ's death on the cross has lasting benefit and this is available and should be experienced by all. As high priest the exalted Christ is continuously making his sacrifice available and effective.

In 6:19–20 the pioneer motif appears again under the corresponding figure of the forerunner (*prodromos*).[36]

> We have this hope, a sure and steadfast anchor of the soul, a hope that enters the inner shrine behind the curtain, where Jesus, a forerunner (*prodromos*) on our behalf, has entered, having become a high priest forever according to the order of Melchizedek (6:19–20).[37]

Although *prodromos* is generally understood as a military metaphor and was used for the one who led others in battle or the foremost runner in a race, its association here with the high priest results in an amazing collocation of images. The preacher is telling his congregation that in the Christian dispensation the high priest is no solitary figure making

35. On the exhortations to enter the heavenly sanctuary see chapter 9.

36. On the pioneer motif see appendix A.

37. On 6:19–20 see more in chapter 9.

his way into an inviolate sanctum but one of a company: the *prodromos* and his followers.[38] This extraordinary picture of the pioneer priest is the basis of the greatest thing the author has to tell his friends, viz. you have direct access to God.[39] Its key importance for understanding the central argument on Christ's atoning work in chapters 7–10 will become clear as we proceed.

The introduction of the veil in 6:19 prepares the way for the revolutionary statement in 10:20 that Christ has thrown open the holy of holies for all to enter. Described here as the veil in front of "the inner shrine" (*to esōteron tou katapetasmatos*) it is very obviously the heavy inner veil that shielded the holy of holies (Lev 16:2, 12, 15. Cf. Exod 26:31–35; Lev 21:23; 24:3; Philo, *Mos.* 2:101; Josephus *Ant.* 8:75; Heb 9:3, 10:19–20).[40] Of the august inner shrine Josephus informs us, "In this stood nothing whatever; unapproachable, inviolable, invisible to all, it was called the Holy of Holies" (*J.W.* 5.219). [41] Into the supremely sacred space that lay behind the veil Jesus has entered as forerunner. There could not be a more forthright statement of his significance.

Lastly in respect to the unit before us, the reference to Melchizedek (6:20) connects with 5:10 and the subject of the preceding verses (5:7–8). Otto Baurernfeind makes the interesting suggestion that *prodromos* in 6:20 looks back to the sufferings attributed to Jesus in 5:7–9 (which he understands to be referring to the whole of Jesus' life and work), i.e., the hardships experienced by the *prodromos* on the way to his becoming "the source of eternal salvation for all who obey him" (5:9).[42] This gives point to Koester's suggestion that the forerunner image is rhetorically effective.

38. On the pioneer as a relative term implying a sequence see appendix B.

39. See chapter 9. Cf. Lindars, *Theology*, 46–47.

40. Käsemann's view that the veil protecting the holy of holies was the gnostic band separating heaven from earth (*Wandering People*, 87–96) is decisively challenged by Hofius, who makes out a convincing case from apocalyptic and rabbinic sources (*Vorhang*). The veil stands for the great distance and inaccessibility separating God from the heavenly agents (Hofius, *Vorhang*, 8). See also Koester, *Dwelling of God*, 163–65. In the *Targum Pseudo-Jonathan* on Gen 37:17 Gabriel tells Joseph that he overheard "from behind the curtain" the date when the slavery in Egypt began.

41. In the case of the Second Temple the inner veil was made from the finest wool shot through with purple and scarlet (*m.Shek.* 8.5; cf. Josephus, *Ant* .8:75). Unlike the outer veil, which had no particular cultic significance and served in place of a door, the inner veil had the greatest possible significance (Schneider, "*Katapetasma*," 629).

42. "It is quite conceivable that the word *prodromos* corresponds to the content of 5.8f if the word refers not just to the final end of the course but to the preceding course itself with all its tests and trials" (Bauernfeind, "Prodromos," 235).

Speakers in antiquity emphasized the deeds that the hero performed, in particular those performed on behalf of others (Aristotle, *Rhetoric* 1.9.38; Quintilian, *Institutes* 3.7.17).[43] The import of the corporate overtones of the *prodromos* concept would not be lost on the members of the community. Joined as they are to their leader they could expect to share his tests and trials.

> They confessed that they were strangers and foreigners on the earth, for people who speak in this way make it clear that they are seeking a homeland. If they had been thinking of the land that they had left behind, they would have had opportunity to return. But as it is, they desire a better country, that is a heavenly one (Heb 11:13–16).

The underlying thought of chapter 11 is akin to the pilgrimage motif. The author summons up a host of individuals who looked beyond their contemporary scene to the future. Some of them do not appear as very obvious examples of faith, and certainly not the best examples the Bible has to offer. The principle of selection is to be found in the relevance of the characters to the experience of those listening to the sermon. Comparisons with similar Jewish and Greco-Roman lists help only up to a point. The heroes and heroines in Hebrews have none of the glory and honor of their counterparts in the other lists.[44] Similarly, attempts to find a source or prototype, possibly from the Hellenistic synagogue, have not had convincing outcomes. If the author used an existing source he subjected it to his own viewpoint and aim. He uses the stories of alienation to speak to people who had themselves experienced alienation, had their property stolen and suffered public abuse because of their faith (10:32–34).

In structure, chapter 11 is a well-defined section, marked out by the reference to faith in the *inclusio* (11:1–2 and 11:39–40), but anticipated by 10:38, "My righteous one shall live by faith."[45]

43. Koester, *Hebrews*, 335.

44. For similar retelling of Israel's history see Ps 78:1–16; Wisd 10:1–19; Sir 44:1—49:16; 1 Macc 2:51–60; 3 Macc 2:2–20; 4 Macc 16:16–23. Cf. Acts 7; 1 Clem 4.1–13; 9.2—12.8; 17.1—19.3; 31.2—32.4. See at length Cosby, *Rhetorical Composition*, 45–106, 111–61.Eisenbaum makes a convincing attempt at profiling the heroes and heroines in terms of the marginalization of the righteous, their separation from the unrighteous and their future orientation (*Jewish Heroes*). For an alternative interpretation of Hebrews 11 see Hays, "No Lasting City," 167.

45. Vanhoye, *Structure littéraire*, 180–81. Subtle rhetorical effect results from the changing of the inverted clause of Hab 2:4 in 10:38 ("anyone who shrinks back") from the expected eschatological deliverer to the Christian believer. Cf. Lane, *Hebrews 9–13*,

There are four well-marked parts to the chapter. The opening one defines faith (11:1–3). Verses 3–31 are artfully connected by anaphora or the repetition of the introductory phrase "By faith." Verse 32 marks an abrupt change, but the rhetorical "what more should I say?" serves to strengthen the argument by referring to countless known and unknown individuals who were not delivered from suffering and death (11:32–38).[46] The closing verses are a form of epilogue (11:39–40). They summarize the examples quoted and at the same time connect the hearers with the witnesses of faith. The way is thereby prepared for the supreme example of faithful perseverance, Jesus the pioneer and perfecter of faith (12:1–2).[47]

The roll call begins with Abel. Commentators have been hard put to explain why God preferred his offering to Cain's (Gen 4:1–16) and why the author of Hebrews chooses him as an example of faith. For our purpose it is interesting to find there is a rabbinic tradition in the Targums that suggests a connection between Abel and the futuristic thrust of Hebrews. It attributes to Abel belief in the world to come and God's just treatment of the righteous and the wicked—things denied by Cain.[48] If this explanation of the story was current at the time of our author he may have included Abel because he saw him as an example of faith looking to the future (11:26; cf. 10:35). Thus the addressees are urged to look beyond the injustices they presently suffer to God's reward of righteousness (11:6, 26; cf. 10:35–36).

Enoch's translation to heaven as briefly reported in Genesis 5:21–24 must have been of more than usual interest to the author since it is mentioned at length (11:5–6). It was also of much interest to Jewish writers who made a great deal of Enoch's travels through the heavenly worlds. As

---

306–7; O'Brien, *Hebrews*, 393.

46. On the significance of the anaphoric "by faith" see, for example, Cosby, *Rhetorical Composition*, 11, 42.

47. On faith as faithfulness in Hebrews see Grässer, *Glaube*; Thompson, *Beginnings of Christian Philosophy*, 53–80; DeSilva, *Perseverance*, 382–87. DeSilva argues for the patron-client connotations of the word faith in Hebrews (*Perseverance*, 61–62). On this reading, Heb 11:6 is translated "[God] is the benefactor of those who diligently seek him" (DeSilva, *Perseverance*, 440). Viewed in this light the blessings God gives entail the obligation to "keep faith" with him. Faith therefore means not only belief in God and trusting him but also a reciprocal faithfulness, i.e., faith in Hebrews involves both faith and works. Cf. Schenck, *Understanding Hebrews*, 65.

48 McNamara, *Targum Neofiti: Genesis*, 66–67. Cf. Dunnill, *Covenant and Sacrifice*, 151.

far as Hebrews is concerned, it is clear that, important as Enoch's ascent to heaven was to Jewish writers, what mattered to our author is the fact that Enoch's way of life was pleasing to God (11:5–6). It is this that the author is commending to his listeners. In spite of all they have to endure they should strive to win God's approval (10:36; 13:15–16).

Noah apparently wins a place in the list of worthies because he looked to "events as yet unseen" (11:7). Despite all the evidence to the contrary, he believed what God said about the impending disaster and built the ark. In other words, Noah did not allow himself to be preoccupied with his immediate concerns but prepared for the future. His faith and resultant action thus secured the future for himself and his family. The message for the listeners is clear. They should pay attention to the warnings they have been given (9:28; 10:25, 37–38; 12:25–29) and join the pilgrimage to the city which is to come (11:10; 13:14).

The extended treatment that Abraham receives indicates his great importance to the author and his hearers (11:8–12, 17–19).[49] It gives eloquent expression to the futuristic orientation of the sermon. The repetition of "he went out" in 11:8 is deliberate. The writer has an eye on his listeners and will return to them in 13:13. For Abraham to leave his home in Haran meant a great deal more than domestic upheaval and the sundering of societal bonds. The importance of one's native country for one's identity and status, and what its loss meant for one's standing in society and the practice of one's religion, is well documented in both Jewish and Greco-Roman literature.[50] Ben Sira gives a pitiful account of the life of the stranger (Sir 29:24–28; cf. 1 Chron 29:15). Philo says that no one easily accepts demotion to the status of a foreigner and the loss of one's rights (*Flacc* 54). Lucian declares that "to sojourn is a reproach" (*My Native Land* 8), and Plutarch says that to have to live away from one's native country incurs reproach and dishonor (*De exil.* 17 [*Mor.* 607A]). The same is the case in the biblical tradition. The psalmist could not sing the Lord's song in a strange land (137:4). While Genesis acknowledges Abraham was a sojourner (*paroikos*) (23:4; cf. 17: 8 LXX), Jewish writers refrain from speaking about this.[51] Philo actually plays down Abraham's alien status by telling us that "he hastened eagerly to obey not as though

---

49. For an analysis of the structure of this passage see Vanhoye, *Structure littéraire,* 186–89; O'Brien, *Hebrews,* 409–17.

50. DeSilva, *Perseverance,* 394–96.

51. Eisenbaum, *Jewish Heroes,* 155–57.

he were leaving home for a strange land, but rather as returning from amid strangers to his home" (*Abr* 62. Cf. Josephus, *Ant.* 1:154, 157).

In marked contrast, Hebrews goes out of its way to emphasize Abraham's alien existence. It describes the promised land as "a foreign land" (*tēn . . . allotrian*) (11:9) and says that even after Abraham and his family were in Canaan they still regarded themselves as aliens (11:9) (*en skēnais katoikēsas*). They knew that Canaan was not their home; they looked for "the city that has foundations" (11:10). They are continuously *en route*, living in tents. Although they had ample opportunity to return to their native land they did not take it, but persisted in acknowledging their status as "strangers and foreigners" (*xenoi kai parepidēmoi*) (11:13).[52] The listeners are urged to view their lives in the same detached way.

The record of the faithful resumes with the anaphoric "by faith" when the writer returns to Abraham to record his supreme test of faith: the offering up of his son—the one upon whom God's promise entirely depended (11:17–19). The story impresses on the listeners Abraham's willingness to do what God asked, however irrational it appeared. Where the modern reader expects the author to attribute to Abraham revulsion and protestations, our author is silent. His interest in Isaac is that he should live to produce offspring.[53] God had promised, "It is through Isaac that descendants shall be named after you" (11:18, quoting Genesis 21:12). Isaac will live.[54] He will invoke blessings *for the future* on Jacob and Esau (11:20). After Abraham's testing is the fulfillment of God's promise. The author hopes his audience will see that God is in their trials. The future looks without hope; but God can be trusted. He will give new life to the faithful.[55]

The faith of Isaac, Jacob and Joseph comes next (11:20–22). It illustrates the truth already stated (11:13): they looked beyond their

52. See the transformation of these demeaning terms in 1 Pet 1:17; 2:11; cf. Phil. 3:20; Hermas, *Sim* 1; Elliott, *A Home for the Homeless*. Elliott takes the *paroikoi* of 1 Peter literally, but regards the "strangers and foreigners" of Hebrews figuratively. I follow Lane in believing the terms in Hebrews are literal (*Hebrews 1–8*, lxiv–lxvi). In any event, our author is anxious that his addressees should see themselves as citizens of God's city and resist conforming to the values and practices of an unbelieving world, whilst accepting its challenges and serving those in need (13:13–16).

53. Eisenbaum, *Jewish Heroes*, 162.

54. O'Brien, *Hebrews*, 424–25.

55. Koester, *Hebrews*, 499. Abraham's obedience when tested by God is commended by God in second temple Judaism (Sir 44:20; 1 Macc 2:52; 4 Macc 16:20; Jdt 8:25–26).

immediate circumstances, and when they died they did so "in faith." By blessing their heirs and pointing them to the future (11:20–21) they demonstrated unwavering trust in the divine promises.[56]

The account of Moses is remarkable for what it does not say.[57] There is nothing on God's call, Moses' intercessory role, or the covenant at Sinai. The only aspect of his role as national leader that receives mention is his institution of Passover (11:28). The fact that Moses did not enter the promised land is ignored by the author. What he dwells on is Moses' concern for God's people (11:25), which led him to spurn the wealth and security of Pharaoh's court and expose himself to the privations and dangers that resulted from his decision to help them (11:27). At a deeper level, his choice was guided by his determination to identify with Christ in his humiliation (11:26). Like Moses, the audience had suffered denunciation themselves (10:33), lost their possessions (10:32–34), and they were likely to do so again (12:7–11; 13:13).[58]

The inclusion of Rahab in the list of worthies (11:31) has puzzled readers from the earliest times. The textual variants for verse 31, which refer to her as "the so-called prostitute," may witness to a tradition that wanted to turn her into a respectable innkeeper (Josephus, *Ant.* 5:5–8). As far as our text is concerned, morality is not an issue. What Rahab had heard about Israel's God impressed her greatly and, with an eye on the future, she was ready to befriend the spies. She identified herself with the journeying people of God and showed she had faith that God would give them the land (Josh 2:8–11). Her daring action, undertaken at great risk to herself, was rewarded. She looked not at the things that are seen, but at what is unseen. When the invading Israelites captured and torched Jericho, Rahab was saved (Josh 6:15–25). The moral of the story is that if this female of ill-repute and a foreigner can exhibit a faith that is oriented toward the future, without regard to the risks, how much more should this be possible in the case of those listening to the sermon.

As the chapter works to a close the tempo rises. The piling up of names and the heightened rhetoric intensify the tension. First, we have the early rulers in Israel, then the prophets (11:32). This is followed by

56. Ellingworth, *Hebrews* (1993), 604–7; Koester, *Hebrews,* 499–500; O'Brien, *Hebrews,* 425–27.

57. Eisenbaum, *Jewish Heroes,* 171.

58. Manson, *Hebrews,* 79. Cf. Koester, *Hebrews,* 503. On the implicit argument from the greater to the lesser (Quintilian, *Inst.* 5.11.9) used in Heb 11 see Koester, *Hebrews,* 509–10, 550.

a graphic depiction of achievements and deliverances, each achieved "through faith." Women follow and are honored (11:35). Next are those whose deliverance lay not in this life but the next (11:36–39). The images that depict their persecution with awful intensity are drawn from the Maccabean martyrs.[59] Their incredible suffering is matched only by their degradation and dishonor. Those who escaped death experienced rejection, public contempt and barbaric cruelty (11:36–38). Whatever the experiences of the recipients they should remember that they are in the company of very many who had suffered before them.

Apart from Us they should Not be Made Perfect (11:40)

The epilogue explains that it was through no fault on their part that the witnesses did not reach the great goal of their hopes; it was part of God's plan (11:39–40). It makes a point of connecting them with the recipients, declaring that "without us" they are not made perfect (11:40). The function of the story of the victories of faith in former times is intended to make the congregation see how urgently faith and endurance are required in their situation and how they will be rewarded.

The message of Hebrews 11 is compelling. God's people of former times looked beyond their difficulties and hardships to what God had promised them. They were at odds with the prevailing culture. The tension that resulted was exacerbated by their being marginalized, ridiculed, and persecuted to the point of death. Their amazing capacity to endure came from their faith in the unseen world and God's promise. All this is impressed upon the congregation. "All these, though they were commended for their faith, did not receive what was promised, since God had provided something better so that they would not, without us, be made perfect"(11:39–40).

Since the thought of chapter 11 runs into 12:1–2 and its call to "run the race that is set before us" a case might be made out for including the latter in the present chapter. However, as we shall argue, the language of 12:1–2, while evoking the forward-looking direction of the previous chapter, denotes athletic activity rather than pilgrimage.[60]

---

59. Tomes, "Heroism," 171–99.

60. Contra Sims, "Rethinking Hebrews 12.1," 54–88, on which see chapter 9.

Summary

The dramatic picture of Christ travelling through the heavens to reach the heavenly sanctuary in 4:14 has numerous parallels in Jewish literature. *T Levi* 3:4–5 is especially apt, since Levi, like Christ, travels to heaven for his consecration to the priesthood. However, the resemblance is no more than formal. What is determinative is the Day of Atonement analogy and the movement of the high priest into the holy of holies. In 4:14 we have a good example of the conflation of the pioneer and priestly motifs that is characteristic of the sermon. It is set in the context of the pilgrimage to Canaan. By making the pioneer/priest's journey follow directly that of the hapless generation of Israelites to their destination (3:7—4:13) the author promises a better outcome to those who follow him. The "rest" follows the Christian pilgrimage and is linked to the pioneer motif. It belongs to the series of forward-looking images that form the structure of the sermon and encourages the community to move out of its perilous position and embrace God's future. The "rest" that is the goal of Jesus' endeavors and theirs is best understood as entry into the heavenly sanctuary. It is both a future hope and a present possibility, the latter anticipating the appeals to pilgrims to "draw near" to the throne of grace. The faith and amazing capacity of the heroes and heroines of earlier times to persevere and endure and never surrender the hope of a better future is intended to motivate the listeners (11:39–40). The way is thus prepared for the presentation of "the pioneer and perfecter of faith" in 12:1–2 as the paradigm for responsible discipleship.

5

A Priest like Melchizedek

The interest Hebrews takes in Melchizedek is remarkable when one considers how little is said about this mysterious figure in Genesis 14 and Psalm 110, but no surprise when one takes into account the great interest in Melchizedek in second temple Judaism.[1] Numerous scholars believe that the author of Hebrews must have known of the extrabiblical traditions on Melchizedek,[2] but this is challenged by others. The latter argue that what the author says about Melchizedek is derived entirely from Gen 14:17–20, approached typologically from Ps 110:4.[3] This will be considered later in this chapter.

The introduction of the high priesthood of Christ "after the order of Melchizedek" is a bold and entirely new concept. It marks an important development in the Christology of the New Testament, not only by giving Jesus a priestly pedigree, but also by providing a basis for understanding his continuing ministry. Its very obvious importance for the author is registered at the outset by his connecting Christ's priestly work ("he made purification for sins") to his leading motif of Christ the eternal Son (1:2–3)[4] and thus with the community's confession of faith. References

1. See appendix C (the Escatological Priest).

2. Yadin, "Melchizedek and Qumran," 152–54; Fitzmyer, "Further Light on Melchizedek," 41; Delcor, "Melchizedek," 126–27. Cf. Jonge and van der Woude, "11QMelchizedek," 320–23; Longenecker, "Melchizedek Argument," 175–79; Rooke, *Zadok's Heirs*, 88; Hofius, "Melchisedek," 951–52.

3 McCullough, "Melchizedek's Varied Role," 52–66; Cockerill, "Melchizedek Without Speculation," 17–24. For the view that Hebrews does not use extrabiblical sources see Koester, *Hebrews*, 340–41.

4. Cockerill, *Melchizedek Christology*, 143–48. A further reference to Christ's priesthood in 1:2–3 is seen by Lane. He writes, "The declaration that the Son has been

to the Son frame the exposition on Christ's unique priesthood (7:3, 28). "It is a reminder of the community's own formal confession (3:1; 4:14; 10:23) as the starting point of all Christological reflection."[5] At the same time, the author is careful not to exalt Melchizedek so that he is equal to or even greater than Christ. Melchizedek is like the Son of God; the Son of God is not like Melchizedek (7:3d). His aim is to present Melchizedek as a prototype of a priesthood that depends not on a genealogical pedigree but a special quality of life (7:1–10, 13–17).[6]

In preparation for the determinative central section on Christ's priesthood in the heavenly sanctuary the author devotes a lengthy exposition to Melchizedek (7:1–28). It is a surprise to many readers of Hebrews that the author introduces his extraordinary claim that Jesus is "a priest after the order of Melchizedek" at 5:6 and 5:10 only to break it off and deal with other matters (5:11—6:18) and not return to the subject till later (6:20—7:22).[7] Longenecker believes that of the different possible explanations for the author's apparent hesitancy the most likely is to think that he is addressing converts (possibly from Qumran) who before their conversion held Melchizedek in high regard. He says, "He (Melchizedek) is at the centre of his argument, but he is also at a crucial point of difference between the Christian faith which he is calling his addressees to reaffirm and their old allegiances to which they are being enticed again. And in such a situation his initial hesitancy to elaborate a Melchizedekian argument is somewhat understandable."[8] This is an attractive suggestion, but a connection with Qumran is contested. The problem that Longenecker and others find here is very likely to be explained by the author's customary rhetorical strategy, preparing his listeners for a subject he intends to deal with at a later stage. As we noted, Christ's priesthood (and thus Melchizedek's) is already introduced in the reference to Christ the Son at 1:2–3, a link acknowledged at 5:6, 8. The

---

exalted to a position at God's right hand bears an unmistakable allusion to Ps 110:1, for this is the only biblical text that speaks of someone enthroned beside God" (*Hebrews 1–8*, 16).

5. Pfitzner, *Hebrews*, 106.

6. DeSilva, *Perseverance*, 288.

7. What the relative pronoun (*hou*) of 5:11 refers back to is ambiguous. If the pronoun is neuter it is the whole subject of priesthood that is in mind, but if it is masculine the reference is to Melchizedek. Hence the NRSV marginal reading "him," and the REB, "Melchizedek."

8. Longenecker, "The Melchizedek Argument," 174. Cf. Hanson, *Jesus Christ*, 70–71.

digression would doubtless serve to ease the strain on those following the argument of the sermon. What it is the preacher wishes to get across to his hearers will become clearer as he proceeds.

More is to be said about the qualification of human experience necessary for the office of high priest, which was touched on fleetingly at 2:17 and 4:15. An illustration is used. "In the days of his flesh, Jesus offered up prayers and supplications, with loud cries and tears" (5:7). This agonized prayer for help distances Jesus effectively from the invincible hero figure of the classics, who, though aided by the gods, is in the final reckoning his own savior. The prayer raises several questions. Is it Jesus' trial in Gethsemane or his experiences in general that are in mind? Does the use of the cultic term *prospherein* ("offered") mean that the writer saw Christ in high priestly terms at this point?[9] What can the author mean by saying that Jesus "was heard because of his reverent submission (*apo tēs eulabeias*)" (5:8)? How may we say God answered Jesus' prayer? But what is not in any doubt is the very obvious point of the passage, viz. to show how fully Jesus shared human experience. He thus acquired a profound capacity for compassion and was thereby qualified to be a true high priest (4:15; cf. 5:1–2).[10]

Irrespective of the difficulties involved in understanding 5:7, most scholars believe it is Gethsemane that is in mind. In its favor is the reference to Jesus' obedience (5:8). Jesus could not have disobeyed on the cross, and there is nothing in the gospels that suggests Jesus elsewhere endured the terror conveyed by 5:7. But whether it is Jesus' trial in Gethsemane or hardships he underwent throughout his life (cf. 2:18), Jesus, in seeking help by appealing to God, is setting an example his followers are urged to follow (4:14–16). This becomes explicit as the exposition progresses (6:19–20; 10:19–25; 12:2–3). The needs of the community are again to the fore. Like

9. Christ's prayer in 5:7 is in the unit encapsulated by the references to the high priest in 5:1 and 5:10 (Guthrie, *Structure*, 82–3) and some exegetes think the prayer is based on the high priest's sacrifice for himself before sacrificing for the people (Stökl Ben Ezra, *Impact of Yom Kippur*, 119; cf. Lane, *Hebrews 1–8*, 119), but this strains the analogy of Christ and the high priest unjustifiably. Christ's sinlessness (4:15) does not necessitate his having to confess sins or to offer sacrifice for himself (Moffatt, *Hebrews*, 64; Attridge, *Hebrews*, 149).

10. Against the virtually consensus view that Gethsemane is the referent in 5:7–8, Richardson sees Jesus' priestly sufferings at Golgotha based on the Day of Atonement ("The Passion: Reconsidering Hebrews 5:7–8," 51–67).

their Lord, its members have to learn the pedagogical value of hardship and obedience and make a point of seeking God's help.[11]

The cultic character of the language in 5:7 (*prospherein*) very likely means that we should find anticipated here the idea of Christ's self-offering (5:1–2).[12] Against this is the fact that the thought of priestly self-offering does not become explicit till 7:27. However, in the mind of our author Gethsemane, the crucifixion, and exaltation are all intimately connected.[13] Thus we find the high priestly and pioneer motifs merging in 5.9: "he became the source (*aitios*) of eternal salvation for all who obey him." The primary meaning of *aitios* is "origin" or "originator,"[14] which is the meaning *archēgos* has at 12:2. Christ is the one who makes salvation possible.[15]

When another Priest arises resembling Melchizedek (7:15)

Why the author introduced a high priestly Christology in the first place has puzzled scholars.[16] However, given the all-important place the high priest occupied in Judaism, the use of the analogy in a document that aimed to convince a largely Jewish audience of the uniqueness of the Christian faith it is no surprise. As we note in appendix C, the analogy is used in early Christian writings outside the New Testament that are quite

---

11. DeSilva, *Perseverance*, 191–92.

12. Lane, *Hebrews 1–8*, 119; Koester, *Hebrews*, 298–99. Eberhart, "Characteristics of Sacrificial Metaphors," 55–56.

13. See, for example, Ellingworth (1993), 289. Cf. Lane, *Hebrews 1–8*, 119; Koester, *Hebrews*, 106, 298–99.

14. See chapter 3 and appendix A.

15. Westcott, *Hebrews*, 129; Hay, *Glory at the Right Hand*, 145. On the connection of the pioneer motif and the priestly ministry of Christ see Johnsson, "Cultus of Hebrews," 104–8.

16. The origins of Hebrews' high priestly Christology are obscure. For the view that the idea of the priesthood of Jesus is implicit elsewhere in the New Testament see Moe, "Priestertum Christi," 335–38. Some scholars find the source in John's gospel. Cf. Heil, "Jesus as the Unique High Priest," 729–45; Schille, "Erwägungen zur Hohenpriesterlehre," 90–91; Attridge, *Hebrews*, 97–103; Mackie, *Eschatology and Exhortation*, 183–85. Stökl Ben Ezra believes that while a direct relationship between Hebrews and 11QMelch cannot be proven "it is clear that both texts derive from a common *imaginaire*" ("Yom Kippur in Jewish Apocalyptic," 358). On the high priest and the eschatological high priest see appendix C.

independent of Hebrews. A specific need that may possibly explain the author's use of the high priestly motif could have been former Jews who felt spiritually and psychologically bereft of the temple of Jerusalem.[17]

A more pertinent question is why the writer went farther and introduced the strange figure of Melchizedek. There are several possible reasons. In the first place, it provided a solution to a problem he had encountered. Having decided to portray Jesus in terms of a high priest, he had to deal with a practical difficulty: "For it is evident that our Lord was descended from Judah, and in connection with that tribe Moses (i.e. the law) said nothing about priests" (7:14).[18] Descent from Judah may have qualified Jesus to become a messiah, but it nullified his chances as a priestly figure. The law was specific: priests could only come from the line of Levi and descendants of Aaron (Exod 40:15; Num 25:13; cf. Jer 33:18). Josephus is adamant that no one "should hold God's high priesthood save him who is of Aaron's blood," and "no one of another lineage, even if he happened to be a king, should attain to the high priesthood" (*Ant.* 20:226).[19] Similarly, Philo described the Levitical priesthood as "that perfect priesthood by which mortality is commended to and recognized by God" (*Sacr.* 132; cf. *Mos.* 2.5; *Spec.* 1.80).[20]

From the perspective of his christological reading of Psalm 110 the author found in Genesis 14 one whose priesthood conveniently predated the Levitical priesthood and who combined in himself the offices of both priest and king.[21] The fact that Melchizedek received tithes from Abraham and gave the patriarch his blessing proved that he was greater than Abraham and, by implication, greater than Abraham's descendant, Levi, who as it were, paid tithes to him through Abraham (7:9). Jesus' office as high priest does not depend on lineage or law. It is directly and solely by divine appointment (7:20–21, 28). This exegetical *tour de force* to make

17. See Lindars, *Theology.* Cf. Isaacs, *Reading Hebrews and James*, 12–13.

18. On the Davidic line of Jesus see Matt 1:1; Luke 1:32, 69; Rom 1:3; Acts 2:29–36; 13:22–23; 2 Tim 2:8.

19. Koester, *Hebrews*, 360.

20. Koester, *Hebrews*, 358.

21. On Ps 110:4 as the sole source of the writer's thought on Jesus as high priest see McCullough, "Melchizedek's Varied Role," 57–58; Lindars, "Rhetorical Structure of Hebrews," 395–96; Isaacs, *Sacred Space*, 150. For the messianic interpretation by the rabbis see Strack and Billerbeck. *Kommentar*, IV, 452–65.

Jesus a high priest who is superior to the Levitical priests is impressive. Isaacs believes that it in fact subverts the Jewish cult entirely.[22]

Melchizedek is also introduced because of his enduring priesthood (5:6; 6:20; 7:3, 17, 22). This served not only to demonstrate the superiority of Christ's priesthood but also his eternal ministry. This was of particular relevance to people who were being made aware of their need of a new commitment to Jesus Christ and the demands of discipleship in an uncertain world. They have the help of one who "remains" (*menei*, 7:3), who "lives" (*zē*, 7:8; cf. 7:24). He arose (*anistēmi*) in the form (*tēn homoiotēta*) of Melchizedek. This is defined in a striking manner as the result of "the power of an indestructible life" (*zōēs akatalutou*) (7:16).[23] "Consequently, he is able for all time to save those who approach God through him, since he always lives to make intercession for them" (7:25). In other words, the acknowledgment that Jesus is a priest "like Melchizedek" means he is priest by virtue of his resurrection (13:20), understood by Hebrews as his exaltation (1:3; 7:26).[24]

But we should be open to the possibility that our alert author may have had a further reason for introducing Melchizedek. As we see in appendix C, numerous Jewish groups took considerable interest in an eschatological and angelic priest, often referred to as Melchizedek. The important text 11Q Melchizedek differs from Hebrews in a number of respects, as we are to see, but it has more points of contact with Hebrews' conception of Melchizedek than do other presentations of this figure in Second Temple writings.

The Qumran text accords to Melchizedek the greatest possible importance, at least comparable to that given to the archangel Michael in other Jewish texts.[25] The fact that the role of executor of the final judgment attributed to Melchizedek (ii:1–12) is the same role that Michael

---

22. Isaacs, "Priesthood," 56. Isaacs writes, "This argument is far more subversive than the Qumran Covenanters' denial of the legitimacy of Jerusalem's current high priestly incumbents. This is no mere argument as to which branch of the Levitical tribe should occupy that office. It does away with the notion of a priestly caste altogether"(57).

23. "The secret of the Christology of Hb. is to be found in 7:16" (Büchsel, "Akatalutos," 339). Cf. Peterson, *Hebrews and Perfection*, 110–11; Moffitt, "If Another Priest Arises," 68–79.

24. On the place Melchizedek has in the sermon's emphasis on the eternal work of Christ see, e.g., Brooks, "The Perpetuity of Christ's Sacrifice," 305–14.

25. For the heavenly priesthood exercised by Michael see *3 Bar* 11; *b.Hag.* 12b; *Zeb.* 62a; *Men.* 110a. Cf. Jonge and van der Woude, "11Q Melchizedek," 305.

has (1 En 10:11–12) leads some scholars to think that Melchizedek in 11QMelchizedek is the archangel Michael in another guise.[26] The nearest Hebrews gets to the role of avenger and judge attributed to Melchizedek in 11QMelchizedek is the passing reference to Christ's enemies becoming his footstool (2:8 = Ps 110:1). Although the Qumran text says nothing of Melchizedek's journey to heaven nor has anything that might indicate that he had an earthly life prior to his exalted heavenly life, we can assume these are presupposed.[27] This is all the more credible if Melchizedek is identified as the Teacher of Righteousness. The same conclusion follows if Melchizedek was Michael, since the War Scroll has Michael present and active in the final battle between good and evil (1 QM 17:5–8; cf. 4 Q544:2.3).[28]

It is hard to believe that our author was ignorant of the prolific traditions that had grown up around Melchizedek. He is interested in angels and makes a point of recording the extrabiblical tradition that angels had the honored role of acting on God's behalf when the law was entrusted to Moses (2:2. Cf. Acts 7:53; Gal 3:19; Jub 1:27; 2:1; Josephus, *Ant.* 15:136; CD 5:18), as well as including them in his great climactic scene (12:24). And we have to explain the fact that for all his interest in Ps 110:4 the author departs from this text to make Christ a *high* priest.

What is particularly interesting to us is the fact that 11Q Melchizedek depicts Melchizedek acting as high priest on the eschatological Day of Atonement. This is indicated by mention of the first day of the tenth jubilee (ii:7), i.e., Yom Kippur (Lev 25:9). Sins are expiated by Melchizedek (ii.8) and the prisoners of Belial are set free (ii:2.4–5, 13, 25). Angels are in attendance (ii:10). Although Melchizedek is not actually called a priest, there is no doubt that he is one, in fact a high priest no less (ii:7–8, 25).[29] Such transcendentalizing of the Day of Atonement and the high priest and his eschatological ministry in the heavenly temple is necessarily of interest to students of Hebrews. Relevant too is the characterization

---

26. Brooke, "Melchizedek (11QMelch)," 687.

27. As Alexander observes, if the Melchizedek of 11QMelch is the same Melchizedek of Gen 14:10–18 and Ps 110:4 then he is very likely to be thought of as another of the human personalities who ascended to heaven and been transformed into an angelic being (*Mystical Texts*, 70).

28. Fitzmyer, "Further Light on Melchizedek," 25–41; Alexander, *Mystical Texts*, 70–71.

29. Puech, "Notes sur le manuscrit," 511–13.

of Melchizedek as a warrior who does battle with Belial (ii:11–13), since this resonates with Christ's conflict with the devil in Heb 2:14.[30]

The similarities which 11QMelchizedek bears to Hebrews cause some students of Hebrews to believe that chapter 7 is an exhortation to converts from Essenism who were hankering after their Jewish beliefs and practices, which included the idea of Melchizedek as a heavenly redeemer figure. Some go so far as to say that the common features make it no longer necessary to think that the conception of a heavenly high priest in Hebrews may have been influenced by Hellenistic Jewish or gnostic traditions.[31] However, the use made of Melchizedek in Hebrews is too positive for it to be construed as an attack on erroneous views attributed to him in this Dead Sea text.[32] Hebrews differs from 11Q Melchizedek in the following ways.[33]

(a) The classic texts in Hebrews, viz. Gen 14:17–20 and Ps 110:4, do not appear in 11QMelchizedek. Instead we have Lev 25:9; Deut 15:2; Isa 52:7; 61:2–3; Pss 2:8–9; 82:2, none of which is used in Hebrews.[34]

(b) Angels are given an exalted position in 11Q Melchizedek (ii:10–11), whereas they are subordinated (1:5–13) as well as honored in Hebrews (1:14; 2:2; 12:22).[35] In Hebrews it is Christ alone who is in the inner sanctum in contrast to 11QMelchizedek which has Melchizedek in the company of the angels.

---

30. Jonge and van der Woude, "11QMelchizedek," 317–18; Aschim, "Melchizedek and Jesus," 140–41.

31. Kosmala, *Hebräer-Essener-Christen.* Cf. Coppens, "Les affinités qumrâniennes," 128–41.

32. McCullough, "Some Recent Developments," 48; Rooke, "Jesus as Royal Priest," 84.

33. Hay, *Glory at the Right Hand,* 138, 152–53; McCullough, "Some Recent Developments," 147–48; Hurst, *Hebrews,* 58–60; Kobelski , *Melchizedek and Melchireša,* 153.

34. The differences in the Old Testament texts used in Hebrews and 11QMelch are taken by Gareth L. Cockerill to mean that the author of the Qumran text did not intend to identify his Melchizedek with the figure in Genesis and Psalm 110, but was using the title in its literal sense of "king of righteousness" ("Melchizedek: or 'King of Righteousness,'" 311–12).

35. On the subordination of the angels in Heb 1 in relation to chapter 7 see Jonge and van der Woude, "11Q Melchizedek," 314–16; cf. Hurst, *Hebrews,* 45–46; Son, *Zion Symbolism,* 105–111. On the disputed question whether angels have a role in the cultus in Hebrews (1:14; cf. 12:22) see Ellingworth, *Hebrews* (1993), 132–33.

(c) Notwithstanding all that Hebrews says about the greatness of Christ, his humanity and suffering are shown in the strongest possible way (4:15; 5:7–10). In 11QMelchizedek all the emphasis is on a being who was not anything other than one who had been transformed into a glorified or angelic being, identified, it would seem, with the *èlohim* of Ps 82:1.

(d) In Hebrews Melchizedek "serves only as the precedent for and prototype of a greater high priesthood."[36] In 11Q Melchizedek occupies center stage.

(e) In Hebrews the decisive eschatological event has taken place and Jesus is already functioning in the heavenly sanctuary. 11QMelchizedek the work of Melchizedek lies in the future in the tenth and final Jubilee (11QMelch ii:7).

(f) Melchizedek is not called a priest in 11QMelch, and although many scholars infer that he was a priest from the role attributed to him in the text (ii:7–8), some do not accept this.[37]

(g) In 11QMelch Melchizedek's role as an avenger and judge (ii:11–14) contrasts with the salvific role of Christ which is emphasized repeatedly in Hebrews.

However, although these differences have persuaded some students of Hebrews to reject the idea that the author knew of 11Q Melchizedek one cannot in all honesty dismiss the very significant parallels: the location is in the heavenly sanctuary, the context is indisputably eschatological, and most importantly the central figure is the high priest who is functioning on the definitive Day of Atonement. Parallels of course do not prove dependence but they do indicate similar traditions.

That our author was familiar with traditions differing from his own is not to be seriously doubted. A glance at the noncanonical texts alluded to in Hebrews that are listed in appendix III of the Nestle-Aland *Novum Testamentum Graece* will prove this. We have already noted the fact that the author draws on a noncanonical tradition when he says that the law was delivered by angels and not, as Exod 20:1 says, directly by

36. Longenecker, "Melchizedek Argument," 178; Lane, *Hebrews 1–8*, 171; Koester, *Hebrews*, 343. "The reader is never allowed to forget that the object of interest is not Melchizedek in himself but the one whom the psalm oracle likens to him" (Hay, *Glory at the Right Hand*, 146).

37. Puech, "Notes sur le manuscrit," 483–513; Kobelski, *Melchizedek and Melchireša*, 64–82; Koester, *Hebrews*, 340.

God himself (Jub 1:27, 29; 2:1; 5:1–2; etc.; Josephus. *Ant.* 15:136). Note also should be taken of Heb 7:8. The reference here to a "witness" or "testimony" (*marturoumenous*) that Melchizedek is living may also be evidence of an extrabiblical source. It is possible of course that it refers to Psalm 110:4 (cf. 7:17), but when we take 7:8 in relation to the fact that it is Melechizedek's never ending priesthood (not his never-ending life) that is referred to in Psalm 110:4 we are obliged to ask whether 7:8 is referring to a source outside the LXX, written or oral. Indeed one must entertain the possibility that the traditions on Melchizedek were so well-known that our author did not need to make explicit reference to them, and in any case he would have had to treat them with reserve.[38]

It is Hay's opinion that "there can be little doubt that the author of the epistle knew more than he chose to elaborate (7:1–3)."[39] Similarly, Attridge says,

> There is something suspicious about our author's reticence and, particularly when he refers to the "life" that Melchizedek is attested as possessing (vs. 8), he presses literary observations to the breaking point. His argument there makes little sense if the Melchizedek whom Abraham encountered were not greater than the patriarch precisely because of the unlimited life attributed to him. It seems likely, then, that his exposition of Gen 14 is not simply an application to a figure of the Old Testament of attributes proper to Christ, but is based upon contemporary speculation about the figure of Melchizedek as a divine or heavenly being.[40]

It is essential that Melchizedek should not be viewed in isolation but in relation to the angelic or heavenly savior beings that were popular in Judaism when Christianity appeared on the scene. These were no longer simply spokespersons of God but priestly figures of great power and influence who acts as intercessors and engage in acts of propitiation for the

38. One must take issue with Cockerill for not commenting on the fact that there is no reference to a *high* priest in Ps 110:4 ("Melchizedek without Speculation," 28–44). It is surprising to find Longenecker saying that Hebrews "found in Ps 110:4 the explicit biblical support he needed for a high-priestly Christology" ("Melchizedek Argument," 177).

39. Hay, *Glory at the Right Hand*, 153. So also Schenck, *Cosmology and Eschatology*, 100.

40. Attridge, *Hebrews*, 191. So also Longenecker, "Melchizedek Argument," 175–79; Loader, *Sohn und Hoherpriester*, 213–15; Kobelski, *Melchizedek and Melchireša*, 126.

human race.[41] The enormous importance attributed to angels in apocalyptic, Qumran, and rabbinic material and the appearance of angels with priestly functions in certain early Christian writings is well documented.[42] Readers of Hebrews cannot fail to notice that the writer no sooner finishes introducing his sermon than he plays down the importance of angels, asserting the superiority of Christ (1:5–13).

However, if the author was familiar with the postbiblical traditions on Melchizedek he made sure that in introducing the subject of Melchizedek it is Christ who stands out as the much more important figure. The fact that this is repeatedly asserted (5:6, 10; 6:20; 7:17) may indicate that he was deliberately distancing himself from traditions crediting greater and greater importance to Melchizedek. It is possible that the hesitation which Longenecker found strange in the author's introduction of Melchizedek may have resulted from the fact that, in Hay's words, "large clouds of speculation swirled about Melchizedek,"[43] and he needed to handle the subject with great care.

A High Priest forever according to the Order of Melchizedek (6:20)

What we have on Melchizedek in chapter 7 is an ingenious and closely reasoned argument. The debate that Hebrews 7 has produced among scholars results to some extent from the figure behind the narrative being taken to be some sort of literal being. Our preacher begins by building up a case for the greatness of Melchizedek. He does this by telling us that (a) the great founding father of Israel paid homage to him (7:1–2) and (b) by saying that Melchizedek is "without father, without mother, without genealogy, having neither beginning of days nor end of life, but resembling the Son of God, he remains a priest forever"(7:3, 21). Psalm 110:4 is used messianically and the reference to the king's living forever is taken to be the priest king who is greater than Abraham (*eis to diēnekes* of 7:3 = *eis ton aiōna* of 7:24).[44] In the normal course of events any significant

41. Bietenhard, *Himmlische Welt*, 135–42; Cody, *Heavenly Sanctuary*, 47–55; Dunn, *Christology*, 151–54; Attridge, *Hebrews*, 97–100.

42. Appendix C.

43. Hay, *Glory at the Right Hand*, 159.

44. As Longenecker says, "For the writer to the Hebrews, the Melchizedek of Genesis 14 is an enigma that finds its solution in Psalm 110:4, but only when Psalm 110 is recognized as having messianic relevance" ("Melchizedek Argument," 176). More

male without an ancestry and genealogy would have been a nobody, but the author adroitly circumvents this and uses the silence of Genesis on Melchizedek's ancestry and genealogy to his advantage. The rabbis said that what is not in the law of Moses does not exist.[45] This may explain the author's reasoning and his crediting eternal life to Melchizedek, but we cannot be certain.

But notwithstanding his greatness Melchizedek is not a definitive model. Jesus is superior. Such is the consequence not only of Jesus' endless life but also, as we shall hear presently, of his unique sacrifice. Consequently, "he has no need to offer sacrifices day after day, first for his own sins, and then for those of the people; this he did once for all when he offered himself" (7:27). "Jesus is a priest 'forever,' not because he continues to exercise the high priestly function of offering the expiatory sacrifice and entering the presence of God in the holy of holies, but because his death and exaltation definitively and finally fulfill the cult's purpose, and therefore needs no repetition."[46] The new priesthood means that the old law has been surpassed. The argument of 7:18–19 is almost Pauline in its *exposé* of the inadequacy of the law of Moses,[47] except that Paul depicts the law failing as a way for people to be put right with God. Consonant with his sacerdotal theme, our author is referring to the law's failure to provide "perfection" (7:11, 19). Against this Lane argues that the author does not deny to the worshippers of the old covenant the possibility of "drawing near" to God.[48] But this is not supported by the language used to describe the law in 7:18[49] since it has in mind the failure of the old system to provide cleansing from sin and thus one's ability to approach God. Supporting this is the thought of 9:9 where "gifts and sacrifices offered (under the old covenant) cannot perfect (*teleiōsai*) the conscience of the worshipper." Since the Levitical priesthood was an integral part of the law this could only result in the law itself being superseded. This was inevitable, for the law (like the priesthood) "brought nothing to perfection" (7:19, REB). The imperfection of the old order and the consequent

---

generally, on the importance of Psalm 110 for understanding Hebrews, see Caird, "Exegetical Method," 44–51; Hay, *Glory at the Right Hand*; Loader, "Christ at the Right Hand," 199–217.

45. Strack and Billerback, *Kommentar*, 3:694.

46. Isaacs, "Priesthood," 57–58.

47. Manson, *Hebrews*, 114–16; Peterson, *Hebrews and Perfection*, 109.

48. Lane, *Hebrews 1–8*, 181.

49. Scholer, *Proleptic Priests*, 114–16.

need for a new and different kind of high priesthood is clinched for the author by Psalm 110:4.

> He holds his priesthood permanently, because he continues forever (7:24)

The dependence of the Levitical system on a never-ending succession of priests is used to good effect by the author. According to Exodus 40:15 (LXX) Aaron and his sons were appointed "forever," but this open statement is immediately qualified by the words that follow: "throughout (their) generations." Josephus states that there were eighty three high priests from Aaron till the high priesthood came to an end with the destruction of the temple in CE 70 (*Ant.* 20:227). The succession of priests in a mortal lineage is taken by our author as conclusive evidence of the incompleteness and defective character of their office. By contrast, the new high priest endures forever since he possesses an indestructible life (7:16). "He holds his priesthood permanently (*aparabatos*)" (7:24). It is unfortunate that *aparabatos* is occasionally taken in the intransitive sense ("without a successor" or "non-transferable") [50] In classical Greek the meaning is "permanent" or "unchangeable" (Plut. *Mor.* 410F, 745D; Josephus, *Ant.* 18: 266; *Apion* 2:293).[51]

The mortality of Levitical priests and the frequent instability this caused were in fact matters of concern within Judaism. *T Levi* promises that "the Lord will raise up a new priest" (18:2), who will endure for all time; "there shall be no successor for him from generation to generation forever" (18:8). Although the Levitical priesthood was believed to be eternal individual priests were not. Capitalizing on the mortality of the priesthood as a deficiency (7:23; cf. 7:8), Hebrews lays the greatest possible emphasis on Christ's never-ending priesthood (5:6; 6:20; 7:17, 21).

The emphasis on the perpetuity of Christ's priesthood has a direct pastoral consequence for those listening to the sermon (7:25, *hothen*). Just as the exposition on Melchizedek began with the declaration that they have an anchor of stability (6:20) it ends with the telling assurance that the one who "lives forever" (7:3, 24) is "able for all time to save those who approach God through him, since he always lives to make intercession

---

50. Moffatt, *Hebrews*, 99; Spicq, *Hébreux* 2, 197; Hughes, *Hebrews*, 269. Cf. Lane, *Hebrews 1–8*, 175; Ellingworth, "Unshakeable Priesthood," 125–26 ; Lane, *Hebrews 1–8*, 175.

51. BAGD, 97.

for them" (7:25).[52] Earlier the hearers were told that their high priest sympathizes with their weaknesses and offers them the mercy and grace they need (4:15–16). Now they are assured that their high priest is in the presence of God for the express purpose of interceding for them (7:25). On this see more fully chapter 8.

Summary

The high priesthood of Christ is introduced in 2:17; 5:6, 10 and expounded at length in 7:1–28. Once introduced, it is developed in terms of Melchizedek. He is of interest not only for the essential priestly ancestry he provides for Jesus but as a foil for Christ's eternal priesthood (7:3). The differences between Hebrews and 11QMelchizedek make it difficult to argue for direct dependence upon the latter, but the parallels cannot be ignored: as the eschatological high priest, he officiates on the decisive Day of Atonement. The locus is the heavenly temple. One has to agree with Hay and Attridge that the author of Hebrews knew more about the extrabiblical Melchizedekian traditions than he divulges. In this case the author had good reason for handling the subject circumspectly. But his reason for doing so was not only the bizarre features in extrabiblical sources. Melchizedek had acquired much greatness. He must not be seen as a heavenly rival to Christ. However, we have our author to thank for what his use of Melchizedek added to the church's understanding of Christ's perpetual ministry. It is this ministry that is of immediate pastoral importance for the suffering members of the church: Christ lives and intercedes for them.

52. Thompson, *Hebrews*, 161.

6

The True Sanctuary

The heavenly sanctuary is the stage setting for the central part of the sermon that is devoted to Christ's priestly ministry.[1] Although it is not the sanctuary but what takes place in it that is of the greatest importance to the author it is vital to his rhetorical strategy that the "true tent," the heavenly sanctuary, should be established as the appropriate setting. The heavenly sanctuary is best understood as the presence of God.

The first thing we have to consider is the fact that it is the tabernacle and not the temple where Christ's priestly ministry takes place. This has puzzled students of Hebrews. Numerous explanations have been offered. A popular view suggests that the author, like Philo (*Mos.* 2:71–79), was concerned to base his argument on the Pentateuch, i.e., the law of Moses.[2] The tabernacle had the distinction of having been made according to a God-given pattern (8:5). Neither the temple of Solomon nor that of Herod had such divine authorization. Also related to the attempt to find an explanation in the formative period of Israel's history is the intimate connection that the tabernacle had with both the historic covenant at Sinai (Exod 24—25) and the pilgrimage to Canaan (Exod 40:34–38; Num 9:19–22). Cody speaks for a number of commentators when he says, "it is only natural that the tent be used rather than the temple because of the association of the tent with the origin of the Old Covenant in the desert

1. Cf. Schierse, *Verheissung und Heilsvollendung,* 26–59; Cody, *Heavenly Sanctuary,* 9–45; McKelvey, *New Temple,* 25–41. See appendix D on "The Sanctuary Not Made with Hands."

2. See, for example, Lindars, "Rhetorical Structure," 395, 403; Koester, *Hebrews,* 52–53.

at Sinai."[3] The focus on the tabernacle and thereby on Israel's wilderness journey may well have served the author's rhetorical aim as a type of the congregation's journey to their promised "rest" (4:6–11).

Some scholars see no great problem here since they believe that the temple of Jerusalem no longer existed.[4] They suggest that by using the image of the tabernacle the author gives his argument a timeless character which would be particularly useful after the temple had been destroyed. Gordon thinks that if the temple had been destroyed the writer to the Hebrews imposes a remarkable "self-denying ordinance" upon himself since reference to this would have served his purpose very effectively.[5]

Other scholars are of the opinion that by omitting reference to the temple of Jerusalem the author is challenging the belief among Jews that the temple of Jerusalem would soon be rebuilt (as it had been after the exile). Dunn thinks that this may well be the chief reason why the writer does not speak about the temple in his exposition of Christ's high priesthood and heavenly sanctuary. "It was the very principle of a special cult and special priesthood and continuing sacrifice which the author wished to contest, thus undercutting the theological rationale on which any renewed or rebuilt Temple might be reconstituted."[6]

We have, of course, to reckon with the possibility that absence of any reference to the temple may simply have to do with the temple never having held very great significance for the community or the writer, especially if they lived in Rome or some other distant location, which would doubtless have been confirmed if the temple no longer existed. It is of course quite possible that we should read the strong attestations that Christians have their own means of atonement (8:1–2; 13:10) to mean that the author had reached the conviction that the temple had in any case been outdated by Jesus Christ, quite apart from whether it still existed or not.[7] He no doubt held the same conclusion about its predecessor,

---

3. Cody, *Heavenly Sanctuary*, 146. The same argument is used by Dunnill, *Covenant and Sacrifice*, 38. Cf. Bruce, *Hebrews*, 198; Lane, *Hebrews 9–13*, 218; O'Brien, *Hebrews*, 307.

4. Rissi, *Theologie*, 12; Brown and Meier, *Antioch and Rome*, 150; Isaacs, *Reading Hebrews and James*, 12–13.

5. Gordon, *Hebrews*, 33.

6. Dunn, *The Parting of the Ways*, 87.

7. Eisenbaum, "Locating Hebrews," 226.

the desert sanctuary. The most he can say about the earthly tabernacle is that it was symbolic, a type of the heavenly reality (9:8–9).[8]

A number of scholars favor the idea that the absence of any mention of the temple is to be explained in terms of the author's rhetorical strategy. Peter Walker is an example of those who believe that in the light of the tension between the Jews of Palestine and their Roman overlords and the devastation the Roman army had caused to the temple the author of Hebrews did not wish to be seen as saying anything that might have appeared devoid of feeling or loyalty, still less of being treacherous. The studied avoidance of reference to the temple is seen by Walker as actually an attack on the very essence of the temple. "By concentrating his attention on the tabernacle in the wilderness, he (the author of Hebrews) could argue that the Tabernacle system of worship, even when considered in its most pristine and pure form under Moses (before any human sin might have twisted the divine intention), had been declared redundant by God through Jesus."[9]

Similarly, Lindars is of the opinion that the choice of the tabernacle rather than the temple was part of the writer's aim in getting across his radical teaching on Christ's ending of the Jewish cultus. He believes that the writer was anxious not to alienate the addressees by speaking disparagingly of Jewish worship.[10] Lindars finds support for his view in what he suggests is the author's diplomatic way of introducing the Jewish priesthood. The "best case" presentation in 5:1–4 suggests that the writer is being careful not to put his hearers on the defensive. He says nothing about the dubious ways in which high priests were elected in his day nor the notorious conduct of some Hasmonaean high priests.[11]

The same line of reasoning is followed by Motyer.[12] He suggests that if the author had mounted a full frontal assault on the temple of Jerusalem and its cultus it would have been entirely counterproductive. Instead what he does is to go about his task indirectly. Motyer sees evidence of a subliminal attack on the temple and the cult in a number of passages (3:1–6; 4:14; 6:19–20; 7:13; 8:1–6, 11; 9:1–14; 10:11–14, 19–25;

---

8. Eisenbaum, *Jewish Heroes*, 129.

9. Walker, *Jesus and the Holy City*, 207–8.

10. Lindars, "Rhetorical Structure," 395, 403.

11. Lindars, "Hebrews and the Second Temple," 425.

12. Motyer, "The Temple in Hebrews: Is it There?," 175–89.

13:13–14). I believe that Motyer makes a plausible case in a number of these texts and I will return presently to what I consider is his strongest case.

Manson sees a connection between Hebrews and Acts 7 that would appear to offer a possible answer to our puzzle. Basing his argument on Stephen's speech, Manson argues that the mobile sanctuary of the wilderness period corresponded with the ongoing call of God to his people in a way that the static temple did not.[13] Whilst this scholar does not attribute the hostility of Stephen towards the temple to the author of Hebrews, he does however see a direct line from the former to the latter. Anti-temple tendencies had a long and well-articulated tradition in biblical and postbiblical literature. However, while there is a case for finding this tendency in Acts 7 it cannot be said that Hebrews shows evidence of it.

In the subject under discussion it is essential to take cognizance of the fact that the description of the tabernacle in Exodus is based on the actual temple (of Jerusalem) and it is likely that the author of Hebrews would have drawn on this tradition. Philo provides a helpful parallel. His expositions of the tabernacle often leave one asking oneself whether it is in fact the tabernacle that is intended and not the temple. Philo obviously made a connection between the two. In one place he says, "The tabernacle was constructed to resemble a sacred temple" (*Mos.* 2:89). Lindars makes a valuable point.

> Though the temple as such is never mentioned in Hebrews, there is a *prima facie* case for the assumption that the argument is conducted in full awareness of the importance of the sacrificial cultus at a time when it was still very much a going concern. It is simply taken for granted that the description of the tent and the regulations for sacrifice in Exodus and Leviticus apply to the present temple. It will now be shown that the existing temple is the real point of reference wherever the tent in the wilderness is mentioned, and similarly all references to priesthood and sacrifice are intended to be seen in relation to the actual practice of the temple service.[14]

13. Manson, *Hebrews*, 35. Cf. Simon, "Saint Stephen and the Jerusalem Temple," 127–42; Ego et al., *Gemeinde ohne Tempel*.

14. Lindars, "Hebrews and the Second Temple," 417. Cf. Beale, *Temple and the Church's Mission*, 93. For the view that Hebrews is not interested in the Herodian temple, see Attridge, *Hebrews*, 8.

In other words, what is important is not the type of sanctuary that is uppermost in the mind of the writer to the Hebrews—for the tabernacle after all was "made with hands"—but the cultus performed therein.

Without doubt the author of Hebrews was familiar with the ritual and the symbolism of the temple of Jerusalem when Christianity appeared on the scene. I take as my first piece of evidence the text which I believe Motyer has convincingly shown does reflect temple worship.[15] It is Hebrews 9:9. This passage follows the writer's comments about the repeated sacrifices of the Levitical priests. The statement that the first or outer tent is "still standing" has featured often in the discussions on the date of Hebrews in relation to the destruction of the temple of Jerusalem. But the connection between the "present time" and the offering of ineffectual "gifts and sacrifices," while it looks to be attractive support for a pre-70 date for the homily, is more apparent than real. The reference to "the present time" presents its own problems. Does it mean the time *then* present (under the old covenant) (AV) or the time *now* present (NRSV, REB, TNIV)? The discussion has now largely settled in favor of the latter. That being the case the allusion is to the temple of Jerusalem. Thus Motyer concludes "The 'parable for the present time,' therefore is suggested to them (the recipients) as a way of understanding the Jerusalem Temple in which this limitation of access is still the case."[16] I believe this is the conclusion that the context demands, otherwise, as Mackie points out, "if the Jerusalem cultus was 'a thing of the past,' the potency of the author's argument would be defused, and it would render his choice of the wilderness cultus even more inexplicable and idiosyncratic."[17]

In similar vein William Horbury finds a number of things in Hebrews which he believes indicate that the author was familiar with the temple of Jerusalem in his day.[18] He cites the fact that what is said about the administration of tithes in 7:5 is following not the Pentateuch (Num 18:21) but first century practice. Similarly, 9:13 connects "the blood of goats and bulls" from the Day of Atonement with the ashes of the red heifer (Num 19:11–21), though the latter in fact has no connection with this festival. In the Mishnah *Middoth* 2:4 tells us the high priest burnt the red heifer on the top of the Mount of Olives so that he "should be

---

15. Motyer, "The Temple in Hebrews: Is it there?," 185–86.

16. Motyer, "The Temple in Hebrews: Is it there?," 186.

17. Mackie, *Eschatology and Exhortation*, 85. So also Montefiore, *Hebrews*, 149.

18. Horbury, "Aaronic Priesthood," 50–52. Cf. MacRae, "Heavenly Temple and Eschatology," 181; Lindars, "Hebrews and the Second Temple, 410.

able to look directly into the entrance of the Sanctuary when the blood is sprinkled." In *Parah*, the tractate devoted in its entirety to the red heifer, we are told that during the seven days when the high priest was kept in isolation from possible defilement (3:1; cf. *m.Yoma*. 1:1) he was cleansed with water containing the ashes from the red heifer (3:1). There is every reason for believing that the mention of the red heifer in Heb 9:13 is evidence that the author was alluding to Second Temple practice.

Horbury believes a similar conclusion can be drawn from the ethical qualities attributed to Christ in 2:17—3.2 and 4:14—5:10, viz. mercy, compassion, sympathy, and solidarity with humanity. Whilst these qualities recall biblical descriptions of the priesthood, they clearly reflect Hellenized accounts of the author's time.[19]

I can only conclude that whilst concentrating on the tabernacle, which suited his pilgrimage theme, it was the temple that the author of Hebrews had in mind. I shall return to this matter in chapter 10 (in regard to Heb 12:22), with further evidence in support of this contention.

The Sanctuary in Heaven (8:2)

The opening verses of chapter 8, describing the sanctuary in heaven to which the pioneer/high priest goes and in which he functions, indicate the main point of what follows (*kephalaion*, 8:1), viz. Christ's work in the heavenly sanctuary on behalf of his people. The significance that the author attributed to the latter cannot be overstated. It is to emphasize this point that the author asserts that Christ is "a minister in the sanctuary and the true tent" (8:2).

The description of the heavenly sanctuary as "true" (*alēthinos*) (8:2; cf. 9:11, 24) and the earthly one as a "sketch" (*hypodeigma*)[20] and "shadow" (*skia*) (8:5; cf. 9:24; 10:1), which aim to demonstrate the superiority of Christianity over the Levitical system, is not saying that the transcendent sanctuary is genuine because what it is contrasted with is false. Its earthly counterpart was certainly not false: God had expressly commanded it to be built (8:5). He had in fact given Moses the actual

19. Horbury, "Aaronic Priesthood," 59–66.

20. In support of the translation "sketch," Hurst writes "'Sketch-plan' remains the best translation of *hypodeigma* in Hebrews, which does not mean, and never has meant, 'copy' (*contra* RSV, NEB, and virtually all modern commentaries on Hebrews")", (Hurst, "'How 'Platonic' are Heb. 8:5 and 9:23f?," 156–65). Also see Gäbel, *Kulttheologie*, 241–42.

plan for its construction, and although what was constructed is referred to as "made by human hands" (9:24; cf. 9:11), i.e., not the same as its heavenly counterpart, it was not idolatrous. The sanctuary in heaven is "true" because it is not a human construction and necessarily subject to the ravages of time. As the writer says of the old covenant, "it is growing old (and) will soon disappear" (8:13). Its high priest, similarly, is not subject to such changes, but lives eternally.

The foregoing is not to say that Platonic categories may not have been at the back of the mind of the author, consciously or unconsciously,[21] even if, as Schenck believes, he did not make a very good job of it.[22] He uses the neutral term "type" (*hypodeigma*) (Exod 25:40) when he could have chosen the indisputably Platonic term "pattern" (*paradeigma*), which was readily available in Exod 25:9.[23] His use of *hypodeigma* in 8:5—wrongly translated as "copy" in numerous versions of the Bible—misled generations of scholars who took it in the Platonic sense of "copy."[24]

A number of exegetes, noting the Stoic concept of a cosmic temple elsewhere in the sermon and the liberal use Philo makes of Stoic ideas alongside Platonic ones (*Plant.* 50; *Her.* 75; *Somn.* 1:215; *Mos.* 2:88; *Spec.* 1:66; *QE.* 2:91), argue that the amalgam of Platonic and Stoic ideas in Middle Platonism provides help not only with the terminological similarities between Hebrews and Plato but also with the cosmological background to the heavenly temple.[25]

---

21. Cf. for example, Spicq, *Hébreux*, 39–166; Williamson, *Philo and Hebrews*; Montefiore, *Hebrews*, 6–9. On the question of the influence of Plato (and Philo) on the sermon see also Thompson, *Beginnings of Christian Philosophy*, 1–16, 152–62; *Hebrews*, 24–25, 168–69, 193–94; Hurst, *Hebrews*, 7–38; Dillon, *Middle Platonists*, 139–45. Hurst correctly argues that the contrast is not between the earthly tabernacle and its archetype in heaven but between the Mosaic tabernacle and the eschatological temple. On this showing, the earthly tabernacle is not the copy of the heavenly but rather its prototype (*Hebrews*, 33–38). For Hebrews and Philo on this subject also see Sterling, "Ontology Versus Eschatology," 190–211; Schenck, "Philo and the Epistle to the Hebrews," 112–35.

22. See Schenck, *Understanding Hebrews*, 84.

23. *Hypodeigma* can mean either model or image (BAGD, 1037). Although Exod 25:40 implies that Moses was shown something like a scale model of the tabernacle (visible according to Heb 8:5) it is not likely that it is this sense of *hypodeigma* that is intended in Heb 8:5.

24. Schenck, *Understanding Hebrews*, 30.

25. Thompson, *Beginnings of Christian Philosophy*, 18–27, 45–52, 109–15; 152–60; Thompson, *Hebrews*, 24–26, 168–69; Meier, "Structure and Theology in Heb. 1.1–14," 168–89; Mackie, *Eschatology and Exhortation*, 105–20.

Still others have made out a robust case for believing that the heavenly tent of Hebrews is the eschatological temple of Jewish apocalyptic.[26]

The view that Hebrews is indebted to Plato goes back at least as far as Eusebius (*Praep. evang.* 12, with reference to Plato's *Republic*). For Plato and his followers material and sensible objects are not ultimate realities but copies of archetypes or "ideas," which can be discerned only by the intellect. Plato writes:

> "I understand," he said, "you mean the city whose establishment we have described, the city whose home is in the ideal (*ēn logois keimenē*); for I think that it can be found nowhere on earth." "Well," said I, "perhaps there is a pattern (*paradeigma*) of it laid up in heaven for him who wishes to contemplate it and so beholding to constitute himself its citizen" (*Rep.* 9:592a, b).

Ideas constitute reality. Eternal, intangible, immutable, and above all true (*alēthes, Rep.* 7:515c, 516a; *Polit.* 300d), ideas form a pattern or model (*paradeigma*) of which all earthly phenomena are a copy (*eikōn* or *mimēma*) or shadow (*skia*) (*Tim.* 29b, 48c–49a; *Rep.* 7:515a, c, 516a, 517d). The phenomenal world is good inasmuch as it is a copy of an eternal and enduring reality, but it is transient and imperfect inasmuch as it is only a copy and nothing more (*Rep.* 7:515c, 516a). "Plato's ideal world is not a heaven that could be entered by Jesus; it can be penetrated only by the intellect."[27]

Philo, who is fulsome in expressing admiration for Plato,[28] obviously found Plato's doctrine of transcendence and immanence congenial to his Jewish presuppositions. He repeatedly describes creation and Israel's cult in Platonic terms.[29] Like Plato, his cosmological orientation is clearly ver-

---

26. Barrett, "Eschatology," 383–89; MacRae, "Heavenly Temple and Eschatology," 182–84. Cf. Hurst, "'Eschatology and 'Platonism,'" 42–48.

27. Williamson, "Platonism and Hebrews," 419.

28. Williamson, *Philo*, 139–41; Dillon, *Middle Platonists*, 140.

29. Although Plato thinks of the Ideas in the celestial world he does not think of them as existing in a particular place. It is because of our finite understanding that we assume that they exist "some place"(*tini topō*), occupying a certain space (*Tim.* 52b, c). What Hebrews is describing is not philosophical at all. For him, the heavenly sanctuary is in a definite place (9:24). It is accessible and it has a living occupant. The one point at which Philo reinterprets the Platonic archetypes in terms of his Jewish heritage is his statement that the archetypes are created (*Opif.* 16). On Philo's use of the Ideas of Plato, see Wolfson, *Philo: Foundations*, 200–225; Cody, *Heavenly Sanctuary*, 26–36; Koester, *Hebrews*, 97–100. On the earlier Neopythagorean belief that the whole world is a copy (*mimēsis*) of the higher world of numbers (*arithmoi*) and Plato's

tical. He says that God made the universe (of sense perception) according to a pattern up in heaven which he fashioned first before proceeding.[30]

> For God, being God, assumed that a beautiful copy (*mimēma*) would never be produced apart from a beautiful pattern (*paradeigma*), and that no object of perception would be faultless which was not made in the likeness of an original (*archetupos*) discerned only by the intellect. So when He willed to create this visible world He first fully formed the intelligible world, in order that he might have the use of a pattern (*paradeigma*) wholly God-like and incorporeal (*Opif.* 16).

On the subject of the tabernacle, Philo says that the "model (*paradeigma*) was stamped upon the mind of the prophet" (*Mos.* 2:76; cf. 1:158; *QE* 2:52, 82).

For our purpose, it is the conflation of Platonic and Stoic traditions in Philo's accounts of the heavenly and earthly sanctuaries that is of special interest.[31] In Stoic belief the thought that God is immanent and present in the world led naturally to the idea of the cosmos as his dwelling. Some Stoics pictured the universe as a great "mystery sanctuary," the house of both gods and humans (*Dio Chrysostom*, 12:33–34; 30:28; 36:29–37); Diogenes Laertius (*Lives of Eminent Philosophers*, 7:156; Cicero, *Fin* 3:64).[32]

As a loyal Jew, Philo does not question the validity of God's earthly habitation. It is the one legitimate place of worship. "Since God is one, there should be also only one temple" (*Spec.* 1:67). It is for Philo, as for the writer to the Hebrews, a copy of the heavenly temple (*Mos.* 2:74–76; *QE.* 2:52, 82; *Somn.* 1:215; cf. Heb 8:5), but he does say that the earthly temple is not really adequate for the worship of God. Revealing clear Stoic influence Philo declares that the entire cosmos is a temple.

> The highest, and in the truest sense the holy temple of God is, as we must believe, the whole universe, having for its sanctuary the most sacred part of all existence, even heaven, for its votive

---

liking for this philosophy see Merean, "Greek Philosophy," 84–106; cf. 141–42. On the cosmology of Hebrews see also Ellingworth, "Jesus and the Universe," 337–50; Adams, "Cosmology of Hebrews," 122–39; Lincoln, *Hebrews*, 45–47.

30. Cf. Cody, *Heavenly Sanctuary*, 26–36; Chadwick, "Philo," 137–57.

31. On the merging of Platonic and Stoic concepts and Pythagorean elements in Middle Platonism see Dillon, *Middle Platonists*, 141–42; Schrenck, *Brief Guide to Philo*, 51–56. On the cosmic temple see also chapter 4.

32. Hahm, *Origins of Stoic Cosmology*, 136–43, 157–65.

ornaments the stars, for its priests the angels who are servitors
to His powers, unbodied souls, not compounds of rational and
irrational nature, as ours are, but with the irrational eliminated,
all mind through and through, pure intelligences, in the likeness
of the monad (*Spec.* 1:66).[33]

Similarly in *Quaesiones in Exodum* 2:91, the holy of holies stands for
heaven and its curtain refers to the division of the lower and the upper
parts of the cosmos.[34] In *De somniis* 1:215 the *Logos* is high priest of the
temple of the cosmos and mediates between humanity and the world of
Ideas (cf. *Somn.* 2:189; *Fug.* 108. See also *Somn.* 2:188–89; *Her.* 205–6).

Returning to the Jerusalem temple, Philo says that it is a "temple
made with hands (*cheirokmēton*)" (*Spec.* 1:67). This has been taken by
Thompson to have a pejorative meaning,[35] but since the context could
not be more positive about the role of the earthly temple it seems necessary to understand Philo to be referring simply to its material character
in contradistinction to its heavenly counterpart. As in Hebrews 8:5, it
is only when the earthly temple is compared with the heavenly that its
limitations become apparent.

The cosmological dualism of Philo's thinking on the temple is described rather differently in *De Somniis* 1:215.

> For there are, as is evident, two temples of God: one of them this
> universe, in which there is also as High Priest His First-born,
> the divine Word (*logos*), and the other the rational soul (*logikē
> psuchē*), whose Priest is the real Man (*alētheian anthrōpos*), the
> outward and visible image (*mimēma*) of whom is he who of-
> fers the prayers and sacrifices handed down from our fathers, to
> whom it has been committed to wear the aforesaid tunic, which
> is a copy and replica of the whole heaven, the intention of this
> being that the universe may join with man in the holy rites and
> man with the universe.

Here the earthly temple has a decidedly Stoic look. Philo who spoke
of the Jerusalem temple in robustly positive terms now can say that the
soul of the rational being is God's habitation on earth. Like the Stoics,

33. On the universe as a temple see also *Plant.* 50; *Rer.Div.Her.* 75; *Somn.* 1:215; cf.
Mos. 2:88; *QE.* 2:91.

34. On the cosmological meanings Philo gave to the different parts of the tabernacle see, e.g., Sowers, *Hermeneutics of Philo and Hebrews*, 56–63.

35. Thompson points to the use of *cheirokmētos,* in Jewish literature for idols, *Beginnings of Christian Philosophy*, 106, 113.

Philo developed this idea and used it frequently as the basis of his ethics (*Sobr.* 62; *Somn.* 1:149; 2:251; *Cher.* 100; *Virt.* 188; *QE* 2:51), but while this individualistic concept found a place in Paul's teaching (1 Cor 6:19), it was not of interest to the writer to the Hebrews.

Cosmological meanings are also given to the tabernacle and the temple in numerous other Jewish writings. Josephus tells us, "Every one of its objects is intended to recall and represent the universe" (*Ant.* 3:180). The temple, he says, "typified the universe" (*eikona tōn holōn*) (*J.W.* 5:212–13).[36] The holy of holies is heaven and the forecourt is earth (*Ant.* 3:181). Similarly, in the Sibylline Oracles, "[God] provided cosmos (*kosmos*) and made a holy house" (5:420). There is another example from Hellenistic Judaism in Sirach 50:19, where the connection is made between the completion of the temple liturgy and the completion of the cosmos (*heōs suntelesthē kosmos kuriou*).[37]

This idea of heaven and earth joined together to form one great temple provided the writer to the Hebrews with an excellent setting for his Day of Atonement analogy. It enabled him to depict Christ offering his sacrifice on the cross in terms of the high priest's offering in the outer part of the sanctuary, followed by his travelling through (*dia*) the heavens in 4:14 (cf. *dia*, 9:11) and entering the heavenly holy of holies with his blood (*dia*, 9:12), corresponding to the high priest taking the blood from his sacrifice into the inner part of the sanctuary. The action is thus all of a piece, thanks to the all-embracing cosmic temple.

But helpful as the cosmology of the Hellenistic world is for interpreting Hebrews,[38] it does not fully explain the metaphysical dualism of the work. Barrett, MacRae, Hurst, Lindars, Lane, Mackie and others have done students of Hebrews a valuable service by drawing attention to the dualism of Jewish cosmology and its influence on Hebrews.

The correspondence between the earthly and heavenly worlds that was the basis of apocalyptic dualism had an ancient and wide-ranging ancestry. This is not the place to say more on this subject than we have already said or to examine how the doctrine of correspondence took on a dualistic form in the apocalyptic writings.[39] We note the fact and proceed to consider its influence on Hebrews. This is well stated by Barrett: "It is

36. Cf. Koester, *Dwelling of God*, 59–63.

37 Hayward, *Jewish Temple*, 79–80.

38. Schenck, "Philo and the Epistle to the Hebrews," 128–32; Mackie, *Eschatology and Exhortation*, 106–15.

39. See appendix D.

worth noting here that apocalyptic in its own nature involves two kinds of (limited) dualism. The contrast between this world and the 'other' heavenly world of supra-sensual reality is often loosely described as 'Platonic' and supposed to be quite foreign to Judaism; but this is not so"[40] Our author's cosmological dualism is introduced by his statement that Moses constructed the tabernacle according to the model shown him by God (8:5; Exod 25:40; cf. 1 Chron 28:11–19; Ezek 40:1–4).[41] For him the relation between the two sanctuaries is essentially a temporal one. The earthly one "foreshadows" the heavenly one inasmuch as the whole Levitical order foreshadowed "the good things to come" (10:1).

Ascent to the heavenly world by visionaries and mystics was a well-established feature of both apocalyptic and rabbinic writers.[42] The goal of all who made the ascent was what Hebrews describes as the "sanctuary not made with hands" (9:11). Let us remind ourselves that what we are studying is metaphor, not cosmological theory.[43]

A Sanctuary not Made with Hands (9:11)

The great importance which the heavenly temple came to occupy in Judaism owed its origin to more than the age-old doctrine of correspondence. Significant among the other contributory factors was the attention paid to the heavenly temple by apocalyptic writers. This was influenced in part at least by the negative associations which the Second Temple acquired.[44] This temple was regarded as a poor substitute for its precedessor (Hag 2:9; *T.Benj* 9:2. Cf. Ezra 3:12; *1Esd* 5:63–65; Josephus *Ant.* 11:80–81). The desecration of the temple by Antiochus Epiphanes, notwithstanding the valiant attempt of Judas Maccabaeus to cleanse it, lingered on in the form of a secret suspicion that the temple had not been quite fully restored to

40. Barrett, "New Testament Eschatology," 139.

41. Wisdom 9:8 tells us that Solomon's temple is "a copy (*mimēma*) of the holy tent that you prepared from the beginning." According to Sirach Wisdom has its tabernacle (*skēnē*) in the "highest heavens" (24:4).

42. Appendix B.

43. D'Angelo, *Moses*, 231. Cf. Schenck, *Understanding Hebrews*, 81.

44. "There is in apocalyptic literature a clear tradition of hostility to the temple of Jerusalem, coupled with a great concern for the temple as a religious idea" (Hamerton-Kelly, "Temple and the Origins of Jewish Apocalyptic," 1). The Qumran literature abounds with criticism of the Second Temple. See CD 1:3; 3:19; 4:1; 5:6; etc. Cf. Davies, "Ideology of the Temple," 287–301, especially 300–301.

holiness. To add to its problems, the temple lacked the ark, the tabernacle, the altar of incense, and other furniture, and had to make do with copies.

Not surprisingly, the heavenly temple was extolled at the expense of its earthly counterpart by the apocalyptic writers.[45] *First Enoch* tells how Enoch sees the heavenly temple and God enthroned in the inner house, i.e., the holy of holies. Its splendor excels description (*1 En* 14:16–18). *Second Baruch* deliberately distances the heavenly temple from its earthly counterpart and, significantly, connects it to ancient tradition by making it the archetype of the tabernacle shown to Moses (4:2–6). Very pointedly the *Testament of Levi* says that the sacrifice offered in the heavenly holy of holies is well-pleasing to God (3:4–6).[46]

The heavenly sanctuary and its superiority over its earthly counterpart have a conspicuous place in the Qumran literature.[47] The *Songs of the Sabbath Sacrifice* are specially relevant. The heavenly temple is used to validate the community, as in Hebrews. The sanctuary in heaven is "the tabernacle of greater height" (4Q 403 II:10), the "wonderful sanctuary" (403 II:22). It oscillates between one sanctuary and seven (403 II:22, 27; cf. I:13). Its magnificent liturgy is described in one song after another until it reaches a climax with the cherubim prostrate before the throne of God (the *merkabah*) (4Q 405:22).[48]

In 11Q Melchizedek we find the heavenly sanctuary is made the venue for the people's full and final atonement. It is a *pesher* on the "Year of Jubilee" in Lev 25:13 and depicts Melchizedek as the high priest officiating at the great eschatological Day of Atonement (11Q13 ii:7–8). Its significance is drawn out by Philip Alexander when he says that 11QMelch 13 "suggests that the Qumran community regarded the heavenly sanctuary as the 'true' sanctuary, the place where atonement would ultimately have to be made for its sins."[49]

The claims being made for the community at Qumran are also evident in passages where the worshippers are described as joining with the

45. See appendix D.

46. On the importance of the *Testament of Levi* as evidence of the increasing interest in the heavenly temple and priesthood see Himmelfarb, *Ascent to Heaven*, 30–46.

47. See appendix D.

48. See also the claims inherent in the connection which the Qumranites made between the worship in heaven and worship in their community (1QM 12:1–2; 4 Flor.i: 4–5; 1QS 9:7–8). Cf. Gärtner, *Temple and Community*, 94–99; McKelvey, *New Temple*, 37–38.

49. Alexander, *Mystical Texts*, 70.

priests and the angels in heaven in offering to God sacrifices of praise and thanksgiving. The question whether the worship which has such an important place in the *Songs* was thought of as actually taking place in heaven rather than on earth is intriguing and without a clear answer,[50] but is immaterial for our purpose. It is the heavenly temple that legitimizes the community.

The rabbis were fond of drawing attention to the connection between the heavenly and the earthly temples (e.g., *B. Ta'an* 5a; *Gen. R.* 55:7). Although there appears to have been a reluctance on their part to follow the apocalypticists all the way in substituting the heavenly temple and city for the earthly one this was eventually done. Strack and Billerbeck supply a number of *midrashim* which show that some rabbis believed that the new Jerusalem and its temple would be the heavenly one come down to earth in the new age. The texts in question are late, but the evidence of Jewish apocalyptic and the Book of Revelation[51] reveal the direction in which cosmological thinking was moving by the turn of the Christian era.[52]

The progression we witness whereby the heavenly temple became the eschatological temple that will one day replace the old discredited temple affected cosmological thinking in a way that is important for us. The spatial contrast of above and below now became a temporal contrast of present and future. In *1 Enoch* we have a graphic description of how the existing temple is torn down and a splendid new temple takes its place (90:28–29), while *2 Baruch* tells us that the new Jerusalem will be the city that God made at the creation of the world (4:2–6). The rabbis consoled themselves with the thought that God would take it upon himself to solve the tantalizing problem of mortals ever providing a temple worthy of him by having the heavenly temple descend to earth (*Bet ha-Midr* 1:55, 23). In the New Testament it is the Book of Revelation that takes the doctrine of God's heavenly dwelling place to the logical conclusion that it reached in Judaism (Rev 21).

The development of temple theology with its increasing emphasis on the heavenly temple and the transformation of the latter into the eschatological temple assist us in finding our way through the maze of the Hebrews' cosmological imagery and dualism by helping us understand

50. On the connection between the worship in heaven and that in the community in the scrolls see 1QM 12:1–2; 4QFlor. 1:4–5; 1 QS 9:7–8. Cf Gärtner, *Temple and Community*, 94–99.

51. Str-B, III.796.

52. McKelvey, *New Temple*, 34–36.

how the vertical hermeneutical line (heaven and earth and thus heavenly and earthly sanctuaries) intersects with the horizontal (this age and the age to come and thus present temple and new/true temple). But important as these juxtaposed contrasts are for our understanding of Hebrews[53] what is more important is the use our author makes of them in portraying the superiority of Christ's priesthood and his heavenly sanctuary.

In the past scholars created problems for themselves by thinking (a) of Jewish apocalyptic in essentially linear terms and (b) assuming that the heavenly/earthly dualism of the epistle was without question Platonic.[54] Barrett's demonstration of the importance of apocalyptic for understanding Hebrews was a necessary corrective. But invaluable as the apocalyptic material is for our understanding of Hebrews it has to be said that Barrett goes too far when he says, "The heavenly tabernacle in Hebrews is not the product of Platonic idealism, but the eschatological temple of apocalyptic Judaism."[55] No single tradition should be singled out to the neglect of the others. Plato's archetypes play a part, as does Stoicism's cosmic temple; but having said that we must register the fact that it is our author's Christian imprint that is most evident.[56] Hebrews 9:23–24 provides a good example of the author's multiple sources and his Christian viewpoint: "It was necessary for the sketches (*hypodeigmata*) of the heavenly things to be purified with these rites, but the heavenly things themselves need better sacrifices than these. For Christ did not enter a sanctuary made by human hands, a mere copy of the true one (*antitupa tōn alēthinōn*), but he entered heaven itself, now to appear in the presence of God on our behalf." And there the great high priest remains. He is high priest "forever."

53. For the earth and heaven contrast see 8:4–5; 9:11, 23–24; 11:13,16; 12:22 and for the now and not—yet contrast see 8:6, 8; 9:8—11, 28; 10:13, 20, 25, 37; 11:13, 39–40; 13:14.

54. As is shown by Hurst, *Hebrews*, 10–11, 16, 41–42; cf. Son, *Zion Symbolism*, 172–73. For an example of the difficulties created by assuming that the author of the epistle is operating within purely Platonic categories, see Wedderburn, "Sawing off the Branches," 400–402. Mackie concludes that Hebrews "reflects a deliberate hybridization of Middle Platonism and Jewish eschatology" (*Eschatology and Exhortation*, 115).

55. Barrett, "Eschatology," 389.

56. Cf. Wedderburn, "It is not the cultic imagery itself which is used here that has brought our author into conflict with the Platonic world-view, but something yet more fundamental, the Christian myth of the Son of God who enters our world and returns to the heavenly one, a myth which is part and parcel of that 'confession' which Hebrews is concerned to safeguard" ("Sawing off the Branches," 402).

The Christian makeover of apocalyptic, Platonic, and Stoic cosmology is thoroughgoing and represents the high point of the doctrinal section of the sermon. To what extent the author's use of the horizontal and vertical contrasts of the cosmological milieu of his times is deliberate or even conscious is hard to tell, but what is not in any doubt is the creative way he makes it serve his purpose. As we are to see, it is this and not the conceptual background as such that contributes most to his argument for the superiority of the Christian faith.

Summary

Why Hebrews refers to the sanctuary in heaven as a tabernacle rather than a temple is not the puzzle it seems. It suits the tabernacle motif, but there is enough evidence in the homily to prove that it is the temple of Jerusalem that is the real point of reference. The description of the sanctuary as "true" reveals the cosmological background of the heavenly sanctuary but the emphasis is on the superiority of the new faith. Acknowledgment of the presence of apocalyptic dualism is a necessary corrective to the overemphasized influence attributed to Platonic dualism, and no less important is the role of the cosmic temple of Middle Platonic and Jewish Hellenistic thought. One cannot say that the author deliberatively keeps in mind the vertical contrast of above and below and the linear contrast of present and future; much of this would have been second nature to him. Helpful as understanding the conceptual background is, what is more important is the imaginative way in which the author uses cosmology to serve his rhetorical aim: the true sanctuary is in heaven, occupied by the superior high priest.

7

The Greater and More Perfect Tent

Understanding the references to the tent/sanctuary in Hebrews is a challenge.[1] The use of the terms (*ta hagia* and *hē skēnē*) lacks consistency. The division of the tabernacle into two rooms or compartments, the separation of the outer from the inner, and the relationship of the one to the other is conceived not only spatially but also temporally: "The way into the sanctuary (*ta hagia*) is not yet opened as long as the outer tent (*hē prōtē skēnē*) is still standing" (9:8). Typological interpretation runs throughout. Sections of the tabernacle are tantalizingly linked with the relationship of the old and new covenants. The author's inspired portrayal of the person and work of Jesus Christ in terms of the Day of Atonement is worked out so extensively and effectively that one could be excused for momentarily thinking that he is speaking literally. We remind ourselves again that the sanctuary in heaven is not a literal construction of some kind, but a metaphorical statement on ultimate reality.

> The sanctuary and the true tent (*tōn hagiōn leitourgos kai tēs skēnēs tēs alēthinēs*), that the Lord, and not any mortal, has set up (*hēn epēxen ho kurios, ouk anthrōpos*) (8:2).

Before we get into the interpretative questions raised by this text we should note that what makes the heavenly temple superior, above all, is the fact that it was God who set it up and not any human being. As a direct creation of God himself, it is beyond all comparison to an earthly counterpart. This is given additional emphasis in the statement that it is "true" and it was, moreover, the template God provided for the earthly sanctuary (8:5).

---

1. The conceptual background of the "true" tent (8:2) is considered in chapter 6.

How is one to understand the relationship between *ta hagia* ("the sanctuary") and *hē skēnē* ("the tent" NRSV)? Is the connecting "and" (*kai*) used to distinguish the two parts of the heavenly sanctuary, or should the second clause be taken epexegetically, so that it is the holy of holies that is solely in mind? In other words, are *ta hagia* and *hē skēnē* to be taken as alternative ways of describing the one and the same thing, most likely the whole sanctuary? The latter interpretation seems more likely to be what is in mind: *ta hagia* embraces the whole of the heavenly sanctuary (cf. 9:8). Further, the author's consistent use of the Day of Atonement imagery is enough to convince numerous exegetes it is the entire sanctuary that is in mind in 8:2.[2]

In contrast to the use of *ta hagia* in 8:2, *hagia* in 9:2 refers to the outer compartment (*skēnē . . . protē*), but the textual variants for the relative clause at the end of 9:2 indicate the uncertainty that resulted.[3]

What we have in the use of terms for the heavenly sanctuary in 8:2 is the flexibility we find in the use of terms for the tabernacle in Hellenistic Judaism. The LXX and other texts similarly alternate between the plural and the singular without any change of meaning.[4]

What follows 8:2 makes it clear beyond any reasonable doubt that it is the heavenly temple *per se* that is being contrasted with the earthly temple, not different parts of the heavenly one.

Through the Greater and More Perfect Tent (9:11)

> But when Christ came as a high priest of the good things that have come (*genomenōn*) (*mg.* good things to come), then through the greater and perfect tent (*mg.* more perfect) tent (*dia tēs meizonos kai teleioteras skēnēs ou cheiropoiētou*) (not made with hands, that is, not of this creation), he entered once for all into the Holy Place (*ta hagia*), not with the blood of goats

2. For the view that it is the sanctuary in general that is intended, "without any reference to the distinction (9.2f) between the inner and outer shrine," see Moffatt, *Hebrews*, 104; Westcott, *Hebrews*, 214; Michel, *Hebräer*, 288; Peterson, *Hebrews and Perfection*, 130–31; Scholer, *Proleptic Priests*, 159; Ellingworth, *Hebrews* (1993), 402; Lane, *Hebrews 1–8*, 200–201; Koester, *Hebrews*, 375–76; Thompson, *Hebrews*, 173; O'Brien, *Hebrews*, 288.

3. See Attridge, *Hebrews*, 233–34.

4. In Lev 16:16 and Ezek 45:18 *to hagion* refers to the holy of holies, while Lev 10:4 and Num 3:28 use *hagia* for the entire tabernacle. Cf. Jdt 4:12; 16:20; 1 Macc 3:43, 59; etc.; Philo, *Fug* 93; Josephus *J.W.* 2:341. Cf. Hughes, *Hebrews*, 283–90.

and calves, but with (*dia*) his own blood, thus obtaining eternal redemption (9:11–12).

This passage is notoriously difficult to unpack. Before we attempt to do so we should note the place it has in the narrative and its general sense. It corresponds in importance to the high point of 8:1–2. In terms of the structure of the sermon the unit (9:11–14) follows closely on the preceding one (9:1–10). There is a close antithetical correspondence between the two units.[5] The emphasis is laid heavily on Christ's cultic work. In mind is the great moment in the Day of Atonement ceremony when the high priest entered into the holy of holies, now represented as being surpassed by the new high priest's entry into the "greater and more perfect tent." "The time of reformation" (ESV) has arrived; the good things that were to come are now here (9:11).[6]

Verses 11–12 are a single sentence which contains several clauses and a suspended main clause, together with a complex number of images. Christ is portrayed as entering into the sanctuary (*ta hagia*) "through the (or *by means of*) the greater and more perfect tent (*skēnē*)." The *ta hagia* in 9:12 is obviously the heavenly holy of holies, but what is the meaning of the Platonizing "greater and more perfect tent" in the previous verse? Does it refer to both the forecourt and the holy of holies or only the holy of holies? Numerous commentators believe that the natural meaning of 9:11–12 suggests that Christ passed *through* (*dia*, local sense) the forecourt of an outer heavenly realm in order to enter the holy of holies (*ta hagia*, heaven itself in 9:24).[7] They draw attention to the idea of movement inherent in the Day of Atonement imagery and implied in the use of "entered" (*eisēlthen* in 9:12; cf. 6:19).[8] Christ is understood as making

---

5. Lane, *Hebrews 9–13*, 237; cf. Westfall, who writes, "When it is recognized that 9.1–10 and 9.11–14 form a cohesive unit because of the cohesive tie of antonymy in contrast, it has a profound effect on the specificity of the topic as opposed to topics that are based on a division between 9:1–10 and 9:11–28" (*Discourse Analysis*, 200).

6. The use of *paraginomai* ("appear," "arrive") instead of the usual and more simple *ginomai* suggests "an official public appearance" (Ellingworth, *Hebrews* (1993), 449). So also Attridge, commenting on the dramatic nuance of the participle, says, "He has 'arrived' (*paragenomenos*) on the heavenly scene as High Priest" (*Hebrews*, 245). Bruce contrasts the Day of Atonement which prescribed fasting and abstention from work (Lev 16:29–31; 23:26, 32) (*Hebrews*, 212).

7. Michel, *Hebräer*, 309–12; Héring, *Hebrews*, 76; Michaelis, "Skēnē," 376–77; Petersen, *Hebrews and Perfection*, 140–44; Ellingworth, *Hebrews* (1993), 446–48; cf. Lane, *Hebrews 9–13*, 235–39; Scholer, *Proleptic Priests*, 163.

8. Thus Young writes, "It is in order to strengthen the idea of movement from one

his way along the passage way created by the double veil. It is argued that the sense that *dia* has in 9:12 does not contradict its use in 9:11 since Hebrews can use the same preposition in different ways in the same place (cf. *pros* in 1:7–8 and *eis* in 7:25). This interpretation has the support of the conception of a cosmic temple.

The other interpretation that has had advocates from the patristic period and still has some support today reads the text as "by means of the greater and more perfect tent" (*dia*, instrumental sense) and understands the reference to be to Christ's body, incarnate or risen and glorified, his eucharistic body, or the church. This view, however, requires us to take 9:11–12 to imply a two compartment sanctuary in heaven, which is not at all certain. Moreover, identification of the "tent" as the physical body of Christ is hard to relate to the portrayal of the "tent" as "not of this creation." In any case, Hebrews nowhere describes the church as the body of Christ.[9]

Schenck suggests that the difficulties of understanding 9:11 are largely overcome if we take the *dia* of 9:11 not instrumentally but modally. He reads it thus, "by way of the greater and more perfect tent . . . Christ entered into the holies."[10] This acknowledges the eschatological nuance of the text, but it cannot be said to be the straightforward sense that follows from the author's use of the Yom Kippur imagery: the high priest passes *through* the tabernacle. The emphasis is not on the way taken; there is no other possible route.

Much of the difficulty encountered in interpreting 9:11–12 results from failure to take account of the antithetical relationship of the passage with the preceding unit (9:1–10). Verses 9:6–10 are obviously allegorical: the outer part of the sanctuary (9:6) stands for the present age, while the inner part (9:7) represents the age to come. The purpose of 9:11b and 12a is to demonstrate why Christ's high priestly work outperforms that of the Jewish high priest on the Day of Atonement: Christ entered the superior sanctuary (the "greater and more perfect tent") and offered a superior

---

sphere to another that our author in chapter nine gives the Mosaic tabernacle the unusual description of being composed of two tents" ("Impact of the Day of Atonement," 167).

9. For bibliography of early advocates of the "instrumental" interpretation see Hughes, *Hebrews*, 283–88; Peterson, *Hebrews and Perfection*, 140–43. Modern-day advocates are Vanhoye, "Par la tente plus grande," 1–28; Cody, *Heavenly Sanctuary*, 155–65; Young, "Gospel According to Hebrews 9," 204; Koester, *Hebrews*, 408.

10. Schenck, *Cosmology and Eschatology*, 164.

sacrifice ("his own blood"). These two crucial points are conveyed in the antithetical clauses which relate to what has already been said in 9:6–8. Similarly, the main clause ("he entered once for all into the Holy Place") connects with the preceding statement describing the repeated entrances of the Levitical priests into the sanctuary (9:6–7). The chiastic structure of the passage reads thus:

> But when Christ came as a high priest of the good things that have come
>
> (a) (then) through the greater and perfect tent (*mg.* more perfect) (*dia tēs meizonos kai teleioteras skēnēs*)
>
> (b) not made with hands, that is, not of this creation (*ou cheiropoiētou, tout' estin ou tautēs tēs ktiseōs*)
>
> (b') not with the blood of goats and calves (*oude di' haimatos tragōn kai moschōn*)
>
> (a') but with his own blood (*dia de tou idiou haimatos*) he entered once for all into the Holy Place (*eisēlthen ephapax eis ta hagia*) (9:11–12).

The positive clauses (a) set out the superior sanctuary Christ enters and the superior sacrifice he offers, while the negative ones (b) demonstrate that his entry was not affected by the imperfections of the Levitical sanctuary and cultus.[11]

The use of the imagery of the Day of Atonement in both 9:11–12 and 9:1–10 proves beyond reasonable doubt that the "greater and more perfect tent" is the tabernacle in its entirety, *skēnē* being used for the whole tabernacle (8:2; 13:10). It is the whole tabernacle that features in 9:2–3 and the antithetical correspondence implies that this is also intended in 9:11–12. The Platonic nuance in 9:11 confirms this (cf. 9:24). Moreover, the antithesis of the statements in 9:11–12 in relation to 9:1–10 shows that *dia* in verse 11 should be taken in a local sense.[12] Christ, the pioneer, passes *through* the sanctuary to fulfill his role as high priest. Scholer comments

> The "local" character of the preposition *dia*, therefore, depicts Christ as walking through or traversing the heavenly sanctuary as he enters into the holy of holies in heaven. Thus the entrance is portrayed as a horizontal movement, paralleling the identical

11. Lane, *Hebrews 9–13*, 237–39.
12. Lane, *Hebrews 9–13*, 237.

practice of the earthly high priest. In fact, at *m.Yoma* 5.1, the high priest is said to have "gone 'through' the sanctuary until he came to the space between the two curtains."[13]

Support for the foregoing interpretation of the *dia* clauses in 9:11–12 is found by a number of scholars in the earlier picture of the high priest passing *through* the heavens in 4:14 and in the statement that he is "exalted above the heavens" in 7:26, which presupposes a passage through the heavens. What Hebrews means by "heaven(s)" in 7:26 is of course somewhat problematical,[14] but given the author's habit for introducing ideas which he intends to return to later it seems safe to think of 9:11–12 in line with the thought of 4:14 and 7:26.[15]

If we take the use of the word "heaven" (singular) in 9:24 (on which see more below), along with the thought of 9:11b, it would appear that what the author is referring to here is the place of the actual dwelling of God and the angels.[16] The lower heavens are thus the forecourt of the heavenly temple. We recall that Philo, in his cosmological allegorizing of the temple, makes the outer precincts stand for the sense-perceptible sphere (including "the heavens"), while the holy sanctuary is the unchanging heavenly realm of ideas where God dwells (*QE* 2:94–96).[17]

We conclude our comments on "the greater and more perfect tent" of 9:11 by endorsing the view that it is the sanctuary at large, embracing what originally were the outer and inner compartments and encompassing heaven and earth. With the removal of the curtain (10:19) the heavenly sanctuary is a single area, open to all who seek the help of the high priest.[18] The pioneer priest, having made his offering on the cross in what

13. Scholer, *Proleptic Priests*, 163. Cf. Hofius, *Vorhang*, 76–78; Schrenck, *Understanding Hebrews*, 85.

14. See e.g., Peterson, *Hebrews and Perfection*, 143; Ellingworth, *Hebrews* (1993), 446; Lincoln, *Hebrews*, 93–94, 99; Mackie, *Eschatology and Exhortation*, 157–64.

15. Moffatt, *Hebrews*, 120; Michel, *Hebräer*, 310–11; Peterson, *Hebrews and Perfection*, 143; Scholer, *Proleptic Priests*, 163–64; Attridge, *Hebrews*, 247; Lane, *Hebrews 9–13*, 237–38.

16. Michel, *Hebräer*, 311–12; Hofius, *Vorhang*, 50–53; Lane, *Hebrews 9–13*, 238. See more generally Stadelmann, *Hebrew Concept of the World*, 49–52. Cody draws a distinction between the cosmological heavens and the axiological heavens (*Heavenly Sanctuary and Liturgy*, 77–84). He defines the axiological as the "place" of God's presence, "the source of reality and the source of salvation"(83).

17. MacRae, "Heavenly Temple and Eschatology," 185; Hurst, *Hebrews*, 27.

18. So Synge, *Hebrews*, 28; Hughes, *Hebrews*, 290; Schrenck, *Understanding Hebrews*, 81, 85.

was once the outer part , has passed through the great cosmic sanctuary to enter the presence of God in its topmost part, formerly known as the holy of holies, and he did this not by means of animal sacrifices, but by virtue of his own sacrificial death, thereby securing an eternal redemption.

It was Necessary for the Sketches of the Heavenly Things to be Purified (9:23)

The next passage to be considered follows very closely the one just completed and takes us into another controversial area.

> Thus it was necessary for the sketches (*hypodeigmata*) of the heavenly things (*ta epourania*) to be purified (*katharizesthai*) with these rites, but the heavenly things (*epourania*) themselves need better sacrifices than these. For Christ did not enter a sanctuary (*hagia*) made by human hands, a mere copy of the true one (*antitupa tōn alēthinōn*), but he entered into heaven itself (*eis auton ton oupanon*), now to appear in the presence of God on our behalf (9:23–24).

Our immediate interest in this passage is the sanctuary (*hagia*), but the opening sentence has caused students of Hebrews such problems that we cannot ignore it. Why should the "heavenly things" need better sacrifices? Moffatt described the idea as "almost fantastic";[19] Montefiore called it an "unhappy comparison";[20] while Attridge thinks it an "almost intolerable paradox."[21] One cannot but wonder whether the doctrine of correspondence, which the author has used to such good effect (8:5; 9:11–12, 23; 12:18–24), has not been carried to absurdity here: since the earthly tabernacle needed cleansing (Lev 16:16; 20:3; 21:23; Num 19:20) logic requires that the same applies to its heavenly counterpart.[22]

The problem is not with the idea of a sanctuary needing cleansing. The Levitical code believed that association with sinful people tainted the tabernacle (Lev 16:16; cf. Exod 29:36). What causes the difficulty is the idea of a heavenly sanctuary needing cleansing. Jerome Smith attempts

---

19. Moffatt, *Hebrews*, 132.

20. Montefiore, *Hebrews*, 160.

21. Attridge, "The Uses of Antithesis in Hebrews 8–10," 8.

22. For a review of the different explanations of 9:23a see Cody, *Heavenly Sanctuary*, 180–92; Hughes, *Hebrews*, 379–82; Cf. Ellingworth, *Hebrews* (1993), 477; Attridge, *Hebrews*, 261–62; Mackie, *Eschatology and Exhortation*, 177.

to get around this problem by saying that it is not heaven itself but the heavenly things (presumably cultic vessels) that are purified,[23] but this is a distinction that the Day of Atonement analogy does not support. Numerous scholars think that what is meant is the cleansing of human consciences.[24] Cleansing of conscience is mentioned elsewhere (9:9, 14; 10:2, 22), but there is nothing in the context of 9:23 to support this interpretation. Another suggestion takes the "heavenly things" to be the people of God who form the church or the temple of God,[25] but this runs counter to the description of the sanctuary as "not made with hands," defined as "heaven itself" (9:24).

A solution to the problem is found by other exegetes in the biblical belief in the pervasiveness of sin and the cosmological ramifications this acquired in apocalyptic cosmology.[26] The heavens as well as the earth are thought of as inhabited by malevolent as well as benevolent beings.[27] Thus, the author of the book of Job says, "The heavens are not clean in his (God's) sight" (15:15; cf. 25:5) and the writer to the Ephesians speaks of "spiritual forces of evil in the heavenly places" (6:12; cf. Col 1:20; Luke 10:18; John 12:31; Rev 12:7–9; *1 Clem* 39:5; Ign. *Smyrm* 6:1). The cleansing of the "heavenly things" is thus understood to mean the removal of the cosmic reality of sin. The problem with this interpretation is that it imports into the text an idea, which although found elsewhere in the New Testament and the early church, is not in Hebrews, unless it is possibly hinted at in 1:13b.

The explanation that commends itself to most commentators understands the author to be speaking not of the purification of the sanctuary but of its dedication or inauguration.[28] In this regard, it is widely agreed that 9:23–28 returns to the discussion which was broken off at

23. Smith, *A Priest Forever*, 124.

24. Attridge, *Hebrews*, 262–63; Montefiore, *Hebrews*, 160; Isaacs, *Sacred Space*, 212; Schenck, "Philo and the Epistle to the Hebrews," 122; Schenk, *Cosmology and Eschatology*, 168; Thompson, *Hebrews*, 192.

25. Manson, *Hebrews*, 140–41; Bruce, *Hebrews*, 228–29; Vanhoye, *Old Testament Priests and the New Priest*, 205.

26. Michel, *Hebräer*, 213–14. Cf. Westcott, *Hebrews*, 270; Moffatt, *Hebrews*, 132; Lane, *Hebrews 9–13*, 247.

27. For the view that in the Priestly understanding gross sins attack and render impure the holy of holies, see Milgrom, *Numbers*, 444–47.

28. Ellingworth, *Hebrews* (1993), 477. Cf. Spicq, *Hébreux 2*, 267.

9:11–14, with verse 23 seen as transitional.[29] It is noted how the author, following the book of Exodus, brackets the inauguration of the covenant with the consecration of the tabernacle (9:18–21; cf. Exod 24–27).[30] Cleansing has the sense of inauguration as well as expiation (Exod 29:9; Lev 8:15).[31] Given the author's use of the covenant analogy throughout, it is concluded therefore that when he says that it was necessary for "the heavenly things to be purified with these rites" he is referring to the inauguration of the heavenly sanctuary resulting from the sacrifice of Jesus. As a new sanctuary (cf. 10:20) it does not need cleansing, but it has to be officially consecrated and commissioned.[32] However, the parallel with the purification of the *earthly* sanctuary in 9:23a makes this interpretation somewhat problematical.

What the cleansing of the "heavenly things" (9:23) means remains a problem. All the proposed solutions contain difficulties. If I were pressed to say which one of the solutions offered approximates to what might seem feasible, I would opt for the view that the author is referring to the consecration and commissioning of the heavenly temple in readiness for the new high priest. Otherwise I seem to have no option but to regard the cleansing of the "heavenly things" as a rather loose statement, pointing to the need for a better cultus. But whatever it was the listeners were supposed to understand they are assured that the cleansing resulted from the offering of "better sacrifices" (9:23), that is, from Christ's offering of himself.

He entered into Heaven itself
(*eis auton ton ouranon*) (9:24)

The measured statement that Christ did not enter the earthly sanctuary but into "heaven itself" indicates, as the contrast with the "sanctuary

29. Vanhoye, *La structure littéraire,* 157.

30. According to Exod 30:22–38; 40:1–15 oil was used for anointing the tabernacle and its contents at its dedication. Hebrews in stating that blood was used (9:21) may be referring an extrabiblical tradition, for Josephus mentions the use of both oil and blood (*Ant.* 3:206) and *b. Yoma* 4a says that oil symbolizes blood (Young, "Gospel According to Hebrews 9," 205).

31. Young, "Gospel According to Hebrews 9," 206. In Ps 45:5 (LXX) reads, "The most high has sanctified his dwelling" (*hēgiasen to skēnōma autou ho hupsistos*).

32. *Katharizein* in 9:23 is synonymous with *enkainizein* ("to inaugurate") in 9:18. Cf. Exod 29:36; Lev 8:15; and 1 Macc 4:36, "let us go up to cleanse (*katharisai*) the sanctuary (*ta hagia*) and dedicate (*enkainisai*) it." Cf. Behm, "Enkainizein," 453–54; Ellingworth, *Hebrews* (1993), 477.

made with hands" shows, that it is the heavenly temple that is signified. The use of heaven in the singular is arresting and has given rise to much discussion.[33] It seems likely that whereas plural forms of *ouranos* refer to "the heavens" that Christ "passed through" (4:14) and has been "exalted over" (7:26), the singular denotes the highest heaven where the heavenly sanctuary is located.[34] Michel speaks for others when he says that we have here an imaginative picture of Christ passing through the lower heavens (the outer tent) and entering into the *hagia*, the highest heaven.[35] Hofius reaches this conclusion by reference to apocalyptic (*T.Levi* 2:6—5:1). The heavens open (2:6) to allow Levi to pass through the different realms until he reaches "the gate of heaven" where he sees the heavenly temple and the Most High enthroned in glory (5:1).[36] In Sirach, Wisdom dwells in "the highest heavens" (24:4). The topmost or most important heaven is the dwelling of God, with the corollary that the lower heavens are part of the tabernacle.[37] In other words, the cosmic temple forms the backdrop to the author's thought.

The final words of 9:24, which tell us why Christ entered the heavenly sanctuary, point to the subject of our next chapter.

Summary

Study of the heavenly sanctuary in Hebrews must allow for the same kind of flexibility in the use of terms for the tabernacle (*hagia* and *hē skēnē*) that one finds in the LXX, often alternating between the plural and the singular without change of meaning. The complex argument of 9:11–12 yields light when we recognize the underlying Day of Atonement analogy and its chiastic structure. Christ's high priestly ministry is superior because he officiates in a superior sanctuary and offers a superior sacrifice. The "greater and more perfect tent" (9:11) is the entire sanctuary, without a dividing curtain (10:19–20). Why it needs cleansing (9:23) remains uncertain. It seems best to interpret it in terms of the consecration and

33. Schenck, *Cosmology and Eschatology*, 164–75.

34. Spicq, *Hébreux 2*, 256; Peterson, *Hebrews and Perfection*, 143; Lane, *Hebrews 9–13*, 248.

35. Michel, *Hebräer*, 312.

36. Hofius, *Vorhang*, 70–71.

37. See Attridge, who sees a link between 9:24 and 9:11: Christ passes through the *skēnē* to the *hagia* (*Hebrews*, 263). Cf. Lane, *Hebrews 9–13*, 248; Mackie, *Eschatology and Exhortation*, 157–58.

commissioning of the sanctuary. "Heaven itself" (9:24) is the heavenly temple that has been in mind throughout, here meaning the highest and most important part of the cosmic temple.

8

He Lives to Make Intercession

Chapter 8 begins the main part of the homily (8:1—10:18). The stress throughout is on what Christ does in the heavenly sanctuary. The focus on Christ and his importance for the community could not be stronger.[1]

The opening words (8:1–6) are as much an introduction of what is to follow as a summary of the preceding argument (7:1–28): the dispirited community is reassured that their pioneering leader has reached his goal and their high priest is interceding for them. The words "we have" (characteristic of the author: 4:14; 6:19; 10:19; 12:1; 13:10) focus the congregation's attention on their inestimable possession—a representative and advocate in the very presence of God. This may be specifically directed at those in the congregation who were suffering cultic deprivation since becoming Christians or, what seems more likely, it may be intended to help the congregation towards a better understanding and appreciation of Christ and a greater commitment to him.

> Now the main point (*kephalaion*)[2] in what we are saying is this:
> we have such a high priest, one who is seated at the right hand
> of the throne of the Majesty in the heavens, a minister in the

1. On the transitional function of 8:1–2 see Guthrie, who writes, "Heb 8:1–2 could be considered the centre point for the great central exposition on the high priestly ministry of Christ (*Structure*, 146). Cf. Thompson, *Hebrews*, 172. The words of 8:1–2 do not in fact summarize the previous argument but proceed to fix attention on the high priest.

2. *Kephalaion* can mean either "summary" or "main point." The latter is common in classical and Hellenistic Greek (BDAG, 541) and is the sense which suits both the immediate and the wider context. Cf. Attridge, *Hebrews*, 217; Ellingworth, *Hebrews* (1993), 400; Koester, *Hebrews*, 374–75; O'Brien, *Hebrews*, 288.

sanctuary and the true tent (*tōn hagiōn leitourgos kai tēs skēnes tēs alēthinēs*) that the Lord, and not any mortal, has set up. For every priest is appointed to offer (*prospherein*) gifts and sacrifices; hence it is necessary for this priest also to have something to offer (8:1–3).[3]

Having completed the lengthy argument on Melchizedek in chapter 7, the preacher is ready to tell his congregation something about the sanctuary in which their high priest functions. He stakes a very significant claim for the new faith by saying that Christ is "a minister in the sanctuary and the true tent" (8:2).[4]

Some commentators have paid so much attention to the origin and meaning of the spatial dichotomy used by the author that the main point of what he is saying is often overlooked. It is not the origin of the spatial dichotomy but its function as the place where Christ carries out his ministry that is uppermost.[5] The emphasis is on what the new high priest does in the sanctuary: the terms "minister" (*leitourgos*) and "ministry" (*leitourgia*) enclose the section (8:1–6).

Christ's installation as high priest introduces us to the cultic theology of Hebrews.[6] We are meant to understand that Christ is ready to officiate in the "true" sanctuary (8:2). From this point onwards in chapters 8–10 attention is focused totally on his ministry in the heavenly sanctuary. As Hay says, "The session is recalled now not for its connotation of supreme honor but for its implication that Jesus is located in the celestial sanctuary."[7] We were alerted to expect this at 5:1: "every high priest . . . offers gifts and sacrifices for sins"[8] and in 7:25 which speaks of his inter-

---

3. The verb *prospherein* is used nineteen times in Hebrews and not elsewhere in the New Testament. On the importance of the cultus in Hebrews, see below and Johnsson, "Cultus of Hebrews," 104–108; Gäbel, *Kulttheologie*, 212.

4. The "true tent" is very likely to be understood as epexegetical to "the sanctuary." So the great majority of scholars (Moffatt, *Hebrews*, 105; Lane, *Hebrews 1–8*, 200–201, 205–6; Hughes, *Hebrews*, 289; Peterson, *Hebrews and Perfection*, 130–31; Bruce, *Hebrews*, 180; Montefiore, *Hebrews*, 132; Ellingworth, *Hebrews* (1993), 400–401; Lane, *Hebrews 1–8*, 200–201, 205–06; O'Brien, *Hebrews*, 288. Other scholars argue on the basis of 9:11–12 that a distinction is required between the *skēnē* (tabernacle), through which Christ passed, and *ta hagia* (the sanctuary), which he entered in 8:2. See Vanhoye, "Par la tente plus grande," 4; Hofius, *Vorhang*, 59–60; Attridge, *Hebrews*, 218.

5. Koester, *Hebrews*, 380.

6. Johnsson, "Cultus of Hebrews," 104–8; Gäbel, *Kulttheologie*, 212.

7. Hay, *Glory at the Right Hand*, 87.

8. Hebrews 8:3 echoes 5:1 (Gäbel, *Kulttheologie*, 250).

cessory role. Not until the *Parousia* will Christ emerge from the holy of holies and appear before his expectant people (9:28; cf. 10:25, 37).

Evidence of the greatness attributed to Jesus is the application to him of Psalm 110:1.[9] This is usually understood in terms of what our author says in 10:12. As the context of this passage shows, the psalm is used in this text in support of the affirmation that Christ completed his priestly work once for all by his unique self-sacrifice, unlike the Aaronic priests who remained standing because their sacrificial work never ended (10:11; cf. 7:27). The context of the central section shows that this is the basic meaning of the statement that Christ is seated. "By a single offering he has perfected for all time those who are sanctified" (10:14). Closer to 8:1 is 1:3 (cf. 1:13), except that in 8:1 the emphasis is not on Christ's exaltation (defined in 1:13 as exaltation over the angels) so much as the *place* of his exaltation. The closing words of 8:1 want us to know that it is in heaven (*en tois ouranois*) that Jesus is enthroned, where the true sanctuary is: the subject of the very next verse (8:2). This presentation of the qualifications of the new high priest may well be intended to help the community appreciate that they have an effective advocate.[10]

The conjunction of priestly and royal prerogatives attributed to Christ in 8:1 is not as surprising as might appear, though the idea of a high priest sitting during his work in the sanctuary stretches the imagination somewhat.[11] Kings undertook priestly roles in antiquity and the Maccabees gave their priests great powers (1 Macc 10:15–20; 13:42; 14:41). Both ideas are present in Psalm 110.[12] Vitally, the psalm sup-

---

9. For the great interest taken in Psalm 110:1 in early Christianity see Mark 12:36; 14:62; 16:19; Acts 2:34–35; Rom 8:34; Eph 1:20; Col 3:1. Cf. Dodd, *According to the Scriptures*, 122; Hay, *Glory at the Right Hand*, 85–91, 143–53.

10. Mackie, *Eschatology and Exhortation*, 182.

11. Timo Eskola equates the throne and the mercy seat and argues that the imagery should be understood as entirely cultic (*Messiah and Throne*, 251–54). This fails to recognize the importance of the throne for Christ's intercessory work, on which see below.

12. For the use of Ps 110 in Hebrews see 1:3, 13; 5:6, 10; 6:20; 7:3, 11, 15, 17, 21; 8:1; 10:12–13; 12:2; Caird, "Exegetical Method," 44–51; Hay, *Glory at the Right Hand*, 85–91, 143–53; Loader, "Christ at the Right Hand," 199–217; McCullough, "Melchizedek's Varied Role," 57–58; Hengel, *Studies in Early Christology*, 133–37. Bauckham can find no trace of Ps 110:1 in Second Temple texts and concludes that its use in the New Testament means that "for early Christians it said about Jesus what no other Jews had wished to say about the Messiah or any other figure: that he had been exalted by God to participate now in the cosmic sovereignty unique to the divine identity" ("The Throne of God," 63). Bauckham does not believe his research is negated by 4Q521:ii.7

plied the writer with the scriptural warrant for finding Christ's entry into the heavenly sanctuary and his session foreshadowed in the high priest's entry into the holy of holies.[13] The *Testament of Levi* shows us Levi receiving sacerdotal and regal functions (2:10; 5:1–2; 8:1–17; 18:2) and 11 QMelchizedek portrays Melchizedek in both priestly and royal terms (ii:8, 14). In Hebrews Melchizedek's kingship makes Jesus a royal priest (7:2c). Although high priesthood is not attributed to Melchizedek in either Genesis 14 or Psalm 110 the preacher describes Jesus as such (2:17; 4:14; 5:5, 10; 6:20), doubtless because a priest who sits at God's right hand was no ordinary priest.

In depicting Jesus as occupying the throne of God on five different occasions Hebrews is attributing the greatest possible importance to him (1:3, 13; 8:1; 10:12; 12:2). For all the apocalyptic and mystical texts of Second Temple Judaism have to say about angelic beings filling the heavenly world they nowhere dare to say that they have the honor of sharing God's throne,[14] even though the ancient world was not unfamiliar with the idea of a *bisellium* or double throne.[15]

One could easily get the impression that in 8:1–3 the preacher in the flow of his sermon is mixing his metaphors, but this is not the case. He is not suggesting that Christ moves from the throne room into the holy of holies. The throne room is the holy of holies. Christ is at one and the same time king and priest.

The statement that Christ is seated at God's right hand (1:3, 13; 8:1; 10:12; 12:2) is fundamental to our understanding of his intercessory ministry in the heavenly temple and should be understood in relation to it.[16] It means that Christ has direct access to God for his intercessory

("For he will honor the devout upon the throne of eternal royalty"), maintaining that the latter reflects the ancient belief that all the righteous will after death be awarded with thrones in heaven (62). Rev 3:21 promises the martyrs a place on God's throne. Rev 20:4 can speak of "thrones" (*thronoi*).

13. Isaacs, *Sacred Space*, 150. It is possible that Hebrews may also have in mind Zech 6.13 (LXX), where the one seated at God's right hand is the anointed priest (Synge, *Hebrews*, 25).

14. Bauckham, "The Throne of God," 60–66.

15. Aune, *Revelation 1–5*, 262. In Rev 12:5 the "child" is taken up to God and his throne, which seems to mean enthronement, while 22: 1, 3 speaks of "throne of God and the Lamb."

16. On the significance of sitting on the right hand side of a person see Grundmann, "Dexios," 37–40. Cf. Collins, *Scepter and the Star*, 136–53; Escola, *Messiah and Throne*, 158–72. See the graphic portrayal of the heavenly enthronement of Moses as

work. This is not to overlook the fact that it is not only the position Christ occupies but the sacrifice he offers that makes him an effective advocate. We already know that his experiences as a human being equip him for the ministry he now undertakes (2:17–18; 4:15).

The thought of 8:1–2 leads naturally to the statement in 8:3 that "It is necessary for this priest to have something to offer (*prosenegkē*)." Since high priests ("every high priest") have the responsibility of "offering gifts according to the law" (8:4), Christ, as high priest, must follow what the law requires. But it is not the fact that since he cannot be a high priest on earth, as there is already a priesthood there, that Christ is obliged to make his offering elsewhere (in heaven). The point is rather: Christ is high priest in the sanctuary that matters, that is, in the "true" sanctuary. He offers a better sacrifice in a better temple. The words of 8:3 confirm the opening statement of 8:1–2: Christ is "a minister in the sanctuary and the true tent." [17, 18]

He Always Lives to Make Intercession for Them (7:25) [19]

Christ's role as intercessor is widely familiar to students of Hebrews. [20] It is no surprise that this is attributed to him. The high priest "prayed with outstretched hands for the whole body of the Jews" (2 Macc 15:12; Josephus *Ant.* 3:189; Philo, *Spec.Leg.* 1:97; 3:131). In *1 Enoch* the angel

---

divine vizier in the Hellenistic Jewish tragedy, *Ezekiel the Tragedian*, 70–89 in Charlesworth, *Old Testament Pseudepigrapha* 2:812. Loader declares, "It is the fact that Christ is at the right hand of God that makes intercession possible" ("Christ at the Right Hand," 206).

17. Gäbel, *Kulttheologie*, 250.

18. As Johnsson says in regard to 8:3–4, it takes us "straight into the heart of the cult, as it were" ("Cultus of Hebrews," 106). The use of the aorist (*prosenegkē),* in contrast to the present, which is used for the constantly repeated sacrifices of the Levitical priests (5:1, 3; 8:4; 9:7, 25; 10:1, 11), is an example of the author's consistent use of this tense for the definitive once-only sacrifice of Christ (1:3; 2:10, 14, 17, 18; 7:27; 8:3; 9:14, 26; 10:12, 14).

19. The conjunctive participle clause in 7:25b can be read causally or modally (BDF 418 (1) and (5). It is best taken here as causal (Zerwick and Grosvenor, *Grammatical Analysis* 2, 669).

20. See, for example, Westcott, *Hebrews*, 193–94; Murray, "The Heavenly, Priestly Activity of Christ," 44–58; Cullmann, *Christology*, 101–2; Loader, "Christ at the Right Hand," 205–7; Hay, *Glory at the Right Hand*, 130–33; Attridge, *Hebrews*, 210–11; Isaacs, *Sacred Space*, 147–53. Along with 7:25 Loader also sees in 8:3 a reference to Christ's intercession (*Sohn und Hoherpriester*, 148–50).

Michael is a heavenly high priest who intercedes for mortals (40:9; 68:2) and angels frequently have an intercessory role (1 *En* 9:1–11; 15:2; 40:6; 47:2; 99:3; 104:1).[21] The attributing of intercession to Christ would suggest itself very naturally to a writer so familiar with the Day of Atonement. Every time the high priest entered the holy of holies he carried with him the names of God's people, engraved on the precious stones on his breastplate. "Aaron shall bear the names of the sons of Israel in the breastplate of judgment on his heart when he goes into the holy place, for a continual remembrance before the Lord" (Exod 28:29; cf. 39:8–21). This means that no significance should be attached to the fact that there is only one direct mention of Christ's intercessory role in Hebrews (7:25; cf. 9:24). The very fact that Christ is in the holy of holies as high priest means that his people's needs are brought before God. Basic to Christ's intercessory ministry are his experiences as a human being (2:17; 4:14), his sacrifice and atoning work (7:23–28; 10:1). Such a high priest may confidently be expected to give help to those who need it (5:9–10; 10:19–21).[22]

It is for the express purpose of interceding "on our behalf" that Christ appears before God. Emphasizing his Christological viewpoint, the author says that it is through Christ that suppliants approach God (7:25). In contrast to the Levitical high priests who appeared before God only once a year and were constantly being replaced, the new high priest is continuously in his sanctuary, "He holds his priesthood permanently, because he continues for ever. Consequently he is able for all time to save those who approach God through him" (7:24–25).

Intercession is implied in the numerous references to Christ's entering into the heavenly sanctuary (7:26; 8:2; 9:11–12; 9:24; 10:19–20) and in the repeated appeals to the listeners to "draw near" (4:16; 7:19, 25; 10:19, 22). We are meant to understand that Christ will respond sympathetically to the appeals of his followers and present them to God.[23] In fact, the author could not be more emphatic in assuring his hearers of Christ's capacity and commitment to intercede for them: "he continually lives in order to intercede for them" (7:25).[24] In this respect Hebrews is

---

21. On the intercessory role of angelic beings see appendix C.

22. Intercession in Hebrews provides no basis for the doctrine of Christ's intercessory activity in terms of propitiation as was sometimes practiced in later times (Hanson, *Image of the Invisible God*, 153, 156).

23. Scholer, *Proleptic Priests*, 108; Mackie, *Eschatology and Exhortation*, 202–8.

24. Lane, *Hebrews 1–8*, 190. Cullmann thinks that Christ intercedes for his people "no longer simply in a collective sense as he did in his unique atoning death; now he

so similar to Romans 8:34 that Michel believes these two texts may be variants of an early confession that acknowledged the exalted Christ as the advocate of the community.[25] However it is more likely to have been developed out of the high priestly theme of the epistle and the author's own profound understanding of the incarnation.

Integral to Christ's intercessory ministry is his experience as a human being (2:17; 4:15–16; cf. 5:2, 7–9). Hebrews could not give greater emphasis to the essential link between Christ's human experiences and his intercessory work: "he had to become like his brothers and sisters in every respect, so that he might be a merciful and faithful high priest" (2:17). In his personal experience of the temptations to which human beings are exposed or prone Jesus remained faithful to his calling. His mercy, made effective because he was faithful, is expressed in his intercession for anxious souls. "In the days of his flesh, Jesus offered up prayers and supplications, with loud cries and tears, to the one who was able to save him from death, and he was heard because of his reverent submission" (5:7). Since this verse is set in a passage on Christ as high priest, Lane says that "Jesus' passion is described in its entirety as priestly prayer."[26] The relationship of Christ's priestly intercession to his experiences on earth is expressed well by Montefiore, "It is in virtue of his glorified and perfected humanity that Christ intercedes."[27] Forever joined with humanity as its representative Christ is able for all time to help those who appeal to him (7:25).[28]

Christ's earthly mission was not only to learn obedience through what he suffered, so that "he became the source of eternal salvation for all who obey him" (5:9), but also that he might be fully prepared to undertake his priestly ministry of prayer and advocacy. There is continuity and interdependence between Jesus' earthly and heavenly ministries. The pioneer who through his trials, suffering, and death opened the way into the heavenly shrine and has received the highest honor that God could give him has not ceased to care for his followers who are still on earth but is active on their behalf. The ministry he now performs in his exalted position is not distinct from or subsequent to what he endured on earth.

intercedes in every moment for each individual" (*Christology*, 102).

25. Michel, *Hebräer*, 296. Note should also be taken of 1 John 2:1.

26. Lane, *Hebrews 1–8*, 120.

27. Montefiore, *Hebrews*, 129. Cf. Cody, *Heavenly Sanctuary*, 199.

28. On the great emphasis Hebrews gives to Christ's ability to help his followers (2:18; 4:15; 7:25, *mg*, "save absolutely," NEB) see especially O'Brien, *Hebrews*, 274.

It is all of a piece; the connecting link is his humanity and his experiences as a human being. The picture Hebrews gives us of Jesus the man—the human being—in the position of greatest influence, interceding for troubled mortals is of immediate importance for theology and worship.

The question whether the writer to the Hebrews thinks of intercession including the forgiveness of sins is not clear. Koester believes that it does, and finds justification in the context of 7:25 in the reference to sacrifices for sins (7:27).[29] Ellingworth disagrees. He thinks that forgiveness is ruled out by the fact that where forgiveness of sins is specifically mentioned (9:22; 10:18) it is linked with Christ's sacrifice on the cross rather than with intercession.[30] Johnsson believes that purgation or cleansing from defilement and not forgiveness forms the conceptual background of Hebrews.[31] Noting Ellingworth's point, and having in mind the fact the writer understood Christ's offering on the cross in Yom Kippur terms (*hilaskesthai tas hamartias*, 2:17), which he viewed as taking place simultaneously on earth and in heaven (as we saw earlier in regard to 9:14), one cannot rule out the possibility that the forgiveness of sins features in Christ's heavenly prayer. Forgiveness of sins is certainly part of the quotation of Jeremiah 31:34 in 8:12 and 10:17. And in 4:15–16 prayer for those facing temptation is undoubtedly implied. It seems wise to conclude that given the varied nature of the problems faced by the congregation all the needs of the members would come within the ambit of Christ's prayers for them.

The prominence and emphasis given to the introduction of the help available to Christians ("we have a high priest," 4:14; 8:1) ("we have an altar," 13:10) indicate that the author is relating to a felt need on the part of his friends. Whether he is writing polemically or not when he says "We have such a high priest" and "we have an altar," he is assuring the listeners of the help that is graciously available. The idea of a heavenly temple with priesthood and intercession was a very prominent feature of different Jewish traditions and had grown in importance as the problems surrounding the earthly temple multiplied with the passage of time.[32] By appropriating this concept and presenting Christ as the eschatological

29. Koester, *Hebrews*, 366, 371.

30. Ellingworth, *Hebrews* (1993), 392. Cf. Loader, *Sohn und Hoherpriester*, 110–11, 144.

31. *Aphesis* (9:22; 10:18) is such a comprehensive term that it can mean different things as well as forgiveness. Cf. Johnsson, "Cultus of Hebrews," 106.

32. Appendix D.

priest in the true temple as the one who offers prayers for the faithful, the writer to the Hebrews is making a bold claim for the new faith.

Now to Appear in the Presence of God on our Behalf (9:24)

Intercession is again in mind in 9:24. In the LXX, "appearing in the presence of God" means seeking help in prayer (Ps 27:8 (26:8)) and "seeing" God's face refers to receiving a favor from God (Pss 17 (16):15; 42(41):2; Matt 18:10; Rev 22:4). Westcott sees emphasis here on the openness or clarity of Christ's appearing before God in contrast to the appearance of the high priest on the Day of Atonement in the dark sanctuary enveloped in a cloud of incense (Lev 16:12–13),[33] but this seems speculative.

Christ appears before God, not for his personal benefit, but solely "on our behalf" (9:24; cf. 6:20; 7:25). What it is that the heavenly priest does "on our behalf" in 9:24 is not specified and has aroused curiosity through the ages. Exegetes of an earlier age were content to say that Christ speaks for his suppliants quite simply by his presence at his father's side.[34] Paul sees the righteousness of Christ imputed to sinners as part of Christ's heavenly ministry (2 Cor 5:21; cf. 1 Cor 1:30; Phil 3:9). What we can say is that his prayer is not the desperate cry of a suppliant but the confident appeal of a well-prepared advocate.

It is "now" that Christ is helping those who appeal to him. The position of the adverb in 9:24 makes it emphatic. It means that Jesus' intercession is taking place at this very moment: "he is now appearing in the

---

33. Westcott, *Hebrews*, 272.

34. Theologians took a particular interest in how Christ intercedes for mortals. Some Roman Catholic theologians, having in mind the humanity which Christ has taken, have tended to depict him as petitioning God in an attitude of humility and submission, while Reformed exegetes, focusing on Christ's exalted position, reacted against the thought of him as an abject, impassioned suppliant and regarded his intercession as an expression of the efficacy of his once for all sacrifice. On this subject see Demerest, *Priest After the Order of Melchizedek*, quoted in Peterson, *Hebrews and Perfection*, 248. The Pauline concept of imputed righteousness finds expression in the view which thinks of the interchange between Christ and God resulting in God's responding to Christ's intercession by looking not at the culpable sinner but at his righteous son. This is memorably expressed in the words "Look Father on his anointed face and only look at us as found in him," in William Bright's hymn, "And Now, O Father, Mindful of the Love."

presence of God on our behalf."[35] This gives force to the perspective of the entire homily by connecting the message of Jesus Christ the high priest "forever" to human need.[36]

Christ enters the heavenly sanctuary "with (*dia*) his own blood" (9:12, 14; 10:19; 13:12), i.e., his saving death.[37] The alternative translation of 9:12, which takes *dia* in an instrumental sense ("by means of his own blood")[38] requires us to believe that the Day of Atonement analogy breaks down at this point.[39] Undoubtedly, the author strains the imagery to the limit, but having used the analogy so consistently throughout it would be very strange if he were to abandon it at the climatic moment. In the Day of Atonement ritual,[40] the death of the victim, the passage of the high priest into the sanctuary, and the offering of the blood are an interconnected series of actions that form a whole (Lev 4:3–7; 8:14–17; 16:11–14, 15; cf. Exod 29:10–12).[41] Thomson helps us follow the author's chain of thought when he says, "The author . . . has collapsed the death and exaltation into one event, bringing together Good Friday and Easter. 'Blood' is not a substance that the exalted Christ brings into the sanctuary but a metaphor for Jesus' sacrifice of himself."[42]

Throughout the central part of the sermon the author has been contrasting Christ's once-for-all sacrifice with the repeated sacrifices of

35. Mackie, *Eschatology and Exhortation*, 182. Cf. Attridge, *Hebrews*, 263.

36. On Jesus Christ "the same yesterday, today and forever" in 13:8 and its relation to the needs of the community see Bruce, *Hebrews*, 375.

37. For the translation "with his own blood" in 9:12 (RSV, NRSV, et al.) see Spicq, *Hébreux 2*, 280; Loader, *Sohn und Hoherpriester*, 176; Scholer, *Proleptic Priests*, 164; Ellingworth, *Hebrews* (1993), 452; Pfitzner, *Hebrews*, 128–29; Thompson, *Hebrews*, 186.

38. So Peterson, *Hebrews and Perfection*, 137; Bruce, *Hebrews*, 213; Lane, *Hebrews 9–13*, 236; Koester, *Hebrews*, 410; Gordon, *Hebrews*, 120.

39. Thus Attridge, *Hebrews*, 263.

40. See appendix C.

41. Nelson, *Raising up a Faithful Priest*, 78–80. "In the popular mind, sacrificing an animal is the same thing as killing it. This oversimplification of the sacrificial act and the overemphasis on the death of the victim has caused all sorts of mischief in the history of Christian thought. In reality, animal sacrifices in the Hebrew Bible were complex ritual events that involved a series of actions" (Nelson, "He Offered Himself: Sacrifice in Hebrews, *Int* 57 (2003), 252). The same point is made by Herbert, "The idea that the death of the victim was the center of sacrifice is simply false. The animal was killed not in order that its life might be destroyed (for 'the blood is the life'), but that the life offered in death might become available for the holy purpose of sacrifice" (*Intercommunion*, 239). The death of the victim was essential, but preparatory.

42. Thompson, *Hebrews*, 186.

the Levitical system (7:27; 9:11–12, 25–26, 28; 10:11–12) and in 9:24–26 he very pointedly compares Christ's entrance into the sanctuary to the Levitical high priest, who having presented the sacrificial blood ("blood that is not his own"), had to leave the sanctuary immediately, only to return and go through the same procedure again and again, year after year. Christ's sacrifice being a real sacrifice, and not a token one, it is perpetually effective and therefore needs no repetition. He appears before God on the basis of "the sacrifice of himself" (9:26), presented and accepted once for all and for all time (10:12). Like the high priest on the Day of Atonement he intercedes for his people, but, unlike them, he does not leave the sanctuary but remains to continue his intercession.

We have a Great Priest over the House of God
(*epi ton oikon tou theou*) (10:21)

The idea of Christ's oversight over the household of God, like his intercession, refers to his continuing ministry in the heavenly world. "House" is taken by some commentators to mean the heavenly sanctuary[43] and by others as the heavenly sanctuary and the earthly church,[44] but it must refer to God's people.[45] The writer nowhere else describes believers as God's temple.

The people of Israel are called God's "house" in Hos 8:1 and this is what is already in mind in Hebrews 3:6 ("we are his house"). The reference in 10:21 may actually refer specifically to the community addressed. 10:21 develops the thought of 3:6. He who was "over God's house as a son" is now "great priest over the house of God." Thus while the use of "house" for the community of believers recalls this use in Eph 2:19 and 1 Tim 3:15, and behind this a long established tradition,[46] it is unlikely that Hebrews 10:21 has the heavenly temple in mind, for the author nowhere speaks of a sanctuary as a "house" (*oikos*) or suggests that believers are themselves a temple.[47] The text before us expands the thought of 3:6

43. BAGD, 698; Héring, *Hebrews*, 91; Vanhoye, *Old Testament Priests and New Priest*, 104.

44. Peterson, *Hebrews and Perfection*, 154.

45. Westcott, *Hebrews*, 321; Pelser, "A Translation Problem," 49; Ellingworth, *Hebrews* (1993), 522.

46. Michel, "Oikos," 125–31. See 2 Sam 1–17. The Jews of Qumran spoke of themselves as a "house," which they understood as a temple (1 QS 5:5–6; 8:4–10; 9:3–6).

47. I no longer think that *oikos* in 10:21 refers to the heavenly temple (contra

so that it conveys Christ's particular role in the church.[48] The assertion that Christ is in charge of God's "house" reminds one of what other New Testament writers have in mind when speaking of Christ's lordship, but our author by connecting Christ's role in God's "house" with his high priestly function suggests that we should think of Christ's responsibility less in terms of authority and more of oversight, expressing itself in care for his people, and evoking in them confidence to approach him (10:21–22).[49]

There is one further point at which some commentators see an allusion to the Day of Atonement analogy. It is in the statement at the end of chapter 9 that Christ "will appear a second time." Just as the reappearance of the high priest on the completion of his work in the holy of holies was a specially welcome sight for the waiting people (Sir 50:5–10; cf. Lev 16:18; m. Yoma. 7:4) since his return would signify God's acceptance of the sacrifice, so it is suggested Christ's return from his work in heaven will be welcomed by "those who are eagerly waiting for him" (9:28).[50] This is possibly what is intended, but it depends upon whether the author is still using Day of Atonement categories at this point, and this is not certain.[51]

New Covenant—Greater Tent

Integrated with the exposition on Christ's work in the heavenly sanctuary is a lengthy discourse on the new covenant in relation to the former covenant (8:8–13; 9:15–22; 10:15–17).[52] This has the effect of making the

---

McKelvey, *New Temple*, 135). I am thus in disagreement with Robinson, who sees in Heb 10:21 a reference to the new temple. He writes, "the whole argument of chapters 9 and 10 leads to the climax that Jesus has now 'opened' the new sanctuary in the temple of his body" (*Twelve New Testament Studies*, 172). Cf. Hofuis, "Inkarnation und Opfertod," 132–41.

48. As Attridge says in regard to 3:6, "That God's 'house' is in fact God's people is made clear from the relative clause that specifies the house as 'ourselves' (*hēmeis*)" (*Hebrews*, 111).

49. For *epi* as oversight see 1 Macc 6:14; 10:69; 2 Macc 12:20; Matt 24:45; 25: 21, 23; Luke 12:42; Acts 6:3; BAGD, 365.

50. So Bruce, *Hebrews*, 232–33; Hughes, *Hebrews*, 388–89; Lane, *Hebrews 9–13*, 250–51; Stökl Ben Ezra, *Impact of Yom Kippur*, 190; Gäbel, *Kulttheologie*, 212.

51. Attridge, *Hebrews*, 266; DeSilva, *Perseverance*, 316.

52. Lehne, *New Covenant*, 123–24; Dunnill, *Covenant and Sacrifice*, 149–87. For the connection of the covenants and the sanctuaries see Vanhoye, *La Structure*, 139–61; Lane, *Hebrews 1–8*, 203–4. On the wider relationship of the two covenants to

subject appear as an irrelevant intrusion since it is the tabernacle that is under discussion. In fact, there is a close connection between covenant and tabernacle. In the book of Exodus the introduction of the tabernacle is made immediately to follow the inauguration of the covenant at Sinai (Exod 24–27) and Hebrews takes the two subjects together (9:18–21).[53] The relevance of the new covenant discourse becomes clear in the contrast between the two covenants and the two sanctuaries in chapters 8–10. The subject is clearly demarcated in the *inclusio* framed by the quotations from Jeremiah 31:31–34 in 8:8–12 and 10:16–17. As in other comparisons in which Christ is said to be "better" (*kreitton*) than his Jewish counterpart (6:9; 7:19; 9:23; 10:34; 12:24), the new covenant is not intended to denigrate the first covenant so much as a way of demonstrating the greatness of the second one, seen as the promised fulfillment of the former (8:8 = Jer 31:31).

The contrast is between the two covenants and the two sanctuaries. There are further antitheses within chapters 8–10: the old cultus and the new (9:1–10), the outer and the inner sanctuaries (9:6–8), internal and external (8:10; 9:9–10; 10:16); heavenly and earthly sanctuaries (9:23–24), copy and true form (9:24; 10:1; cf. 8:2), the one sacrifice and the many (9:7, 26–28; 10:11–14), those who looked forward to the fulfillment of the promise and those who received it (11:1–40), the fearsome experience of Sinai and the joyful assembly on the heavenly Mount Zion (12:18–24).

Throughout Hebrews 8–10 there is a play on the words "first" (*prōtē*) and "second" (*deutera*).[54] There are two covenants (8:7, 13; 10:9), two tents (9:2–10) and two dispensations (10:9).[55] The contrast that these couplets introduce is striking. In the case of the tabernacle it is only its twofold nature which is of interest to the writer (9:6–8). Everything else about the tabernacle is of secondary importance (9:1–5). The author concentrates on the division of the sanctuary into two compartments in chapters 8–9.

the epistle at large see Schenck, *Cosmology and Eschatology,* 91–111.

53. For the chiastic structure that scholars see in Heb 8–9 and the connection between the covenant and the sanctuary and priesthood see Lane, *Hebrews 1–8,* 203–4. On the important place that Gäbel believes the covenant has in the narrative see his *Kulttheologie,* 242. Gäbel agues that the two covenants are intimately connected with the two-fold meaning of *hypodeigma* "sketch," (8:5; 9.23) (*Kulttheologie,* 242).

54. The play on words suggests that the difference between the earthly and the heavenly sanctuaries has at least as much to do with the typological relationship between the two covenants as with Platonic dualism. Cf. Lane, *Hebrews 1–8,* cxxiii.

55. Cf. Schenck, *Cosmology and Eschatology,* 78–111.

This distinction is crucial for understanding what is said in chapter 9. The author works his metaphor with such enthusiasm that clarity suffers. The standard designations *hagia*, "holy place" and *hagia hagiōn*, "holy of holies" (9:3, 12, 24) are juxtaposed with the numerical terms *prōtē*, "first" (9:2, 6, 8) and *deutera*, "second" (9:7). But what is meant is clear enough without following Synge and D'Angelo, who argue that the author was thinking not just of two parts of the single construction but two separate tents.[56] The words "first" and "second" do not signify two separate tents, but adjoining rooms of a single sanctuary. Figuratively speaking, the first tent symbolizes the present age (9:9), the time in which the first covenant was in force, and serves as a spatial metaphor for this time, but it is no longer operative once the second was introduced (8:7, 13; 10:9).[57] The play upon the words in the context (9:6–7) suggests that we can read 10:9 to refer to both covenants and sanctuaries: "He abolishes the first in order to establish the second."

The author has now completed his theological exposition. He has gone to considerable lengths to describe the ministry of Christ the "great high priest" who "lives forever." As we are to see in the final section, the so-called *peroration* or conclusion of the sermon (10:32—13:25), the preacher is ready to apply what he has said by urging his friends to avail themselves of this great means of grace. It is an extended application to the life and worship of the hearers which develops points touched upon earlier and concludes with a new and vigorous challenge. The author's use of the Day of Atonement analogy and the symbolic world of Leviticus, which has served his purpose so well, is all but finished. Intricate and extensive as his arguments in the doctrinal sections are, the immediate needs of the congregation are kept constantly in view. The comparison of the pioneer's passage through the heavens to the entrance of the high priest into the holy of holies has these needs in mind throughout, and this will be given dramatic expression in the final section. The writer is fully aware of the human condition and people's need of something or someone greater than themselves. The one who is both human and divine—Jesus *pontifex* the bridge builder—spans the yawning divide that

56. Synge, *Hebrews*, 26–27; D'Angelo, *Moses*, 225–31. Synge writes, "It is clear that in 9.2f Hebrews is distinguishing between two tabernacles" (*Hebrews*, 26). So also Lehne, *New Covenant*, 100–101. See the critique by Young, "The Gospel According to Hebrews 9," 200, and Lane, *Hebrews 9–13*, 219.

57. Hofius, "'Das 'erste' und das 'zweite' Zelt,'" 271–77; Young, "Gospel According to Hebrews 9," 200–202; Lane, *Hebrews 9–13*, 224.

separates sinners from God. His once and for all self-sacrifice achieves what the sacrifices of the old order labored to achieve, but failed. It is available for all time.

Summary

The main point of the sermon for the community is the assurance that they have a representative and advocate in the presence of God. They should look beyond the reality of their situation to the unseen reality of Christ's ministry in the heavenly sanctuary. In depicting this sanctuary as a "true" (8:2) the author is impressing upon the listeners the great significance of Christ and his priestly work (8:3–5). Christ's session at God's right hand facilitates his work as intercessor (7:25). Both his experiences as a human being and the efficacy of his sacrifice qualify him for such a ministry. It is intercession without limit and available for all time. Coupled with it is Christ's role as head of God's household (10:21). In the section describing Christ's contemporaneous ministry "for us" (8–10), the part devoted to the contrast between the old and new covenants is not the interruption it appears to be when one sees it in relation to the twin idea of the two sanctuaries. What the author says in chapters 8–10 about the ministry in which Christ is now engaged completes his theological exposition. He leaves the listeners with his compelling presentation of Christ as the one whose unique self-sacrifice saves humankind and whose intercession is undertaken on behalf for all who appeal for help.

9

Confidence to Enter the Sanctuary

We return to 4:14–16 to consider it from another point of view. It is the first of a number of passages in which the author encourages those following the pioneer on the pilgrimage of faith to "draw near" (*proserchesthai*) to their high priest in the heavenly sanctuary and find the help they need (4:16; 6:18–20; 10:19–22; 12:22–24; cf. 7:19, 23).[1] Very importantly, it is on the basis of what Christ has done and continues to do that they are encouraged to approach God. "Drawing near" to God is all but universally understood to refer to prayer or prayer and worship.[2] It bears no relation whatever to the mystical transportation to heaven that is so common in apocalyptic and mystical writings described in appendix B.

The significance of what Hebrews says about "drawing near" to God or the "throne of grace" cannot be overstated.[3] Access to God was a matter of the greatest possible importance to the people of the Bible (Pss 26:8; 42:1–4; 48:8–9; 61:4; 63:1–2; 65:1–2; 66:13–15; 84:1–2, 7–10; 100:4),

1. On the strong cultic associations of "drawing near" in the LXX see Scholer, *Proleptic Priests*, 93–94. The phrase is used for priestly access to God (Lev 9:7–8; 21:17–24; 22:3) and the approach of the people in worship (Exod 16:9; Lev 9:5; Num 18:4). On the prerogative and privilege of the high priest entering the holy of holies on the Day of Atonement see appendix C.

2. Scholar, *Proleptic Priests*, 11, 144–46, 201; Isaacs, *Sacred Space*, 218–19; De Silva, *Perseverance*, 329, 337; Thompson, *Hebrews*, 105. Scott Mackie makes an unconvincing attempt to interpret the "drawing near" texts (4:14–16; 10:19–23) in terms of mystical ascent to heaven ("Heavenly Sanctuary Mysticism," 76–117).

3. Lindars says, "The leading thought for Hebrews is *direct access to God*" (*Hebrews*, 46, author's italics).

but such was their intensely acute sense of God's holiness and majesty this was only possible by means of a specially chosen proxy who carried out his responsibilities within strictly defined limits.[4] So great was the desire to reach God, however, that a more direct means was devised by venturesome apocalyptic visionaries and Heikhalot mystics. These were prepared to go to great lengths to prepare themselves for the mystical journey whatever its perils.[5]

One can well believe that those who received Hebrews must have found the idea of the heavenly sanctuary thrown open to all startling, to say the very least. This groundbreaking change has been brought about by Christ, the new high priest. His atoning work enables suppliants to have forgiveness and cleansing from sin (1:3; 2:17; 8:12; 9:14; 10:17, 18, 22) and gain entrance into what had been for the listeners the most sacred place imaginable (4:16; 6:19; 10:19; 12:22).

"Drawing near" is a corporate act, to be undertaken by the community. This is to be inferred from the fact that in 10:19–21 it is linked with "our confession" (*homologia*) and an appeal to the community to keep together.[6] It was one thing for the troubled community to hear the good news that their leader had reached his destination and opened up the way into the sanctuary, but it may well have been quite a different matter for them to act on this. The fact that the exhortation is repeated so frequently and given such prominence in the final appeal of the sermon suggests not only the importance of the subject but the likelihood that the invitation to enter to enter the presence of God was so novel and startling that the listeners hesitated in responding to it. Undertaking it on a congregational basis would have been particularly important.

If my suggestion is near to the mark it is further evidence of the christological deficit in the church. Viewed alongside the great concentration on Christ as high priest it suggests a failure to understand or appropriate his saving work in relation to inherited Jewish beliefs and practices. The author endeavors to allay any fears his hearers may have by showing that thanks to Christ the throne of God is now the "throne of grace." Later he will give a graphic picture of the "new and living way that Christ opened for us" to enter the presence of God (10:19–20). The repeated claim "We have a (great) high priest" (3:1; 4:14; 7:26; 8:1; 10:21),

4. On the high priest see appendix C
5. See appendix B.
6. Thompson, *Hebrews*, 210.

asserting that what was once the special prerogative reserved for a very privileged individual is now offered to all believers, is central to the overriding argument of the sermon.

> Since, then, we have a great high priest who has passed through the heavens, Jesus, the Son of God, let us hold fast to our confession. For we do not have a high priest who is unable to sympathize with our weaknesses, but we have one who in every respect has been tested as we are, yet without sin. Let us therefore approach (*proserchōmetha*) the throne of grace with boldness (*parrēsia*), so that we may receive mercy and find grace to help in time of need (4:14–16).

This passage bears such close resemblance to 10:19–23 that a number of scholars believe these two exhortatory passages to be connected. Weiss regarded them as "decisive control centres."[7] Guthrie believes the parallels between 4:14–16 and 10:19–23 "represent the most striking use of *inclusio* in the book of Hebrews."[8]

The parallels are

4:14–16	10:19–23
Jesus	Jesus
(the Son) of God	(the house) of God
Since we have	Since we have
a great high priest	a great priest
through the heavens	through the curtain
let us hold fast to our	let us hold fast to the
Confession	Confession
let us approach with	let us approach with
Boldness	Boldness

The parallels take us to the heart of the sermon, setting forth Christ's work as pioneer and high priest and its import for Christian belief and access to divine grace. They give clear expression to what Isaacs calls "a new and powerful theology of access," since both portray the pioneer opening the way into the holy of holies and the high priest welcoming his suppliants.[9] These texts are integral to the Christian cultus as set out in Hebrews and especially relevant to the pastoral needs of the community.

---

7. Weiss, *Hebräer*, 52.

8. Guthrie, *Structure of Hebrews*, 79; Westfall, *Discourse Analysis*, 133–39; 230–40.

9. Isaacs, *Sacred Space*, 127–77. See the detailed study of the language of "access" in Hebrews and its cultic overtones in Scholer, *Proleptic Priests*, 91–149, 150–84.

The here-and-now meaning of the texts to be examined complements the futuristic thrust of the sermon but in no way weakens it. Dahl
writes of the recipients, "Having in prayer access to God through Christ
they have already a share in the life of the new, eschatological world. In
worship the eschatology is 'realized,' but only proleptically."[10] The writer
is obviously anxious to impress upon his readers that as Christians they
are God's people *now*. Because they have Jesus as their high priest Christians' access to God is possible *now*. This is not apart from the earthly
pilgrimage, but essential to it, directing and sustaining it. In Johnsson's
expressive phrase, Christians are "a cultic community on the move."[11]

The throne of grace to which the recipients are invited is the antitype
to the "mercy seat" in the earthly temple (9:5, *hilastērion*. Cf. 4:16; Lev
16:2).[12] It was before the earthly mercy seat that propitiation was made
on the Day of Atonement and the grace of God extended to the people.[13]
Fascinatingly, one rabbinic source says that God has two thrones: the
throne of justice and the throne of grace. Special prayer was required for
God to move from the throne of justice to the throne of grace (*Midr R.
Lev* 29:1).[14] As we saw, the throne of God had irresistible appeal for the
apocalyptic and mystical writers. Our author's compressed mention of
the throne of grace is in striking contrast to the gigantic throne in the seventh heaven surrounded by millions of angels in the Jewish writings so
graphically described in the material produced by Gershom Scholem.[15]
In particular, Hebrews very pointedly directs attention to the sole occupant of its sanctuary. As a result of what Christ, the true high priest,
has accomplished God's throne is now above all the throne of grace.[16]
The christological emphasis so characteristic of Hebrews is now clearer
than ever.

Since Hebrews thinks of Christ reigning in heaven (1:3, 8, 13; 8:1;
10:12; 12:2) one naturally thinks of the throne of grace as his special
throne, but it is more likely to be the throne of God (though shared by

10 Dahl, "New and Living Way," 409.

11. Johnsson, "Pilgrimage Motif," 249.

12. It is odd that Heb 9:5 does not highlight the mercy seat. The emphasis is on
Christ offering his blood (9:12–14; 10:19; 13:12).

13. Compare the "throne of mercy" of Isa 16:5 (LXX) and the "throne of judgment"
of Pss 9:4, 7; 122:5; Prov 20:8. See the use of propitiatory language in Heb 2:17c.

14. Goodenough, *By Light, Light*, 235–36, 263–64.

15. Scholem, *Major Trends*.

16. Michel, *Hebräer*, 209–10.

Christ) in view of the fact that the word "approach" (*proserchesthai*) is used in the homily for approaching God (7:25; 10:1; 11:6).[17] In point of fact it is Christ's throne as much as God's. And since the one who was the first to approach the throne of God, having made himself the offering for sin, the throne he shares is the place of mercy to which all are now urged to draw near. They have nothing to bring; they only receive. The importance of "drawing near" is seen from its repetition (4:16; 7:19, 25; 10:19, 22; cf. 12:22).

The high priestly motif is much to the fore in the references to "draw near, " but this is not to say that the pioneer figure is neglected. Attridge rightly sees its presence in the exhortation to "draw near" (*proserchesthai*), which we shall find repeated beside its companion verbs *eiserchesthai* (6:19–20; 9:12, 24) and *engizein* (7:19).[18] He says, "Through that exhortation the addressees are urged to follow the path 'through the heavens' that Christ blazed and take advantage of the access to God that he provides."[19] Similarly, Ellingworth notes how the language of drawing near "complements that of the journeyings of God's people (2:10; 4:1, 9; 12:2; 13:14)." [20]

Let us Approach the throne of Grace with Boldness (4:16)

"Drawing near" means appearing in the presence of God (*emphanisthēnai tō prosōpō*, 9:24).[21] It has its beginnings at least in Israel's pilgrimage to Mount Zion and God's temple. It features prominently in the graphic

---

17. Koester, *Hebrews*, 284.

18. See the repeated use of *proserchesthai* (7:25; 10:1, 22; 11:6; 12:18, 22). Cf. Scholer, *Proleptic Priests*, 91–149, 150–84.

19. Attridge, *Hebrews*, 141.

20. Ellingworth, *Hebrews* (1993), 270.

21. The verb "draw near" is used of worshippers approaching God (Exod 16:9; Lev 9:5; Num 10:3–4; 1 Sam 14:36; Sir: 1:28, 30) and of priests going to the altar (Lev: 9:7; 21:17; 22:3). Cf. Schneider, "Proserchomai," 683. Hebrews uses this form of expression consistently throughout (4:16; 7:25; 10:1, 22; 11:6; 12:18, 22). The Israelites are referred to in Heb 10:1 as the *proserchomenoi*, "those who approach God." See Peterson (*Hebrews and Perfection*, 78–79) and at length Scholer (*Proleptic Priests*, 91–149). According to DeSilva "drawing near" contrasts with "shrinking back" (10:38; cf. "failing to reach" (4:1; 12:15) (*Perseverance*, 339). Mackie is to be questioned, however, when he says that the author intended his exhortations to "draw near" to "provide an exact rhetorical foil to his graphic depictions of disobedience, which repeatedly employ the language of movement to denote rebellious withdrawal from God" (*Eschatology and Exhortation*, 207).

picture of the festival assembly at the heavenly Mount Zion in 12:22–24. The cultic terminology is revamped by the author and applied to the congregation so that the work of Christ is efficacious not only in the future, but now in the present.[22]

The exhortations to "draw near" are in the present tense (*proserchōmetha*) (4:16; 10:21). Even if this means that the readers were not altogether unfamiliar with such a break with religious practice,[23] it is still possible that they were hesitant or reluctant to follow their leader priest all the way by entering into the most holy place of all (5:11–14). The elites of apocalyptic and mystical circles and the Jews at Qumran might not be deterred by the awesome majesty and inapproachability of God and claim to worship with the angels, but it may well have been a very different matter for the average worshipper.

The "confidence" (*parrēsia*) which the congregation is exhorted to have in approaching God means courage, fearlessness, and freedom of speech or authority to undertake some task.[24] It applies to one's approach to figures of authority, especially in approaching God. Job is a good example. His fearless tenacity in appealing to God, despite persistent opposition and ridicule (7:11–21; 13:13–28; 23:1–17), influenced much later thought on one's approach to God (*1 En* 104:2; *T.Levi* 4:2–3; 4 Ezra 7: 98–99; Philo, *Her.* 5–7; Josephus *Ant* 2:52; 5:38). The recipients of Hebrews are urged to overcome the reserve and fear they had inherited from Jewish belief and practice and approach God without hesitation. As in the case of Job, our author thinks particularly of approaching God in prayer. We shall find this line of thought developed in 10:19–20. Confidence is on the one hand an internal assurance that one is welcomed by God and on the other hand visibly expressed in prayer and fearless witness.[25]

---

22. Scholer, *Proleptic Priests*, 108. Note the use of the present tense (*proserchōmetha*) in 4:16 and 10:21.

23. So Scholer, *Proleptic Priests*, 106. Lane translates the Greek as "let us continue to draw near" at 4:16 and 10:22 (*Hebrews 9–13*, 286), i.e., assuming that the members of the church were already doing so. I suggest that the continuous action implied by the present tense of the verb and its repeated use indicate that the author wants the congregation to make a practice of availing themselves of this means of grace.

24. Vorster, "Meaning of PARRHESIA," 54; Schlier, "Parrēsia," 871–86; BAGD 781 (3). "In content *parrēsia* is freedom of access to God, authority to enter the sanctuary, openness for the new and living way which Christ has restored for us (10:19)" (Schlier, "Parrēsia," 884). For *parrēsia* as courage, see especially Acts 4:13, 29, 31. Cf. 2 Cor 3:12.

25. On the subjective and objective character of *parrēsia* see Käsemann, *Wandering People,* 43; Scholer, *Proleptic Priests*, 109–110; Attridge, *Hebrews*, 284. Käsemann

The exhortations to "draw near to the throne of grace" are taken by numerous commentators to mean that Christians are the new priesthood.[26] The Levitical priesthood is believed to have funneled into the priesthood of Christ and through him into the priesthood of all Christians. Bourke says, "What the Old Testament reserved to the priesthood is attributed to all believers."[27] This is contested by Isaacs who says that any idea of a priestly succession, which passes from the Levitical order to Christ and his followers, flies in the face of what Hebrews is saying. It is the uniqueness of Christ's priesthood that is argued, not its inclusiveness or transmission.[28] We shall return to this question.

Key to the confidence human beings are encouraged to have in approaching the throne of God is Jesus Christ. He is the merciful and faithful high priest. He shares humanity and because he experienced human weakness and genuine human temptation himself he is able to sympathize with those who are weak and vulnerable to temptation, especially weakness that leads to sinning (4:15; cf. 7:26). "We have one who in every respect has been tested as we are, yet without sin" (4:15).[29]

> We have this hope, a sure and steadfast anchor of the soul, a hope that enters (*eiserchomenēn*) the inner shrine behind the curtain, where Jesus, a forerunner (*prodromos*) on our behalf (*huper hēmōn*), has entered (*eisēlthen*), having become a high priest for ever according to the order of Melchizedek (6:19–20).[30]

says, "One 'has,' (10.19) *parrēsia*, not merely as a subjective attitude, but as an approximation of something already given" (43).

26. See Westcott, *Hebrews*, 187, 318, 321; Congar, *Mystery of the Temple*, 175; Best, "Spiritual Sacrifice," 280–86; Floor, "General Priesthood," 73, 77. Vanhoye thinks Hebrews is tending in the direction of the priesthood of all the faithful (*Old Testament Priests and New Priest*, 230). Cf. Scholer, *Proleptic Priests*, 91–184, who believes that the priesthood of the faithful is not more than implicit in Hebrews. Westfall, by contrast, has no doubts that believers are priests in Hebrews (*Discourse Analysis*, 200, 205, 233).

27. Bourke, "Hebrews," 933.

28. Isaacs, "Priesthood," 58.

29. On the sinlessness of Jesus (4:15) see Williamson, "Hebrews 4.15 and Sinlessness of Jesus," 4–8; Koester, *Hebrews*, 293–95. The fact that Christ was without sin does not affect his solidarity with humans. "Authentic solidarity with sinners does not consist in becoming an accomplice of their faults, but in bearing the whole weight of the penalty that results from these faults" (Vanhoye, *Old Testament Priests and New Priest*, 114).

30. On 6:19–20 also see chapter 4.

The dynamic language of movement that we noted earlier is conveyed very effectively in this passage by the term "forerunner." The metaphors flow in rapid succession, becoming mixed in the process and problematic for the interpreter, but the effort of the author to impress upon his hearers the importance of Jesus Christ is not in any doubt.

Gordon serves us well by drawing attention to the extraordinary presentation of Jesus as the forerunner who has gone into the sanctuary with the intention that others will follow him there.[31] "Nothing in the Old Testament cult prepares us for this idea—adumbrated here, to be developed in 10.19ff—that the entry of this high priest paves the way for others."[32] Once again the solidarity of Christ and his people is in mind. And doctrinal exposition is again followed by pastoral encouragement. Those in danger of drifting from their Christian moorings (2:1) are assured that their faith is secured, anchor-like, by virtue of their pioneer having entered the heavenly sanctum and is on duty as high priest.

Is it the "anchor" or the "hope" that penetrates behind the veil and what precisely is meant? Since the anchor connotes stability the thought of its moving into the holy of holies is incongruous. In any case, the relative pronoun (*hēn*) is the complement of the immediately preceding word ("hope") in 6:18b and there cannot be much doubt that it is the "hope" that enters the sanctuary. The other question immediately follows: what does "hope" mean? The answer is seen in the parallel use of the verb "enter" (*erchomai*) in the next verse. It is Christ in his atoning and intercessory capacity. This gives stability to those who are wavering. The christological intent of the passage surfaces in the author's statement that it is expressly "on our behalf" that Christ became forerunner and entered the holy of holies (6:20; 9:24). Which veil it is that is in mind in 6:19–20 is not a problem; it is obviously the inner one (Lev 17:2, 12, 15). The veil that features in 10:19–20 is considered later in this chapter.

How 6:19–20 connects with the practical needs of the readers is not certain. Commentators have been in the habit of taking the figure of the anchor in relation to 2:1, which they have understood to be a nautical metaphor (*pararrein*, NRSV, "to drift away"). The congregation or some members of it were believed to be in danger of abandoning their Christian faith.[33] However, the word *pararrein* has a much more general sense

---

31. Gordon, *Hebrews*, 79.

32. Quoted by Motyer, "The Temple in Hebrews: Is it there?," 184.

33. Cf., for example, Hughes, *Hebrews*, 73–74.

(Prov 3:21 [LXX]),[34] so that the danger the author is warning against may refer to losing contact with the teaching they had received (3:6; 4:11; the "confession," 10:23). If those who are described in the context as having "taken refuge" (6:18) are literal refugees there may be something to be said for those who adopt a sociological approach to the text and take the "hope" to be offered to people who are rootless and in need of security.[35] What is not in any doubt is the assurance given to the members of the church: their pioneer and forerunner has successfully completed the journey and taken up his position in the presence of God. The whole purpose of the forerunner is bound up entirely with those on whose behalf he functions, that is, those following him, while the presence of a merciful and faithful high priest in the sanctuary forms the basis of the exhortations to the hearers to "draw near" (4:16; 10:19–22; cf. 7:25).

Hebrews 6:19–20 thus has a particularly influential place in the author's strategy for leading the listeners forward in the direction in which he wishes to move them. Verses 9:12, 24, 25 are parallel with 6:20. Chapter 10 repeats and develops what we have seen are the leading ideas of the sermon, but now the emphasis is on the practical consequences resulting from Christ's opening up the heavenly holy of holies: God's anxious people can enter his presence.

> Therefore, my friends, since we have confidence to enter (*eisodon*) the sanctuary (*tōn hagiōn*) by the blood of Jesus, by the new and living way (*hodon prosphaton kai zōsan*) that he opened (*enekainisen*) for us through the curtain (that is, through his flesh) (*estin tēs sarkos autou*), and since we have a great priest over the house of God, let us approach with a true heart in full assurance of faith, with our hearts sprinkled clean from an evil conscience and our bodies washed with pure water (10:19–22).

These verses are a climax of the entire central section of the sermon.[36] They are the final exhortation on the Christians' free access to God. Manson calls them "the supreme expression of the writer's thought

34. Moffatt is quite sure that the nautical sense is not intended and thinks that *pararrein* simply meant "going wrong" (*Hebrews*, 18).

35. DeSilva, *Perseverance*, 252. Cf. Koester, *Hebrews*, 334. Some of the recipients had houses and resources (13:1–6), but this does rule out the possibility that they were not fully accepted by society (Koester, *Hebrews*, 334).

36. On the question whether 10:19–22 summarizes the preceding argument or plays a transitional role in introducing what follows or has both roles see Guthrie, *Structure*, 103–4;Westfall, *Discourse Analysis*, 231; O'Brien, *Hebrews*, 361.

of the Christian life as worshipful approach through Christ to God."[37] What follows is the most intensely practical part of the sermon.

The language of 10:19–20 is graphic and startling.[38] It conveys the intensity of the preacher's concluding appeal, first by reminding the listeners of Christ's revolutionary action of opening the way into the holy sanctuary and then by urging them to enter. Both Jews and Platonists would have been aghast at what the author did to their respective traditions. Those listening to the sermon would at least have been prepared by what the preacher has already said about Christians as people who follow their pioneer (2:10) and forerunner (6:19–20), but the end result of following Christ right into the presence of God would have caused them serious heart searching.

We could scarcely have a clearer statement of the importance of the pioneer motif to the community and the conjunction of the pioneer and priestly motifs. Commenting on the way into the sanctuary is opened by Christ, Attridge says, "here the full significance of Christ's evocative titles *archēgos* and *prodromos* becomes apparent."[39] He quotes the striking passage from Lucius Annaeus Florus' *Epitome* on the legendary devotion of Decius Mus, who hurled himself into the thick of the battle in order that "he *might open up a new path to victory along the track of his own lifeblood*" (1.9.14).[40] It is an impressive picture, but it diverts attention from the cultic character of the passage. The author is still using Day of Atonement categories. As in 2:10, 17; 4:14–16; and 6:20, the pioneer image coalesces with that of the high priest, and it is he and not the hero figure, who enters through the veil. The cultic imagery of the text is further illustrated by the use of the verb translated "opened" (*egkainizein*) in 9:18. This is used in relation to the sanctuary in numerous LXX passages where it means "consecrated" (1 Kgs 8:63; 1 Macc 5:1; cf. Num 7:11, 88; Heb 9:18).[41]

The unit begins with what is the final appeal to the listeners to "have confidence to enter the sanctuary" (10:19, cf. 4:14). Since *parrēsia*

37. Manson, *Hebrews*, 66. On the significance of 10:20 see also Lindars, *Hebrews*, 46.

38. On the visual impact this part of the sermon (10:19–20) would have had on the hearers "when hearing is turned into sight" see what Mackie suggests ("Heavenly Sanctuary Mysticism," 112).

39. Attridge, *Hebrews*, 285.

40. Attridge, *Hebrews*, 285. The italics are Attridge's.

41. Dahl, "New and Living Way," 403.

here has the meaning of authorization, i.e., right of entry,[42] the author is obviously anxious that his friends should know for certain that the prohibitions that once prevented them from approaching the sanctuary on pain of death no longer apply. They have God-given permission to enter the sanctuary. This permission has been made possible "by means of the blood of Christ," i.e., Christ's self-sacrifice. The community now possesses the hitherto impossible and unimaginable right of access to God himself (10:19, 22; cf. 4:16; 7:25; 9:24). This is the unquestionable basis of their confidence.

Particularly expressive are the writer's words about the way into the sanctuary and how it is entered.[43] In an eloquent wordplay, *eisodos* ("entrance") is followed by *hodos* ("way" 10:19–20). The words are similar in meaning but not synonymous. *Eisodos* is parallel with *hodos* in verse 20 and this gives it the dominant sense of "means of entering."[44] This is borne out by the appeal to "draw near" in verse 22. But while the emphasis is on the entrance into the sanctuary, the sanctuary itself is also in mind. It is the inner sanctum. In other words, the listeners are free to follow Jesus who pioneered the way into the holiest place on earth that ancients could imagine. This is "the goal of the listeners' pilgrimage of faith (10:19–20)."[45] Presently we shall find that from this point of the sermon the order of things is dramatically reversed. The call to follow Christ into the sanctuary, which has featured so prominently and reaches a climax in the passage under consideration, is followed by the call to go out into a dangerous world in the section that follows (11:1—12:29). It is a movement from going in (10:19) to going out (13:13). The idea of movement continues throughout.[46]

One imagines oneself visualizing the entrance to the sanctuary and proceeding to view its magnificent veil. We remind ourselves again that the writer is not thinking of a literal building but speaking metaphorically. As Attridge says, "Our author ultimately suggests . . . that Christ entered that realm (the heavenly sanctuary) and made it possible for others to do so, not by a heavenly journey through a supernal veil, but by means

---

42. Vorster, "Meaning of ΠΑΡΡΗΣΙΑ," 56; Lane, *Hebrews 9–13,* 274, 283; Koester, *Hebrews,* 442. Cf. Schlier, "Parrēsia," 884.

43. Dahl, "New and Living Way," 403.

44. Westcott, *Hebrews,* 318; Pelser, "A Translation Problem," 47.

45. Koester, *Hebrews,* 413. It is always the goal, but never in this life is it the final experience when believers enter Christ's presence. See below on 12:23.

46. Attridge, "Use of Antithesis," 222.

of his obedient bodily response to God's will."[47] The "way" is the way that is opened by the pioneer (cf. 6:19).[48]

The description of the way as "new" (*prosphatos*) (10:20) is apt since such access to God was not possible so long as the old system was still functioning (9:8).[49] Koester draws attention to the practice of the Romans who on completing a new road displayed a dedicatory inscription. For example, the emperor and high priest Hadrian opened "the New Hadrian Way."[50] The cultic character of the imagery is foremost. The way is inaugurated in the same way as a sanctuary was inaugurated (*egkainizein*) (9:18). Moreover, the way has been recently opened (*phosphatos*) (cf. 9:8). This puts it in sharp contrast to the old way into the earthly sanctuary, on which Behm makes the suggestion that the Greek (*egkainizein*) may mean "to make a way which was not there before,"[51] but this runs counter to the writer's contrast between the two cultic systems and the continued existence of the first covenant (8:13). The way is qualitatively new by virtue of the new covenant: see the use of *egkainizein* in relation to the new covenant at 9:18.[52] And as Bengel points out in respect of the use of the verb, one is expected to follow in the way that Christ has inaugurated.[53] It is "for us" that the way into the sanctuary has been opened (10:20; cf. "on our behalf," 6:20).

It is tempting to relate the description of the way as "living" to the "I am the way" saying in John 14:6, but our author's use of the word "living" suggests that the pathway to life was opened by the one who himself lives forever (7:17, 24).

The statement declaring the opening of the curtain by the pioneer (10:20) is particularly effective. The curtain in question is the inner curtain, the "second curtain" mentioned in 9:3, even though the two parts of

---

47. Attridge, *Hebrews*, 287.

48. Jewett, *Letter to Pilgrims*, 174–75.

49. Although *prosphatos* owes its origin to the idea of slaughtering in advance (of a sacrifice) it referred to "a wide range of 'fresh' objects and 'recent' events" (Ellingworth, *Hebrews* (1993), 518).

50. Lewis and Reinnhold, *Roman Civilization*, 154. Quoted by Koester, *Hebrews*, 445.

51. Behm, "Egkainizein," 454.

52. Maurer, "Prosphatos," 766–67; Westcott, *Hebrews*, 319; Lane, *Hebrews 9–13*, 283.

53. Bengel, *Gnomon*, 435. Cf. 12:1 where the Christian race is the race "that is set before us."

the sanctuary are no longer in mind. One naturally wants to ask whether the writer is thinking of the rending of the veil that the synoptic gospels depict as happening at the moment of Jesus' death (Mark 15:38 and *parr.*).[54] The latter has in mind the inner curtain and is similarly intended to portray the opening of the way to God. But if there is any such dependence it is more likely that Hebrews reflects a common underlying tradition rather than direct dependence on Mark, though we have no means of knowing. The curtain in the synoptic gospels is an obstacle that has to be torn away, but one does not get this impression where the curtain in Hebrews is concerned.[55] It is referred to quite neutrally (6:19; 9:3; 10:20), unless we are to think the reference to Christ's flesh in 10:20 implies laceration and this parallels the tearing apart of the curtain. Since the context (chapters 8–10) suggests that the sanctuary in heaven is a single compartment it follows that it does not have a curtain and this applies in the case of 10:19–20, whether its imagery means that we should think of the curtain as ripped apart, pulled down, or drawn to one side.

Other questions remain. Should we take the parenthetical phrase "that is, his flesh" of 10:20 to refer to the curtain or to the way? The word order and the parallel use of the genitive case for "curtain" and "flesh" convince a number of scholars that "flesh" refers to the curtain.[56] The phrase is thus understood to signify "passage through the curtain, that is, through his flesh." This interpretation raises its own problems. Attractive as the comparison of the tearing of the curtain and the tearing of Christ's flesh may be, it creates the visually difficult problem of understanding how Christ may be said to pass "through" his own flesh. It is also theologically questionable. As Westcott comments, "It remains surprising that 'the flesh' of Christ should be treated in any way as a veil, an obstacle, to the vision of God in

54. Cf., for example, Bruce, *Hebrews*, 251; Lindeskog, "Veil of the Temple," 132–37.

55. I find myself in agreement with Michaelis, who says, "In the two passages in which the curtain is mentioned in Hb. (6:19: 9:3), it is not designed to bar access but to mark off the innermost part of the sanctuary, cf. Ex.26:33 . . . The thought is that there can be access only after the first tent is set aside (the curtain, which is the second curtain in 9.3, does not belong to the first tent at all). It thus seems advisable not to take the curtain as a hostile barrier but as the border beyond which the sanctuary begins (and to take the *sarx* of Jesus similarly: beyond His *sarx* = after his death" ("Hodos," 124 n 77).

56. See appendix B for the difficulties in regard to Käsemann's interpretation of the curtain as the gnostic partition between heaven and earth and chapter 4 for the case made out by Hofius for believing that the interest taken in the inner veil in apocalyptic and rabbinic sources helps us understand its importance in Hebrews.

a place where stress is laid on His humanity (*en tō haimati Jēsou*)."[57] When the word "flesh" is used in Hebrews it refers to Jesus' becoming a human being (2:14; 5:7) and when his exaltation is referred to it is assumed that he ascended in his glorified humanity (3:1; 4:14; 6:20).[58] Further, as Hurst points out, it is the obfuscation that results from this interpretation that is its greatest weakness. "(But) the problem is far greater; it requires the grotesque corollary that Christ's flesh *is a barrier which he himself had to penetrate, and which he helps others to penetrate*."[59]

The other possibility is to understand "his flesh" to be dependent on and explanatory of the "new and living way."[60] There is much to be said for this view since this is one of the passages in which we have found that the controlling idea is that of the pioneer/forerunner who opens the way for his followers. Interpretation is eased when we take into account the links between verses 19 and 20.

10:19	10:20
to enter	the new and living way
the sanctuary	through the curtain, that is
by the blood of Jesus	through his flesh

Verses 19 and 20 are joined by the relative pronoun (*hen*) (i.e., the access which he opened). Verse 20 serves as an elucidation of verse 19. Both verse 19 and verse 20 conclude with reference to Jesus' sacrificial death as the means by which the way into the heavenly sanctuary is opened.[61] "His flesh" is very likely a metonym for Jesus' sacrificial use of that flesh (10:5–10). Through the sacrifice of Jesus' body, of his flesh and blood (9:12; 10:5, 10, 19), the way into the presence of God has been thrown open. The mention of Jesus' body in relation to his sacrifice in 10:10 means of course that the incarnation is presupposed, and the implicit reference to his humanity here, like its mention elsewhere in Hebrews (2:14; 5:7), is correctly noted by a number of commentators.[62]

The message of the sermon is of fundamental importance to the congregation. The hiddenness and inaccessibility of God that marked the

57. Westcott, *Hebrews*, 320.

58. Hofuis, "Inkarnation und Opfertod Jesu," 132–41.

59. Hurst, *Hebrews*, 28–29. The italics are Hurst's.

60. Westcott, *Hebrews*, 320; Spicq, *Hébreux 2*, 316; Héring, *Hebrews*, 91; Montefiore, *Hebrews*, 173; Hofius, *Vorhang*, 81; MacRae, "Heavenly Temple and Eschatology," 188; Buchanan, *Hebrews*, 168; Hurst, *Hebrews*, 28–29.

61. Lane, *Hebrews 9–13*, 275–76. Cf. Pfitzner, *Hebrews*, 141.

62. Westcott, *Hebrews*, 320; Hofius, "Inkarnation und Opfertod Jesu" 138–41.

old order have gone. Christ has opened up the way into the very presence of God. In the new order of things Christians have the inestimable privilege of being able to approach God.

The unit very naturally leads up to the final appeal to the hearers to avail themselves of this privilege and "draw near" (10:22). The goal is not mentioned, but in the light of the parallel in 4:16, as well as what is said in 7:25; 10:1; and 11:6, it is obviously God who is to be approached. As in 4:15, the basis of the appeal to "draw near" is made clear. There it was Christ's experience of being a human being; here it is the assurance that "we have a great high priest over the house of God" (10:21). That the listeners are exhorted to approach God "in full assurance of faith" may be directed at any lingering doubts they may have about breaking age-old taboos. The basis of the appeal, once more, is the "great priest" and the efficacy of his ministry (cf. 4:14–16; 6:19–20; 7:24–25).

Christians are able to respond to the petition to approach God because they have been "sprinkled" and "washed" (10:22b). This echoes what is said in 10:10, 14 about believers being "sanctified." The language is cultic and is widely explained by reference to the consecration of Aaron and his sons to priestly service when they were sprinkled with blood and washed with water (Exod 29:4; 40:30–32; Lev 8:6, 30; Num 8:6–7; etc. T.Levi 9:11). The high priest was required to wash his body before proceedings on the Day of Atonement (Exod 29:4; Lev 8: 6; 16:4; m.Yoma 3:3).[63] The mention of Christians being "sanctified" in 10:10, 14 is interpreted by numerous scholars as implying that believers have undergone a priestly consecration and approach God as consecrated priests.[64] Justin Martyr was sure that Hebrews ascribes priesthood to all Christians. He quotes 6:16–20 and 10:19–20 and says that Christians, by virtue of the death of their high priest, have become "the true high priestly people of God" (Dialogue 116:1–3).[65] Calvin sees in 10:19 the "royal priesthood" of

63. Peterson, Hebrews and Perfection, 155; Attridge, Hebrews, 288; Lane, Hebrews 9–13, 287. Most scholars believe that there is a reference to baptism in the text. Best sees the baptism of Christians as their ordination ("Spiritual Sacrifice," 281).

64. So Westcott, Hebrews, 318; cf. 187; Moe, "Gedanke des allgemeinen Priestertums," 62–63; Dahl, "New and Living Way," 406–7; Best, "Spiritual Sacrifice," 281; Lane, Hebrews 9–13, 284–85; Westfall, Discourse Analysis, 233, 236, 241. Scholer is more cautious and speaks of Christians as "proleptic priests" (Proleptic Priests, 91–184).

65. Quoted by Hofius, Vorhang, 96 and Lane, Hebrews 9–13, 285.

1 Pet 2:9. However, the most that we can safely find in 10:10, 14 (cf. 9:19c) is an implicit priesthood of believers.[66]

The author comments on worship at length in 12:18–24, but the brief point he makes in 10:25 throws important light on how he construes drawing near to God. Access to God is understood in terms of the corporate life of believers as they worship together. The intimate connection the author makes between theological understanding and worship and its relation to the problems within the congregation is well expressed by Lane. "The neglect of worship and fellowship was symptomatic of a catastrophic failure to appreciate the significance of Christ's priestly ministry and the access to God it provided."[67]

The passage just considered is a good example of how easily exposition moves into pastoral application. Not for one moment does the exhortation to enter the presence of God mean that one is to attempt to turn one's back on the world. Life in the world remains the writer's concern and in the final section he will give extended attention to faith's relation to practice (11:1—13:25). In keeping with that and in the expectation that he has said enough about God's provision for pilgrims, the writer allows the high priest to retire from the scene and concentrates once more on the pioneer, the underlying theme of chapter 11. Attention is directed to the journey of faith, already introduced in chapter 4. But as if to make absolutely certain that in the trials that lie ahead his friends have the help they need the author finishes the unit (10:23–25) by urging them not to neglect worship—worship, as he will presently tell them, that unites them with the "spirits of the righteous made perfect and to Jesus the mediator of a new covenant" (12:23–24). For the moment, however, the author wants to say more about the need for faith and perseverance. His final words in chapter 10 thus prepare the congregation for what is to follow in chapter 11.

The aim of Hebrews 11, as we saw in regard to what is said to the congregation in chapter 4, is integral to the message of the entire sermon: the congregation, like God's people of former times, should look beyond their present concerns and troubles to the future God wills for them. Linking the faithful of the past and those now on the journey of faith is Jesus Christ, the pioneer and perfecter of faith.

---

66. Moffatt, *Hebrews*, 144; Peterson, *Hebrews and Perfection*, 155; Attridge, *Hebrews*, 288; Ellingworth, *Hebrews* (1993), 511; Isaacs, "Priesthood and Sacrifice," 58.

67. Lane, *Hebrews 9–13*, 290.

Therefore, since we are surrounded by so great a cloud of witnesses (*marturōn*), let us also lay aside every weight and the sin that clings so easily, and let us run with perseverance the race that is set before us (*hupomomēs trechōmen ton prokeimenon hemin agōna*), looking (*aphorōntes*) to Jesus the pioneer and perfecter of our faith (*lit.* perfecter of faith) (*eis ton tēs pisteōs archēgon kai teleiōtēn Iēsoun*), who for the sake of the joy that was set before him endured the cross, disregarding its shame, and has taken his seat at the right hand of the throne of God. Consider him who endured such hostility against himself from sinners, so that you may not grow weary or lose heart (12:1–3).

These verses stand in close relation to chapter 11. This leads Colin Sims to argue that they should be interpreted, not in terms of an athletic metaphor, as has been traditionally done,[68] but of pilgrimage.[69] This resonates with the forward-looking orientation of the sermon. However, a number of things are against it. The emphatic position of "endurance" in 12:1c and its repetition at 12:7 suits athletics better (12:1, 2). Verse 12:3 grows out of 12:1–2, while 12:4 is a fresh appeal to the hearers. The athletic metaphor is already used to depict the "hard struggle" his listeners have endured (10:32–35)[70] and it reappears again in 12:12–15 to inspire runners in danger of failing to reach the finishing line,[71] so it would be strange if it were dropped in 12:1–2. It is true, as Sims says, that the words *trechein* ("run," NRSV) and *agōn* ("race" NRSV (12:1)) have a broad meaning,[72] but in this context their meaning is made precise by three things. First, the exhortation that participants should get rid of impediments fits the athletic metaphor admirably but is less applicable to pilgrimage, since clothing and other items are essential for all except

68. Westcott, *Hebrews*, 391–94; Moffatt, *Hebrews*, 192–96; Bruce, *Hebrews*, 333–36; Montefiore, *Hebrews*, 213–14; Hughes, *Hebrews*, 519–21; Attridge, *Hebrews*, 354–56; Lane, *Hebrews 9–13*, 406–10; Ellingworth, *Hebrews* (1993), 637–39; Koester, *Hebrews*, 521–23; 534–35.

69. Sims, "Rethinking Hebrews 12.1," 54–88. However, Westfall's attempt to connect the imagery of 12:1–2 with the festival assembly of 12:22 is forced (*Discourse Analysis*, 269–70).

70. *Athlēsis* is used for the intense efforts of athletes in the stadium (Polybius, 5.64.6; 7.10.2–4; 27. 9.7.11); Lane, *Hebrews 9–13*, 298.

71. For the athletic allusion in the "drooping hands and weak knees" at 12:12 see Philo, *Prelim. Studies*, 164; Lane, *Hebrews 9–13*, 298, 426–27. On the use of athletic imagery in 10:32 and 12:12–15 see also Bruce, *Hebrews*, 270, 347; Attridge, *Hebrews*, 298; Koester, *Hebrews*, 459, 530; O'Brien, *Hebrews*, 449–54.

72. Sims, "Rethinking Hebrews 12.1," 61–67.

the very shortest pilgrimages. Second, the fact that runners ran naked (on which, see below) makes it highly unlikely that the reference is to pilgrimage. Third, 12:1–2 is redolent of forerunner (*prodromos*) imagery.

The passage in front of us is striking for its rhetorical finesse, arresting images, and theological content. Leaving aside Jewish analogies for the moment, the writer goes to the Greek classical tradition to make use of the popular topos of the athletic *agōn*. He employs the imagery to depict Jesus both as running the course appointed for him by God and as forerunner opening a new way into God's presence for those with him. By taking faith to its ultimate goal Jesus is the example Christians should follow.[73]

The point the sermon is making could not be clearer. Living by faith, persevering and enduring, the members of the community are to run their race, enduring their share of hardship and shame. The focus has thus moved from the attested witnesses of history to the hearers and the struggle in which they themselves are engaged (12:3, 5, 7–11, 12–13; 13:13).

The athletic imagery suggests an amphitheater with ascending tiers of spectators who are watching the race, but at the time in question most stadiums were not elaborate affairs.[74] They were rectangular in shape and enclosed by an embankment, natural or artificial. Sizeable crowds of spectators were usually present; they stood or sat on the embankment. Races were measured in stadium lengths (*stades* of 200 yards or 183 meters), of two, seven, twelve, or twenty *stades*. The longest that we hear of was twenty-four *stades* (4.80 km).

Athletic imagery was extended easily into metaphorical use.[75] It is used in 4 Maccabees 17:11–16 in a way comparable to Hebrews.[76] It makes clear the real nature of the struggle. "Truly the contest (*agōn*) in which they were engaged was divine" (17:11). But while it seems permissible to see evidence of martyrological traditions in Hebrews 12:1–3 this

73. Koester, *Hebrews*, 536.

74. On the subject of games and stadiums in the classical period see Gardiner, *Athletics*, 128–29. Competitors ran to and fro, turning round markers at either end of the track each time. The track at Olympia was 192.27 meters long, whilst that at Pergamum was 210 meters (Gardiner, *Athletics*, 128–43).

75. Pfitzner, *Paul and Agon Motif*, 134–38; Michel, *Hebräer*, 425–26; Harris, *Greek Athletics*, 51–95; Lane, *Hebrews 9–13*, 408; DeSilva, *Perseverance*, 361–64, 426–30.

76. DeSilva, *Perseverance*, 363. The Greek of 12.1c (*trechein agōna*) is best translated "run the race" (NRSV), though *agōn* has the wider meaning of enduring a struggle or contest (Moffatt, *Hebrews*, 195–96; Spicq, *Hébreux* 2, 382–83).

is not to suggest that martyrdom rather than the agonistic tradition is the controlling idea in our text or that *martus* had acquired the technical meaning of one who gives public testimony to his/her faith before a tribunal and is put to death. As Croy notes, the narrative lacks a number of the chief features of the Maccabean martyrdoms. "Jesus is not adduced as an example of courageous defiance, righteous opposition in the face of pagan oppression, nor (as I will argue) self-renunciation. He is the champion of enduring faith."[77] In his case it is the shame of Jesus' manner of death as much as the intense physical pain that is emphasized.

The "cloud of witnesses" consists of those who according to chapter 11 have received witness (acknowledgment) from God because of their faith (*emarturēthēsan*, 11:2; cf. 11:4, 5, 39). Their presence and role are of a great encouragement to the participants. The Greek participle *perikeimenon* ("surrounded") very likely means that they are more than simply spectators. Having taken part in the contest themselves they are well aware of its demands and the importance of encouraging participants. They are not passive onlookers but actively participating as they follow the performance of the contestants.[78] The runners, for their part, owe much to the encouragement of those who at great cost to themselves finished the race of faith and are expected to acknowledge this by their performance. Since "witnesses" in court testify to the truth (10:28), the preacher may be giving the listeners a subtle reminder of their accountability in the race of life, surrounded as they are by the great company of witnesses whom he has summoned in chapter 11.[79]

But above all, those listening to the sermon must pay attention to Jesus. As the heroes and heroines of chapter 11 had to persevere by faith, so the Christian runners must keep going until they reach their goal. They

---

77. Croy, *Endurance*, 40.

78. Müller, *ΧΡΙΣΤΟΣ ΑΡΧΗΓΟΣ*, 304; Lane, *Hebrews 9–13*, 408; Strathmann, "Martus," 504. Croy shows how the word *martus* often appears along with *theatēs* ("spectator"). A *theatēs* observed games or war on the battlefield (Isorates, *Evangoras* 79; Diodorus Siculus 13.15.5; 13.60.4; 13.72.8). Dio Chrysostom says that the king must practice virtue because he "has all people as spectators and witnesses (*theatas kai marturas*) of his own soul" (3.11). Lucian records an imaginary conversation on the subject of athletics between Solon, the Athenian law-giver, and Anacharsis, a Scythian sage. The latter is upset by the way wrestlers and boxers abused one another for sport "among so many spectators and witnesses (*theatais kai martusi*) of violence (*anacharsis* 11)" (Croy, *Endurance*, 60–61).

79. Koester, *Hebrews*, 522; Croy, *Endurance*, 59. Ellingworth does not think that "witness" (*martus*) has a legal nuance in Heb 12:1 (*Hebrews* (1993), 638).

have much greater incentive and encouragement since they have Jesus the pioneer and perfecter of faith.

But before the writer proceeds to speak of Jesus he has some practical advice to give to the runners. They are to strip off "every weight and the sin that clings so closely (12:1)." The language is highly expressive, not to say intriguing. The "weight" (*ogkos*) cannot refer to clothing since Greek athletes ran in the nude.[80] It may refer to excess body fat or to weights carried by the runners to build up their stamina.[81] The "sin" may be something else or it may be a more specific definition of "weight." If the latter is the case the meaning is "every weight, that is, the sin that clings so easily." Two good manuscripts suggest something that "easily distracts" the runner, which suits the athletic imagery. One only has to imagine the allurements of the prevailing culture and the ever-present temptations that beset believers to appreciate the relevance of such an admonition.

The foot race is a popular metaphor.[82] Since the runners are depicted as taking part under the watchful eye of the spectators the race in question must be one that takes place within the stadium and it is obviously a race that has repeated runs. The definition "set before us" can simply mean that the race "lies ahead of us" (REB), but it is more likely to be a specifically designated race since the expression is used in classical writers for a race whose course is determined by the officials.[83] This meaning is well expressed in the TNIV ("the race marked out for us"). In other words, the race in question is the race God planned for Jesus and his followers. The thought of the passage connects with the introduction of the pioneer image in 2:10–18. "Jesus' course conformed to the needs

80. "To be ashamed to be seen naked was to the Greek the mark of a barbarian . . . (The custom) served as a valuable incentive to the youth of Greece to keep themselves in good condition. The Greek with his keen eye for physical beauty regarded flabbiness, a pale skin, want of condition or imperfect development as disgraceful" (Gardiner, *Athletics*, 57, 58).

81. Bruce, *Hebrews*, 335–36; Croy, *Endurance*, 63, 171.

82. For classical uses see Attridge, *Hebrews*, 355. Cf. Rom 9:16; 1 Cor 9:24. Some scholars take the reference to endurance to mean that the race in question was long-distance, but this is not necessarily required. It could have involved numerous runs to and fro.

83. Attridge produces numerous references to show that "the race set before us" is "a fixed classical expression" (*Hebrews*, 355). So also Héring, *Hebrews*, 111; Lane, *Hebrews 9–13*, 399, 410; DeSilva, *Perseverance*, 429. Lane says, "Because the race has been prescribed for us (*ton prokeimenon hēmin agōna*), we can rest assured that it will bring us to the desired goal" (*Hebrews 9–13*, 410).

that God knew the 'many sons and daughters' would face (2:10–18). That is to say, God, having knowledge of the conditions in which his children would find themselves along their journey home, fitted Jesus beforehand to be their pioneer and helper by means of sending him through the course first."[84]

What the contestants need especially is endurance.[85] The word *hypomonē* has many nuances: perseverance, steadfastness, fortitude, and patience. In view of the allusions earlier to the Maccabean martyrs the primary meaning of our text is endurance (4 Macc 17:10, 12, 17). What Philo says about those who faint early in the contest of life (*Deus* 12–13) recalls those our author says had failed to make progress (5:11–14; the weak-limbed of 12:12). Whatever happens, the participants must not drop out of the race, but make every effort to reach the finishing line, whatever the pain. The Maccabeans endured suffering by "looking to God" (4 Macc 17:10). Christians are to look to Jesus for their inspiration and leading (12:2).[86]

Pioneer and Perfecter of Faith (12:2)

The use of "pioneer" in 12:2 bears such a close resemblance to 2:10 that an allusion may be intended.[87] But any suggestion that 12:2 and 2:10 are structurally meant to complement one another weakens the very close connection that 12:1–2 has with chapter 11 and thereby harms its climactic force.

The designation "pioneer and perfecter of faith" (*archēgos kai teleiōtēs*) is a remarkably compact and expressive christological statement. It conveys the essential thought of the whole sermon. It is closely connected with the examples of faith of the preceding verses, and it is presenting Christ as more than an example of faith. He is the one who initiates faith and takes it to its fulfillment. The fact that the two nouns

---

84. DeSilva, *Perseverance,* 429.

85. On the important place endurance has in Hebrews see 6:15; 10:32, 36; 12:1, 7, 20.

86. The expression *aphoran eis* means "to look away from all others towards one," LSJ. 292; Zerwick and Grosvenor, *Grammatical Analysis,* 2, 684. Cf 4 Macc 17:10; Epic. *Ench* 2.19. The personal name "Jesus" in 12:2 (cf. 2:9; 5:7; 7:22; 13:12, 20) puts the emphasis on his human life and what is said about his suffering and disgrace on the cross.

87. For example, Ellingworth, *Hebrews* (1993), 640.

are linked by a single article (*ton*) and the common genitive attribute (*tēs pisteōs*) means that pioneer and perfecter are dual christological titles.[88] *Archēgos* is used here in the sense of "initiator" or "founder," whereas *teleiōtēs* means "completer." To translate *archēgos* in 12:2 as "champion," as Lane does,[89] fails to express the strong communal or familial overtones that *archēgos* possesses and are present in this passage by virtue of Jesus being leader of the entire company in chapter 11. There is no thought in this text of Jesus as the mighty warrior who defeats evil on the cross and wins a place at God's right hand by his prowess. It is God who exalts Jesus, the Jesus who was "beset with weakness" (5:2) and fear (5:7), and suffered the most painful and shameful death (12:2).

The arresting collocation *archēgos-teleiōtēs* has puzzled exegetes.[90] However, Croy discovered help in Dionysius of Halicarnassus, a historian of the second century BCE. In this writer *teleiōtēs* is used in a doublet with *heuretēs* (close in meaning to *archēgos*) where it refers to one who refines or perfects what another has invented or originated (*On Dinarchus* 1).[91] In Hebrews 12:2 *teleiōtēs* serves very effectively to convey the dynamic character of *archēgos*.

The application of both terms of the doublet to a single person, Jesus, so that he is at one and the same time initiator and consummator of faith, produces a remarkable christological statement. Croy points to the all-too-familiar fact of human life that a person or group of persons often starts something, but it is left to others to refine or perfect it.[92] Jesus does both things. He is initiator in the sense that he brings in the epoch of fulfillment that the heroes and heroines longed to see. He is its perfecter or consummator because he completed the journey of faith himself and leads others to do the same. There is a useful parallel for 12:2 in Aelius Aristides produced by Delling. "Zeus, who has power over all things, is

88. Some scholars take *teleiōtēs* as an adjective and therefore epexegetical (Delling, "Teleioun," 86–87). Johnston renders 12:2 as "The Prince of our faith who is also its Perfect Example," ("Christ as Archēgos," 385), but this has no basis in the text.

89. Lane, *Hebrews 1–8*, 56–57; Lane, *Hebrews 9–13*, 411. So also Knox, "The Divine Hero," 229–40; Manson, *Hebrews*, 102–5; Montefiore, *Hebrews*, 61. As noted in appendix B, the translation "champion" has some justification in the context of 2:10 but it is quite unsuitable in the case of 12:2.

90. For the play on the *arch-* and *tel-* stems in the epistle see Attridge, *Hebrews*, 356. As the stems suggest, the "pioneer and perfecter" (*archēgos kai teleiōtēs*) is the one who initiates a particular undertaking and sees it through to its conclusion.

91. Croy, *Endurance*, 175–76; "A Note on Hebrews 12.2," 117–19.

92. Croy, *Endurance*, 176.

the only author and finisher of all things (*archēgetēn kai teleion monon
... tōn pantōn, Or.* 43.31)."[93] Jesus is both the originator or source of faith
and the one who brings faith to full expression, i.e., its perfecter.[94]

The way in which 12:2 echoes 2:10 is brought out by Müller when
he says "He (Jesus) strode ahead of all believers in faith and led faith to its
definitive end."[95] The relationship of the two key words and the primacy
of *archēgos* is highlighted by Peterson, who says, "*Archēgos* obtains its
meaning through *teleiōtēs*, implying priority or leadership in the exercise
of faith because of his supremacy in realizing it to the end."[96]

It is surprising that 12:2 is still rendered as "Jesus the pioneer and
perfecter of our faith" in some modern translations of the Bible. There is
no textual justification whatever for including the possessive pronoun.
Happily, the REB and the TNIV have "Jesus, the pioneer and perfecter of
faith." The faith that Jesus initiates and brings to full or perfect expression
is not the faith that Christians confess,[97] but his own faith in God, which,
for example, helped him in the testing situations in which he found
himself (e.g., 5:7–10).[98] Jesus is thus the Christian's model, embracing in
himself the actual quality he wants his followers to maintain.

But while the author thinks of the many who lived faithful lives
(chapter 11) and sees Jesus as the first one to have reached faith's ultimate
goal, it is clear that for him Jesus is more than an example for his followers. He leads them to their destination by way of his cross. Although the
author does not think here of Jesus' death on the cross as redemptive (as
in 1:3b), he underlines what he said earlier, viz. that Jesus was made the
pioneer of their salvation through suffering (12:2; cf. 5:9; 9:13, 28a; 10:12,
19). This, as we saw from 2:10–17, is what qualifies him to become high
priest. Hence 12:2 proceeds immediately to connect the pioneer and perfecter of faith with Jesus' enduring the suffering and shame of the cross.

93. Delling, "Teleioun," 86.

94. Koester, *Hebrews*, 523; O'Brien, *Hebrews*, 454.

95. Müller, *ΧΡΙΣΤΟΣ ΑΡΧΗΓΟΣ*, 310.

96. Peterson, *Hebrews and Perfection*, 171–72.

97. It is not helpful to use 5:9 (*aitios sōtērias*) to explain *pistis* in 12:2. "In Hebrews
pistis is not to be equated with *sōtēria*, since it does not specifically denote the content
of Christian faith" (Delling, "Teleioun," 86).

98. On the exemplary character of Jesus' faith, see Grässer, *Glaube,* 60; Peterson,
Hebrews and Perfection, 171–72; Still, "Christos as Pistos," 746–55. See Peterson's discussion on the qualitative distinction which Du Plessis draws between Jesus' faith and
the faith of his followers (*Hebrews and Perfection*, 172). Cf. Lane, *Hebrews* 9–13, 412.

The exemplary purpose of Jesus' faith and faithfulness is expressed poignantly in the summarizing words (12:2).

> (Jesus) who for the sake of (*anti*, margin, instead of) the joy that was set before him endured the cross, disregarding its shame, and has taken his seat at the right hand of the throne of God (12:2).

How this statement is to be construed depends upon the meaning of *anti*, which is ambiguous. It can be either (a) "instead of," "in place of," or (b) "because of."[99] The use of the preposition in 12:16 for Esau selling his birthright in exchange (*anti*) for a meal, where it clearly means "in place of," suggests that in 12:2 the writer is referring to what Christ surrendered in becoming a human being.[100] This is often compared with Philippians 2:6–11; cf. 2 Cor 8:9, and taken to have a substitutionary meaning (*anti*), except that the latter concept has no support in Hebrews. The majority of translators (NRSV, REB, NJB, TNIV, CEV) and commentators take *anti* in the sense of "because of," "for the sake of."[101] In support of this is (a) the athletic imagery that governs the whole of 12:1–4; (b) the parallel between "the joy that was set before him" and "the race that its set before us"; (c) the fact that the paraenetic aim of the author is better served by the inference that as Jesus was sustained by the thought of the joy that lay beyond the cross so the suffering experienced by Christians is made more tolerable by the prospect of future glory 2:10;[102] (d) the pilgrimage motif of chapter 11. See 11:26 where Moses endured abuse by looking forward to a reward; (e) many classical texts refer to prizes that are "set before" those who compete (Polybius, *Hist.* 3.62; Plutarch, *Mor.* 8D; Philo, *Mut.* 88).[103] "Because of" or "for the sake of" seem generally preferable.

What 12:2b conveys is all of a piece with not only the immediate but also the wider context of the homily. Jesus the pioneer is made perfect through suffering (2:10), which included the shame associated with crucifixion. Crucifixion was regarded as such a cruel and shameful form of

---

99. BAGD 88 (3).

100. Lane, *Hebrews 9–13*, 399; Thompson, *Hebrews*, 248.

101. Moffatt, *Hebrews*, 196; Windisch, *Hebräerbrief*, 109; Spicq, *Hébreux 2*, 387; Bruce, *Hebrews*, 339; Michel, *Hebräer*, 434; Hughes, *Hebrews*, 522–23; Attridge, *Hebrews*, 357; especially Croy, *Endurance*, 177–85; DeSilva, *Perseverance*, 436.

102. Attridge, *Hebrews*, 357.

103. Attridge, 357, Croy, *Endurance*, 66; Ellingworth, *Hebrews* (1993), 641; Koester, *Hebrews*, 524; O'Brien, *Hebrews*, 455–56.

execution that civilized people were not even encouraged to think about it (Cicero, *In Verr.* 2.5.62, 162–65; cf. *Pro Rab.* 5.16).[104] The author is providing a paradigm for the church. He wants the members to see their experiences in the light of what Jesus went through. They had personally undergone suffering (even if it had not yet meant martyrdom, 12:4) along with the shame of public abuse and the loss of material goods (10:32–34), and they would face further trouble (13:13).[105] As in the gospels, discipleship is prefaced by cross-bearing (Mark 8:34; Matt 10:38).

But beyond the threat of suffering and shame to which Christians are exposed there is the glory to which their leader is taking them (2:10). He has completed the race and has taken the seat of honor "at the right hand of the throne of God (12:2)." This is the joy for the sake of which he endured the cross, the prize that was awaiting him on the completion of his struggle (*agōn*). He achieved this not for himself alone but for all those following in his train. Thus Bruce comments, "The throne of God, to which he has been exalted, is the place to which he has gone as his people's forerunner. That is the goal of the pathway of faith; the Pioneer has reached it first, but others who triumph in the same contest will share it with him."[106]

The culmination of the passage in the depiction of Christ seated at God's right hand uses Ps 110:1 for the final time. Commentators draw attention to the fact that the verb is in the perfect tense (*kekathiken*).[107] Some think it suggests the posture of one whose work has been completed.[108] Spicq likens it to "the rest of an athlete after effort."[109] The reason for the use of the perfect in Hebrews is not always obvious (4:14, 15; 7:28), but the fact that in all the other uses of Ps 110:1 the aorist is consistently used (1:3; 8:1; 10:12) does suggest that its use in 12:2 is significant. Spicq's

104. For other classical texts see Schneider, "Kathairein," 411; Hengel, *Crucifixion*, 1–10, 22–32. Cf. Phil 2:8: "even death on a cross."

105. On the shaping of the Jesus tradition to the paraenetic purpose of the author in 12:2 and the following verses (12:1–13) see Croy, *Endurance*, 192–209. For the possibility that 12:1–2 reflects the shame culture of the times see DeSilva, "Despising Shame," 446; DeSilva, *Perseverance*, 434–35; Lincoln, *Hebrews*, 48–49.

106. Bruce, *Hebrews*, 339, where attention is drawn to 4 Macc 17:18: those martyred under Antiochus "now stand beside the divine throne and live a life of eternal blessedness" (cf. Rev 7:9, 15).

107. Attridge, *Hebrews*, 358; Ellingworth, *Hebrews* (1993), 642; Lane, *Hebrews* 9–13, 414.

108. Isaacs, *Sacred Space*, 183.

109. Spicq, *Hébreux 2*, 388.

comment on Christ's posture (12:2) leads one to ask whether Koester is not correct in suggesting that the text is conveying the idea of Christ as the victor.[110] The use of the perfect is against this possibility, since it connotes what pertains to the future as well as the present. Interestingly, Lane, who translates *archēgos* in 12:2 as "champion,"[111] does not subscribe to the foregoing interpretation of the seated Jesus, as one would expect. The title of *leitourgos*, "minister," given to Christ at 8:2 suggests activity rather than repose. But that raises a fresh problem, viz. the difficulty of visualizing how Christ operates as high priest from a seated position. However, this is more imagined than real and results from failing to recognize the multilayered nature of the imagery in which regal and priestly nuances coalesce. This throne also functions as a mercy seat.

The paraenetic purpose in reminding the addressees of the endurance of Jesus (12:3–17) aims pointedly at making the congregants compare their experiences with that of Jesus so that they "may not grow weary or lose heart" (12:3). Grievous though their trials may have been they do not come anywhere near to what their leader suffered (12:4). Like a true father, God disciplines them (12:5–11). What they should do is to turn their disciplinary sufferings into training that will make them fitter for their contest (12:11–14).The author then proceeds to the last section to draw attention to particular ways in which they should do this (12:14—13:2).

Summary

Access to God made possible by Christ is an outstanding if not the outstanding feature of Hebrews. Pilgrims on their way to their heavenly destination are urged to draw near to God because their pioneer and forerunner is now installed as high priest and is able and ready to help. The repeated exhortation to the community to enter the heavenly sanctuary reflects the great importance of the subject (4:14–16; 6:19; 10:19–22; cf. 7:25) and possibly a certain reluctance to break old taboos. The statement that Christ opened up the heavenly sanctuary for all would have shocked both Jew and Platonist. Very properly it is regarded as a leading thought of the sermon. Is "his flesh" in 10:20 a reference to the "curtain" or the "way"? The latter seems the more preferable interpretation. By

---

110. Koester, *Hebrews*, 188.

111. Lane, *Hebrews 9–13*, 411.

means of the sacrifice of Jesus' body, his flesh and blood (10:5, 10, 19), the way into the presence of God has been opened up. The "great cloud of witnesses" encourages the followers of the pioneer. (It is an athletic event, not a pilgrimage, that is in mind). They are to keep their attention fixed on their leader, who is not only faith's supreme example but its initiator and consummator. He leads his people to their destination by way of the cross and thus is savior as well as example. Following Jesus means suffering for those who come after him, but beyond this lies the glory to which their leader is taking them (2:10). Once again exposition is followed by application. Girded with the example Jesus sets them, the hearers are urged to engage in the race with fresh resolution (12:3, 12–13).

10

You Have Come to Mount Zion

The sermon is brought to its conclusion in 12:14—13:21. The appeal for endurance gives place to exhortations in the form of pastoral directives that are meant to clarify the life of the pilgrim community. But first as a final incentive there is a vision of worship on the heavenly Mount Zion (12:18–24).

> You have not come to something that can be touched, (*psēlaphōmenō*), a blazing fire, and darkness, and gloom, and a tempest, and the sound of a trumpet, and a voice whose words made the hearers beg that not another word be spoken to them. (For they could not endure the order that was given, "If even an animal touches the mountain, it shall be stoned to death." Indeed, so terrifying was the sight that Moses said, "I tremble with fear"). But you have come (*proselēluthate*) to Mount Zion and to the city of the living God, the heavenly (*epouraniō*) Jerusalem, and to innumerable angels in festal gathering (*panēgyris*), and to the assembly (*ekklēsia*) of the firstborn who are enrolled in heaven, and to God the judge of all, and to the spirits of the righteous made perfect (*pneumasi dikaiōn teteleiōmenōn*), and to Jesus, the mediator of a new covenant, and to the sprinkled blood that speaks a better word than the blood of Abel (12:18–24).

One's immediate reaction is surprise. It is the heavenly Mount Zion and (therefore) the temple, not the tabernacle, where the worshipping hosts are gathered. This will have our attention presently.

The sensory character conveyed by the passage is palpable. The antithesis is striking: "You have not come to (*ou gar proselēluthate*) . . . but

you have come to (*alla proseleluthate*. . .).[1] The earthly Mount Sinai and
the heavenly Mount Zion are juxtaposed in order to contrast the old and
new covenants and their respective mediators (cf. 8:6–13; 9:15–22).[2] The
contrast does not, as one might expect, compare the heavenly Zion with
the earthly Zion but with Sinai, the latter being chosen no doubt because
it marked the inauguration of the covenant. The juxtaposition is highly
effective. On the one hand is Sinai, the place of dread, which people dare
not approach (Exod 19:12–13), and on the other hand Zion, the place of
joy, where the pilgrims join in the jubilant assembly. The negative character of the one very effectively gives place to the positive character of
the other in what is the preacher's final and dramatic statement of the
superiority of the faith he is commending.

The city is a transcendent reality, like the "true tent." Thompson
makes an attempt to interpret it in Platonic terms.[3] He argues that the
word *pselaphomenos* translated as "something that can be touched," is a
descriptive term for the sense-perceptible nature of the Sinai event, contrasting with the word "heavenly" accorded to Zion (12:22). According
to Thompson, the writer sets the new covenant over against the old by
comparing the "tangible" with the "intangible" and the "earthly" with the
"heavenly." The great significance this places on a single word is contested
by other scholars, who believe the contrast is to be explained by the vertical imagery of apocalyptic favored by the author.[4]

What is described in 12:22–24 is very obviously a cultic assembly.
The Zion image draws on the great gatherings of pilgrims at Jerusalem for
the annual festivals. It evokes the joy and the sense of fulfillment associated with the arrival of the pilgrims in the city and their joining together
in worship.[5] Jerusalem was never so truly the city of God, and Israel never

1. See, for example, Son, *Zion Symbolism*, 77–93. The perfect tense in 12:22 is taken
by Barrett ("Eschatology," 376) and Peterson (*Hebrews and Perfection*, 79) to locate
this new approach to a decisive moment in the past experience of the hearers, their
baptism or conversion. On *proseleluthate* ("you have come to") see further below.

2. Sinai is not mentioned by name. Is this intended to indicate that it, like its covenant (12:24), has been superseded? Cf. Spicq, *Hébreux* 2, 403. In the introduction to
1 Enoch Sinai is named as the venue of God's coming revelation (1:4).

3. Thompson, "That Which Cannot Be Shaken," 582–84; Thompson, *Beginnings of
Christian Philosophy*, 45–47. See also Cody, *Heavenly Sanctuary*, 78–84.

4. For a detailed criticism of Thompson's interpretation of Heb 12:18–22 see Hurst
"Eschatology and 'Platonism,'" 69–73.

5. In both Jewish and secular sources the word *panegyris* signifies joyful assemblies
(Spicq, "Panégyrie de Hébr. XII.22," 30–38). It is correctly translated "festal gathering"

so truly the people of God, as at the festivals (Isa 30:29; 33:20; 35:10; Pss 48:12–14; 122:3–9; etc.). As the city and the temple acquired ever greater significance it was raised to a level of supra-historical importance (Isa 2:2; Mic 4:1; Pss 78:69; 122; etc.).[6]

The heavenly Jerusalem, the counterpart of the earthly, which became the eschatological city of God, is a popular theme of apocalyptic (*1En* 14:16–18; 26:1–2; *2En* 55:2; 2 *Bar.* 4:1–7; *T Levi* 3:4; 4 Ezra 7:26; 8:52; 10:26–27; 1Q32. Cf. Rev 3:12; 14:1; 21:2, 10). Thus Hebrews has Abraham looking forward to the city God has prepared for pilgrims (11:16; cf. 11:10; 13:14) and now depicts the pilgrims proleptically assembled in "the city of the living God" (12:22).

The vision in 12:18–24 is so arresting that one could be excused if we momentarily failed to notice the dramatic change in the imagery. The tabernacle has been displaced by the temple! But, in fact, the change of imagery is not the surprise it appears to be. A (heavenly) Jerusalem necessarily implies a (heavenly) temple. The three designations, Mount Zion, the city of the living God and the heavenly Jerusalem are synonymous and form a single unit so that it is impossible for the author to have thought of Zion without having the temple in mind.[7] One has only to take note of the presence of the worshippers (12:22–24) to realize this.[8] Thus, as Norman Young says, "The switch to language about a city in v.14 is only a linguistic change, not a conceptual shift, for Jerusalem was the holy city, for within it was the holy place, the temple."[9]

The temple imagery implicit in this passage comes as a surprise only if we suppose that the author's use of tabernacle imagery meant that he has completely shut out of his mind any thought of the temple. I do not think this is the case. As we have seen, it is the temple that is the real point of reference when the author is speaking of the tabernacle (chapter 6). I suggest that what we have in 12:22–24 is the kind of semantic overlap that is a familiar feature of Jewish writing on Jerusalem and its temple. In *1Enoch* the "house" that refers to the city in 89:41–50 is the temple in

---

by the NRSV. Cf. BAGD, 753–54. The same corporate sense is conveyed by *ekklēsia*.

6. McKelvey, *New Temple*, 9–24.

7. The Psalms abound with examples of Zion, Jerusalem and the temple as interchangeable ideas (48:2; 74:2; 76:2; 78:68–69; 128:5; 132:13–14; 147:12).

8. As Strack-Billerbeck remark ,in commenting on the statement in Rev 21:22 that the New Jerusalem does not have a temple, "Das zukünftige Jerusalem ohne Tempel—ein für alte Synagoge unvollziehbarer Gedanke" (Str-B, *Kommentar*, 3:852).

9. Young, "'Bearing His Reproach,'" 257.

90:28–36. In 2 *Baruch* 4:1–6 we find that the inviolability that God promises to Zion turns out to refer to the tabernacle, the archetype that was shown to Moses (4:2–6). Similarly, in 4 Ezra 10 the lamentation for Zion (vv. 1–18) is lamentation for the temple (vv. 19–22).[10] Already in Jeremiah 3:17 "Jerusalem" and the "throne of the Lord" are interchangeable designations. In our text, Jerusalem is described as the city of the living God and the dwelling of God, even though it is actually the holy of holies that is the place where God is enthroned.[11] God is called "judge" (12:23), i.e., he is on his throne, which means the holy of holies. The image of "drawing near," employed so consistently for approaching the heavenly tabernacle, is used for the heavenly temple in the words "you have come to" (12:22). Finally, the presence of angels points to God's throne room in the temple, as in Jewish writings and Revelation 5:7.

The backdrop of the presentation of God on his throne in 12:23 is the author's depiction of heaven as a temple. As we saw at an earlier stage of our study, heaven is the throne room of a royal court and this forms the setting for the presentations of the throne.

> The Lord is in his holy temple; the Lord's throne is in heaven
> (Ps 11:4 (LXX 10:4).[12]

Members of the congregation who were following the sermon closely would not have been surprised by the presentation of the city in 12:22. They had heard about it already, for it is the city which Abraham looked forward to, "the city that has foundations, whose architect and builder is God" (11:10), the city God has prepared for his people (11:16). These earlier references are a further instance of the author's penchant for introducing ideas that he plans to develop later.

What appears to us as a terminological mystery is clarified once we realize that our author has been using parallel concepts: tabernacle and city (temple). Here as elsewhere his rhetorical strategy is designed to serve his pastoral aim. Each image conveys its own particular aspect of the author's message. The tabernacle imagery is addressed to those on pilgrimage (4:1, 11), while the "city that has foundations" is directed to those who find themselves "living in tents" (11:9) or less desirable accommodation (11:38). Both images reflect the varied experiences of the

---

10. Bietenhard, *Himmlische Welt*, 193–95; Barrett, "Eschatology," 373–76; Scholer, *Proleptic Priests*, 141.

11. Scholer, *Proleptic Priests*, 141.

12. Isaacs, *Sacred Space*, 208–9.

listeners. They are set in the context of the pilgrimage motif. Pilgrimage in the biblical tradition always leads to Jerusalem, for it is where God is. However much our author reworks traditional material he must connect the pilgrimage with Jerusalem. "[The] city thus becomes an eschatologically charged image for Hebrews."[13]

The overlap of the twin themes of tabernacle and city in the final vision takes place without explanation. No explanation is necessary. The pilgrimage is over; the tabernacle theme has served its purpose and gives way to Zion, the temple and its worship, the ideal (not to say necessary) goal of the pioneer and his pilgrim people.

You have come to Mount Zion (12:22)

The note of eschatological fulfillment in 12:22–24 could not be more vibrant. Whether the author was responsible for this unit or used an already existing source, he made it his own by expressing it in terms of his favorite theme of "drawing near" (*proserchomai*) and had it serve his rhetorical purpose.

How exactly 12:22 (*proselēluthate*) should be translated is debated. "You have come . . ." is questioned by some scholars on the grounds that it does not suit the futuristic viewpoint of the epistle.[14] One must acknowledge that in the final analysis the heavenly Jerusalem is the city which is to come (13:14),[15] but both the immediate and wider context require one to treat *proselēluthate* as "have come":[16] (a) 12:22–24 parallels the preceding verses (12:18–21), the point of which is that Israel had come to the holy mount; (b) the imagery of these verses describes people at worship; (c) *proselēluthate* is itself a cultic *terminus technicus* throughout the homily for the access of worshippers to God (4:16; 7:25; 10:22; 11:6; cf. 10:1; 12:18).[17] The thought of the passage is thus in line with the ear-

---

13 Pursiful, *Cultic Motif,* 106.

14. So Montefiore, *Hebrews,* 229–30; Koester, *Hebrews,* 544; Wilson, *Hebrews,* 230–31.

15. Ellingworth, *Hebrews* (1993), 677.

16. So Peterson, *Hebrews and Perfection,* 160–61; Scholer, *Proleptic Priests,* 143–45; Lane, *Hebrews 9–13,* 465; Isaacs, *Sacred Space,* 58, who quotes Jewett, "the perfect tense of the verb 'you have approached' makes this one of the most dramatic and radical statements of realized eschatology in the N.T." (*Letter to Pilgrims,* 223).

17. M-M, VGT, 547; Spicq, *Hébreux,* 1:281; McKelvey, *New Temple,* 153; Lane, *Hebrews 9–13,* 465. Cf. in general, Scholer, *Proleptic Priests,* 137–49.

lier exhortations to "draw near." On their long and arduous journey the pilgrims have their strength and vision renewed by moments when they are in the presence of God and the heavenly ones. In such moments when the faithful on earth "draw near" and worship alongside the "righteous made perfect," futurist and realized eschatology coalesce in a remarkable configuration.

All this is not to say that the writer means that his listeners have arrived at the heavenly Zion in a physical sense or that a mystical sharing with the worship of heaven is in mind. What Dahl says in relation to 10:19 is applicable here.

> The idea is not that we should ascend to heaven—for example, in mystical experiences—but that we should come before God who is in heaven. This means prayer, as in the parallel 4.16 . . . worship through thanksgiving and prayer is the sacerdotal service to which the "consecrated" of the new covenant are exhorted (7.25; 9.14; 12.28; 13.16).[18]

The worshippers "are even now still standing in a heavenly presence, not material but spiritual."[19] What the author is saying is that the worship in which they momentarily engage while on their earthly pilgrimage is a foretaste of the worship continuously offered to God in heaven. The pilgrim people still seek "the city which is to come" (13:14). They are given this vision for their inspiration and encouragement.

In the passage before us the pilgrimage motif in the Old Testament goes a good way towards explaining the thought of the writer. Where Jerusalem was the goal of the annual festivals in Jerusalem the heavenly Jerusalem is the goal of the Christian pilgrimage. Not only the sense of fulfillment and joy but also the inclusive character associated with the former helps us understand the latter. The great pilgrimage festivals at Jerusalem assembled representatively the whole of the nation. Synagogue services were timed to coincide with the temple services (*B.Ber.* 26b; *J Ber.* 4.i.7b) and representatives of the dispersion took part (*mTa'an* 4.2). Commingling with this is the idea of participation with the angels in worship which we saw is so familiar in the Qumran writings (1QS 11:7–8; 1QM 12:1–2; 1QH 3:21–22; etc.).[20] Our author's picture of the

---

18. Dahl, "New and Living Way," quoted by Scholer, *Proleptic Priests*, 108.

19. Westcott, *Hebrews*, 412.

20. Cf. appendix B. For the parallels between Heb 12:22–24 and the fellowship of the Qumran worshippers with the heavenly hosts see Gärtner, *Temple and Community*,

"righteous made perfect" and their pioneer/priest enjoying what for his hearers was life's most valued experience represents his greatest appeal to his hearers. It is asserting the superiority of the Christian faith over its Jewish counterpart.

The festive mood of the gathering inspires the pilgrims to join the worshipping company. In many ways the thought of 12:22 is similar to that of the texts on "drawing near" to the throne of grace and points to the already-not yet paradox of Christian living. In contrast to Mount Sinai, access to God and proximity to him characterize this vision. Along with the earthly pilgrims are those who have been made perfect (12:23).[21] This is their foretaste of what will be their eternal joy when their own pilgrimage is finally completed.[22]

The picture of the heavenly gathering is arresting. The social and relational character of the worshippers, so reminiscent of the pilgrim festivals of Jerusalem, which is not mentioned in the other texts on drawing near to the heavenly sanctuary, is specially prominent. But what is not clear is the number and identity of the groups depicted as worshipping.[23] However, noteworthy of all of them is their corporate nature: innumerable angels, assembly of the first born, and spirits of the righteous.

The angels that were conspicuously absent from the holy of holies in the earlier part of the epistle are now present and acknowledged. In fact, they head the list. One is instantly reminded of the hosts of angels seen by the apocalyptic and mystical travelers to the heavenly temple and particularly significant is the fact that, as at Qumran, they are depicted

---

88–99.

21. Peterson writes, "If 12:22–4 is indeed a picture of the ultimate, eschatological encounter with God, 'the spirits of just men made perfect' will refer to the saints of all ages as those who have been perfected by the work of Christ. Looked at in this light, 12:23 speaks of the fulfillment of 11:40, so that believers of pre-Christian days and Christians together enjoy the consummation of their hopes" (*Hebrews and Perfection*, 164).

22. One cannot doubt that the writer's description of the convivial community on Mount Zion owes something to his experience of Christian community on earth. The classicist Dodds believes that the vitality of the early Christian communities and their rapid expansion had much to do with a sense of belonging and togetherness they engendered (*Pagan and Christian*, 137).

23. See, for example, Ellingworth, *Hebrews* (1993), 679; Lane, *Hebrews 9–13*, 467 on the question whether *panēgyris* should be connected with the preceding phrase (the angels) or the following phrase (the assembly of the firstborn). Cf. at length Hughes, *Hebrews*, 552–55.

as joining in worship with the people of the new covenant (12:24).[24] Our text resembles passages like 1QM 12:1–2 in expressing a vivid sense of the unity of the faithful on earth with those in heaven. Since Qumran made much of the claim that God and his angels dwelt in their midst (e.g., 1QS 11:7–8; 1QM 12:1–2; 1QH 3:21–22; 1Q28b 4:24–28) it is possible that the great gathering so eloquently portrayed in Heb 12:22–24 is intended not only to encourage pilgrims, but aims to legitimate the claims the author is making for the new faith. The fact that Hebrews puts the angels at the head of the liturgical assembly suggests that they lead the celebrations marking the arrival of the pioneer and his followers—the climax of the text (12:24). As is the case in 1:6, they are honoring the Son. In the Qumran text 1Q28b the central figure, the eschatological priest, is set in the midst of the angels (3:25) and is described as "serving in the temple of the kingdom, sharing the lot of the angels of the face (i.e., the presence)" (4:25–26). In Hebrews we get the impression that Jesus relates more to his followers from earth (the firstborn) than to the angels. Compared with the mediatorial role one finds attributed to angels in the apocalyptic and *Hekhalot* literature Hebrews is markedly restrained (1:14; 12:24).[25] Most significant is Jesus the eschatological priest; Melchizedek, or Michael for that matter, are nowhere to be seen.

The "assembly of the first born" who are described as "enrolled in heaven," which must be pilgrims from earth.[26] Their "enrollment" corresponds to the final stage of pilgrimage, described by Johnsson as the arrival at the sacred place in his comparison of the pilgrimage motif in Hebrews with the phenomenology of religious pilgrimages.[27] They are

24. Appendix B. Strugnell, "Angelic Liturgy at Qumran," 318–45; Gärtner, *Temple and Community*, 89–99; McKelvey, *New Temple*, 36–38. On the differences between Qumran thinking and Hebrews on this subject, see Klinzing who thinks that the sectarians and the author of Hebrews both drew on a common apocalyptic tradition (*Umdeutung des Kultus*, 201–2).

25. On the angels in 12:22 and their relation to those in 1:6 see, for example, Pursiful, *Cultic Motif*, 104–5, 110–13.

26. For the view that it is human beings, not angels, who are in mind see Westcott, *Hebrews*, 415; Moffatt, *Hebrews*, 217; Hughes, *Hebrews*, 553–55; Attridge, *Hebrews*, 375; Pfitzner, *Hebrews*, 185. Scholer strangely restricts the "assembly of the firstborn" to deceased believers (*Proleptic Priests*, 146). If the reference is not to the living it would conflict with all the author says about Christians being able to "draw near" while on earth and offer little encouragement to them to "run with perseverance the race that is set before (them)."

27. Johnsson, "Pilgrimage Motif," 246–47.

"firstborn" because they are the followers of him who is the first-born *par excellence* (1:5–6), who has many siblings (2:10, 12).

God is in the midst; "a judge who is God of all."[28] Peterson's suggestion that the description of God as judge indicates that the multitude is assembled for judgment runs counter to the exuberant spirit that habitually marked the arrival of the pilgrims at Zion and the joyful tenor of Heb 12:22.[29] The thought of God as judge signifies the throne and therefore the holy of holies. It is essentially a worship scene that is portrayed. God is in the midst, accessible to all. Consonant with all the writer has said about Christ making God accessible, there are no barriers separating him from the worshippers.[30]

Next to God are "the spirits of the righteous made perfect" who had to await the sacrifice of Christ before they could be perfected (11:40; 12:24). They have finally arrived at their destination. Appropriately, they are placed next to their forerunner and share in worship along with the church on earth.

Jesus the Mediator of a New Covenant (12:24)

Attention is very obviously directed to Jesus, "the mediator of the new covenant."[31] "Jesus, perfected, having led many 'sons' to glory, stands in the congregation of his many followers. What had been anticipated liturgically at Heb 2:12 is spelt out with programmatic precision in this context."[32] This is the eschatological priest surrounded by his redeemed people. He is no Herculean figure who has achieved glory through his prowess, but the one whose blood "speaks more graciously than the blood of Abel." And he has not entered heaven alone but accompanied by his followers.

Very fittingly, Käsemann compares 12:24 with Revelation 14:1–5 and its depiction of the Lamb at the center of the throne, surrounded

28. This follows the RSV translation. The writer is not thinking of the final judgment, contra Bruce, *Hebrews*, 359. As Ellingworth points out, the judgment "is not yet realized" (*Hebrews* (1993), 680). Cf., Koester, *Hebrews*, 545.

29. Peterson, *Hebrews and Perfection*, 162–63.

30. DeSilva, *Perseverance*, 467.

31. Ellingworth comments, "This verse (12.24) is the climax of vv.18–24 and thus rhetorically of the whole epistle" (*Hebrews* (1993), 681). For the important place the new covenant occupies in the narrative see chapter 8.

32. Dumbrell, "Spirits of Just Men Made Perfect," 158.

by his followers.[33] And, as this scholar observes, the paranaetical aim of the passage is "to show to the people of God still wandering on earth the greatness of their promise and their goal."[34] But even though the writer to the Hebrews does not join the author of Revelation in promising the congregation that the holy city will descend to earth he is far from commending a world-denying outlook to them, as he will make strikingly clear in what we are to consider in the closing part of the sermon.

The vision of the heavenly Zion assures people who are no longer certain of their place in this world that God has a great future for them. They are prompted to make a supreme act of faith and look to what is in store for them and to embrace it now, as if it were a present reality (11:1). Having given them this assurance the preacher is ready to make his final appeal (13:1–25).

Summary

The climactic contrast between the two mountains and the two dispensations they represent, with its vision of the joy of the worshipping host of the heavenly Mount Zion, is the future hope that is proleptically experienced by the faithful on earth. It corresponds to the earlier references to "drawing near" to the throne of grace. To the reader's surprise the followers of Jesus are assembled not at a tabernacle but at a temple (part of the heavenly Mount Zion complex). In fact there are enough hints throughout the sermon (11:10, 16; cf. 13:14) to prepare us for this apparent *volte-face*. The scene is a reconstruction of the great annual pilgrimages to Jerusalem. The presence of the angels recalls Qumran accounts of the faithful worshipping with the heavenly beings, but the whole is given an unmistakable Christian configuration, with Jesus the pioneer-cum-priest made the preeminent figure and next to him those he set out to lead to glory, his "many sons" (2:10). Given this perspective, the community can devote itself to its everyday responsibilities and trials (13:1–25).

33. Käsemann, *Wandering People*, 55–56.
34. Käsemann, *Wandering People*, 56.

11

Outside the Camp

The final challenge to the congregation comes in the appeal to them to go to Jesus "outside the camp" (13:13). This is part of a complex and tightly integrated passage that has been variously interpreted, and we need to begin by surveying the unit.[1]

> Do not be carried away by all kinds of strange teachings; for it is well for the heart to be strengthened by grace, not by regulations about food (*lit.* not by foods), which have not benefited those who observe them. We have an altar from which those who officiate in the tent have no right to eat. For the bodies of those animals whose blood is brought into the sanctuary by the high priest as a sacrifice for sin are burned outside the camp. Therefore Jesus also suffered outside the city gate (*pulē*) in order to sanctify the people by his own blood. Let us then go to him outside the camp (*parembolē*) and bear the abuse he endured. For here we have no lasting city, but we are looking for the city that is to come (13:9-14).

The view that chapter 13 was not originally part of the letter has been canvassed by some scholars,[2] but this has not been generally accepted. The chapter has many points connecting it with the earlier chapters, recapitulating the argument.[3]

---

1 Isaacs, "Hebrews 13.9-16," 268-84; Young, "Bearing His Approach," 243-61; Westfall, *Discourse Analysis,* 288-91.

2. For example, Wedderburn, "The 'Letter' to the Hebrews," 390-405.

3. See Attridge for the similarities that chapter 13 shares with the preceding chapters (*Hebrews*, 384-85). Cf. Isaacs, "Hebrews 13.9-16 Revisited," 270-72.

In this complex collage of images, doctrinal statements jostle with paranaetical exhortations, and indicative verbs combine with subjunctives and imperatives as the author brings his letter to its conclusion in a powerful plea to his friends to follow their leader "outside the camp."

What "all kinds of strange teachings" means is not very clear. The phrase has a gnostic ring (cf. Col 2:20–23), but what follows about food points to Jewish practices.[4] Lane suggests that the "strange teachings" may mean that some people believed that participation in the meals in question evoked eating at the altar in Jerusalem.[5] The "regulations about food" (*lit* "foods"), followed, as it is, by the "altar" suggest that the food in question had a sacrificial meaning for some members of the congregation (see 9:10).[6]

The "altar" (13:10) itself has occasioned a great deal of discussion. The emphatic indicative with which it is introduced ("we have an altar") may possibly imply that it is a reply to the charge that Christians did not have a proper means of atonement.[7] Interpretations of the altar have tended to divide exegetes along confessional lines, with Roman Catholics seeing a reference to the Eucharist and Protestants believing it refers to Christ himself or more specifically Christ and his death on the cross; but this is a difference that is no longer clear-cut. Recent times have seen a convergence of views, even though some scholars still maintain that the "altar" refers strictly to the Eucharist.[8] If we take "altar" in relation to what follows, as the closely integrated nature of the context obliges us to do, the word is seen to have an inclusive meaning and not refer exclusively to Golgotha but also to its outworking in the heavenly world. The verb "we have" (*echomen*) is frequently used in Hebrews for the possession of a heavenly blessing (4:14–15; 6:19; 8:1; 10:19). Thus "we have an altar"

4. The reference is possibly to synagogue meals held at festival times to create a sense of solidarity with the worship of the temple of Jerusalem. Cf. Josephus, *Ant.* 14:214. See Attridge, *Hebrews*, 395.

5. Lane, *Hebrews 9–13*, 539; cf. 530–31.

6. Montefiore, *Hebrews*, 244; Hughes, *Hebrews*, 577–78; Loader, *Sohn und Hoherpriester*, 179; Bourke, "Hebrews," 941; Attridge, *Hebrews*, 396; Koester, *Hebrews*, 567.

7. Moule, "Sanctuary and Sacrifice," 37–39. Against the view that 13:10 is polemical, see Isaacs, "Hebrews 13.9–16 Revisited," 280–81. Cf. O'Brien, *Hebrews*, 520–22. See also Lindars, *Theology*, 10–15.

8. Thurén, *Lobopfer der Hebräer*, 49–247; Swetnam, "Christology and Eucharist," 74–95. For discussion on the subject see Williamson, "Eucharist and the Epistle to the Hebrews," 300–312; Isaacs, "Hebrews 13.9–16 Revisited," 277–81; Daly, *Christian Sacrifice*, 262–63.

parallels "we have a high priest" (4:14; 8:1; 10:21). It is hard not to see a polemical intent in the claim however mild.

Koester expands on the claim in 13:10 and draws attention to a neglected point of the context (13:16).

> The altar has two aspects of meaning (Aquinas, *Ad Heb.* 744). In one sense, the altar is the place where Jesus was crucified (13:12). The community meets at this altar, not by assembling at Golgotha, but by gathering for the proclamation of Christ's self-sacrifice. In a second sense, the listeners' altar (*thysiastērion*) stands wherever they offer through Christ their own sacrifices (*thysia*) of praise to God and of kindness toward others (13:15–16).[9]

Very importantly, the assertion that "we have an altar" prepares the way for the daring reinterpretation that follows. Employing a feature of the Day of Atonement imagery which he has not so far used, the author begins by making the startling Christological statement in verse 12: "Jesus also suffered outside the gate in order to sanctify the people by his own blood."[10] This uses the Levitical ruling on the disposal of the remains of animal sacrifices outside the camp (Lev 16:27) to dramatize Jesus' death "outside the city gate" (13:12). That is to say, Christ made his offering for the sins of the world not on holy ground, but on unholy ground, right outside the sacred enclosure (Lev 16:27–28; cf. Heb 13:11). Members of the church who were familiar with the procedure in Leviticus must have found the argument astonishing, not to say repulsive and offensive. The "camp" was where God was (Deut 23:14), but the place "outside"(Lev 16:27) was where blasphemers and other grievous offenders were stoned to death (Lev 10:1–5; 24:14, 23; Num 15:32–36) and lepers were assigned (Lev 13:45–46).[11]

Persons who left the camp to incinerate the carcasses became ritually unclean and required ceremonial cleansing before they could reenter the camp. It is precisely the author's use of the phrase "outside the camp" that makes a potent contrast between the Day of Atonement ritual and the sacrifice of Jesus on the cross. "Jesus also suffered outside the gate," i.e., Jerusalem, surrounded by walls, was analogous to the Israelite camp

9. Koester, *Hebrews*, 575.

10. That "outside the (city) gate (*pulē*)" in 13:12 means "outside the camp" is shown by the use of *parembolē* in 13:11, 13.

11. Elsewhere there were "clean places" which were "outside the camp" (Lev 4:12; 6:11). Cf. Exod 33:7.

with its boundary. Jerusalem is called "the holy camp" in the Qumran text 4QMMT. "Jerusalem is the camp; and outside the camp is [outside of Jerusalem] . . . because Jerusalem is the holy camp, the place which he has chosen from among all the tribes of Israel" (4QMMT 29–30, 60–61). Cf. *Num R* 53; *b Yoma*. 65ab, which equate Jerusalem with the camp in the wilderness.

The intention of the author is even more explicit than at 12:2 when he referred to the shame Jesus suffered by crucifixion. But the full impact of the author's analogy is still to come. It appears as he presses home his point by saying that Christ carried out his great atoning work quite independently of the Jewish system, "in order to sanctify the people by his own blood" (13:12). But before his mention of Jesus' death the author says Jesus "suffered outside the gate" (13:10), presumably to remind the listeners of his solidarity with all who suffer (2:9–10). The sermon of course has numerous references to Jesus' atoning work but here it is highly significant that his suffering and death are positioned in the profane world. For the death of Jesus to be described not only as the death of a common criminal but as a sacrilege of the worst possible kind must have caused profound shock and offence. And that was not all. To depict Jesus as having become a corpse in the course of pursuing his priestly work would have been totally incomprehensible and abhorrent to those who knew that on the Day of Atonement the high priest had to be in a state of absolute Levitical purity and particularly have nothing whatever to do with a corpse (Num 19:13; Lev 21:11; 22:4; *m Sanh.* 2:1; Philo, *Spec.* 1:113).[12] In the starkest possible contrast to the high priest who was removed from all human contact and whatever else might cause defilement in preparation for his offering (*mYoma* 1.1; *Parah* 3.1), Jesus makes his offering on unholy ground and between two criminals. This is nothing less that the subversion of the entire Levitical system.

It is not difficult to imagine what this would say to the recipients, not simply because of their possible attraction to Judaism but also in regard to their place in the world. The sermon's portrayal of the "outsider" character of Jesus' atoning work, seen in the context of the heroes of Hebrews 11 as "outsiders,"[13] helps us as we now approach the crucial exhortation to go to Jesus "outside the camp" in 13:13. Commenting on

12. Jeremias, *Jerusalem*, 152. Cf. Radcliffe, "Christ in Hebrews," 499. Lane writes, "It was as an outcast that he offered his sacrifice to God" (*Hebrews 9–13*, 542). Cf. Thurén, *Lobopfer der Hebräer*, 76–78.

13. Eisenbaum, *Jewish Heroes*, 184. Cf. Dunning, "Alien Status and Cultic Discourse," 189.

Jesus' suffering "outside the gate" and its rhetorical use in the appeal to go "outside the camp," James Thompson says, "That the author's memory of Jesus' suffering 'outside the gate' is not only a historical fact but also a metaphor becomes clear in the exhortation 'Therefore let us go out to him outside the camp'" (13:13a).[14]

> Let us then go to him outside the camp and bear the reproach
> he endured (13:13).

The importance of these words is universally recognized though understood in different ways.[15] Before we examine the ways in which the challenge has been understood we note the suggestion of a number of scholars that the "going out" in 13:13 is the converse of the appeals that called the hearers to go into ("enter into") the heavenly rest (3:7—4:11) and the heavenly sanctuary where the forerunner has gone ahead of them (4:16; 7:25; 10:19, 22).[16] This is an intriguing suggestion but it could be misleading, unless the "going out" is prefaced by or accompanied by the "entering into."[17] In the mind of the author of Hebrews what the "going out" of 13:13 involves can only be undertaken as one "goes into" Christ to receive his help. The direction of the movement keeps alternating, but it is always a double movement, and the objective is always the same: Christ. The "going into" Christ is accompanied by a "going out" to Christ, "outside the camp," and similarly the converse is true. Gift is accompanied by responsibility; responsibility is discharged through the gift received.

The general sense of the thought behind 13:13 is clear enough: it is movement from sacred to profane space. What the preacher means by the "camp" is what causes debate. In terms of the pioneer theme in the wider context, 13:13 relates to 2:10, as Thompson says, by "challenging the community to maintain solidarity with the one who demonstrated his solidarity with them (cf. 2:10–18)."[18] The importance of 13:13 is universally recognized though understood in different ways.

A popular interpretation takes "outside the camp" to mean "outside Judaism" and regards 13:13 as a call to leave behind the institutions and practices of Judaism and be totally committed to Jesus Christ. Attention

14. Thompson, *Hebrews*, 283.

15. Ellingworth, *Hebrews* (1993), 716–17.

16. Attridge, *Hebrews*, 398–99; Dunn, *Parting of the Ways*, 299; Nelson, *Raising Up a Faithful Priest*, 152.

17. DeSilva, *Perseverance*, 501.

18. Thompson, *Hebrews*, 283.

is drawn to the fact that the "camp" in 13:13 is a parallel to the "tent" in 13:10, which is very likely associated with the reference to foods in the previous verse (13:9; cf. 9:10), and is therefore Jewish.[19] This interpretation is frequently taken to mean that the recipients were finding Christian discipleship in a hostile world too exacting. Fear of further persecution (10:32–34) or weariness from sustaining their commitment to Christ (6:11–12; 12:12) had resulted in their maintaining their links with the established religion in the hope of a less dangerous or demanding way of life. The community is therefore challenged to face up to the responsibilities of Christian discipleship.

Other scholars regard 13:13 as an appeal to leave the cultic world of ritual requirements and embrace the life of the secular sphere.[20] Helmut Koester believes the author is saying that the sacrifice of Jesus, which cleanses people, was offered not in a sacred place but outside in unsanctified ground. Christians should abandon the supposed security of familiar routines and follow Jesus into an unhallowed and dangerous world.[21]

DeSilva, following up his view that the basic problem of the congregation was fear of the loss of honor and status because of their Christian confession, believes that the author is quite deliberately urging it to embrace an existence on the margins of society.[22]

Along somewhat similar lines is the interpretation which takes 13:13 to be an adaptation of the gospel call to take up one's cross and follow Christ in any situation regardless of the danger (Mark 8:34 and parr.). Typical of a popular interpretation of the passage is Floyd Filson. He writes,

> The exhortation to "go forth to him outside the camp" urges the Christians addressed to break ties with whatever would prevent full loyalty to the Christ who offered himself as the once-for-all sacrifice for sins . . . it makes no difference whether their city is the earthly Jerusalem or imperial Rome or any other earthly city in which Christians now dwell, it is not *the* city, the perfect

19. Westcott, *Hebrews*, 441–42; Bruce, *Hebrews*, 380–82; Hughes, *Hebrews*, 580; Montefiore, *Hebrews*, 246; Lindars, *Hebrews*, 11; Lane, *Hebrews* 9–13, 545–46; Pfitzner, *Hebrews*, 200, O'Brien, *Hebrews*, 525.

20. Koester, "Outside the Camp," 299–315; Trudinger, "Gospel Meaning of the Secular," 235–37. Cf. Bruce, *Hebrews*, 381–82; Hughes, *Hebrews*, 582.

21. Koester, "Outside the Camp," 301.

22. DeSilva, *Perseverance*, 501–4.

home for God's people; that perfect home will only be found in "the city which is to come."[23]

A quite different view is proposed by Thompson.[24] He holds that "outside the camp" does not mean "outside Judaism," but is a call to leave behind earthly securities and seek the eternal world where Jesus is. In support Thompson cites Philo's allegorization of Exod 33:7–8 and Moses' erection of the tent of meeting outside the camp of Israel (*Spec.Leg.* 2:54–55; 3:46; *Gig.* 54), which he interprets to mean that "Moses left the whole array of bodily things."[25]

Mackie suggests that 13:13 is a warning not to depend on the status and false sense of security offered by the *Pax Romana*.[26] In his view, it is "an implicit polemic subtly and suggestively lodged against the Roman Empire."[27] Mackie believes the author drew on his personal experience of marginalization as a Jew of Alexandria affected by the ruling of Claudius that Jews had to accept that they lived in "a city that belongs to others" (Suetonius, *Claudius*, col.v.95). He writes, "If the recipients are located in Rome, as some have argued, then the claim that 'here we have no lasting city' (13:14) potently counters the characterization of Rome as the "eternal city" (*urbs aeterna*), the capital of the 'eternal empire' (*imperium sine fine*)."[28]

Again a different proposal is made by Randell Gleason.[29] He believes the letter was written to a community in Palestine and interprets 10:26–31 as a literal warning of the imminent destruction of Jerusalem

---

23. Filson, *"Yesterday,"* 61, 68. The italics are the author's. Lane similarly writes, "The task of the community is to emulate Jesus, leaving behind the security, congeniality and respectability of the sacred enclosure, risking the reproach that fell upon him" (*Hebrews 9–13*, 543). For the "camp" as urban life see Koester, *Hebrews*, 571.

24 Thompson, "Outside the Camp," 53–63; Thompson, *Beginnings of Christian Philosophy*, 141–51.

25. Thompson, "Outside the Camp," 61. Moffatt says that the text "makes a broad appeal for an unworldly religious fellowship, such as is alone in keeping with the *charis* of God in Jesus our Lord" (*Hebrews*, 235).

26. Mackie, *Eschatology and Exhortation*, 145–50.

27. Mackie, *Eschatology and Exhortation*, 148.

28. Mackie, *Eschatology and Exhortation*, 149. For Rome as "the eternal city" see Ovid, *Fasti* 3:72.

29 Gleason, "Eschatology of the Warning," 97–120. Somewhat similar is the view of Stökl Ben Ezra, who thinks that the author "is asking his audience in a concrete, geographical sense to leave Jerusalem and its temple for the real, future space" (*Impact of Yom Kippur*, 192).

by the Romans. He argues that 10:25b shows that ominous events were already evident to the hearers. It is for their personal safety they are urged to leave the "camp."[30]

The prolific number of readings of 13:13 is indicative of the difficulty of determining what exactly it is that the writer was urging upon his friends. Some things are reasonably clear. The everyday concerns mentioned in the context (13:1–7, 17–19) show that he was not advocating the other-worldly orientation that Thompson believes is his intention. On the other hand, while one must agree with Helmut Koester that a this-worldly involvement is what Hebrews has in mind, this is not to be undertaken at the cost of blurring the boundaries between the sacred and the profane (12:4–11, 14–17). Gleason's suggestion that the author is concerned for the physical safety of the recipients of the sermon does not fit the way in which they are commended for their previous endurance of suffering (10:32), hostility from the public (10:33) and their cheerful acceptance of the plundering of their possessions (10:34). Mackie's suggestion that Rome represents the prevailing culture within which the recipients live and operate cannot be contested, but when Roman culture (the benefits of the *Pax Romana*) is placed alongside Jewish culture (the security of an established religion or its means of atonement) as the issue at stake this is not a convincing argument: the context of 13:13 deals with Jewish matters.

This leaves us with the first possibility, viz. that the solution lies in the area of the church's relation to the local Jewish community and this is to be dealt with by an unreserved commitment to Christ.

In the first place, the natural interpretation of 13:13 understands it as a call to leave behind the institutions and customs of Judaism. "Outside the camp" in 13.13 parallels both "outside the camp" in 13:11 and "outside the gate" in 13:12. The reference is to Jesus' atoning death, undertaken independently of the Jewish sacrificial system and in contradistinction to all it meant. There are other allusions which point to a Jewish background. The admonition not to be "carried away by all kinds of strange teaching" in 13:9 is anticipated in 9:9–10 and refers to the gifts and sacrifices offered under the Levitical system.[31] The reference to the "foods" in 13:9, while capable of different interpretations, should most likely be taken as cultic meals on account of its proximity to the "altar from which

30. Gleason, "Eschatology of the Warning," 97, 103, 120.

31. Lane, *Hebrews 9–13*, 536.

those who officiate in the tent have no right to eat" (13:10). Similarly, in the case of the "altar," the fact that this is immediately followed by reference to the Day of Atonement indicates that it, like the "camp," has to do with Judaism.

In the second place, "going out" to Jesus "outside the camp" is one of the most forthright christological and paraenetic statements of the whole sermon. The pioneer motif is worked to maximum effect. It may well be developed here in terms of the cross-shaped form that discipleship has in the synoptic gospels (Mark 8:34 *parr.*). To keep following Christ, leaving behind whatever has been impeding or harming commitment to him, calls for the fuller appreciation and espousal of Christ and his saving work that is consistently commended throughout the sermon. It may also have in mind the community's confession of faith (the *homologia*) and its core Christological confession; "Jesus, the apostle and high priest of our confession (*homologia*) (3:1; cf. 4:14; 10:23).[32]

The writer is fully aware of the costly nature of what he is saying to his friends. He prefaces it by reminding them of Jesus' ignominious death on their behalf (13:10) and shows great empathy by indicating that he is alongside them, facing the same challenge ("let *us* go to him"). What is more, he reminds them of their great transcendental hope ("the city that is to come" 13:14).

The call to follow Jesus "outside the camp" challenges the community to reaffirm their commitment to be the pilgrim people of God. It is the climax and conclusion of the sermon. Like the conclusion of a good sermon, it grows out of what has already been said and it is driven home with persuasive effect. It has in mind Abraham who went out into the unknown (11:9) and Moses who left behind the security and comfort of life in Egypt for the wilderness (11:26–27), and it draws together all that has been said about Jesus Christ by directing attention to the emotive figure who is pushing ahead into a threatening world—their leader who endured the worst for their sakes (13:12–13). The race that is set before

---

32. "In the community addressed, the core (of the confession) was the acknowledgment of Jesus as the Son of God (4.14)" (Lane, *Hebrews 1–8*, 75). So also Thompson, *Hebrews*, 79–80. Cf. Moffatt, *Hebrews*, 41. Montefiore believes that Hebrews was not thinking of confession before unbelievers (1 Tim 6:12) but of "open acknowledgment of faith (cf. 2 Cor 9:13)" (*Hebrews*, 70). However, bearing in mind what the community had suffered and was likely to suffer again, one cannot but consider Alexander Nairne's suggestion that reference to confession in 1 Tim 6:12 helps us understand *homologia* in Heb 3:1. He proposes that we translate 3:1 as "the creed which you are destined to confess courageously" (*Epistle of Priesthood*, 48–49).

them is the one God has marked out for them. They will have to bear the abuse their Lord endured and share his obloquy, antagonism, and suffering. But the pioneer is their leader still, and he will take them through the new and untried ways that lie ahead. The vision disclosed to them of "the city that is to come" will not only sustain them but inspire them to praise God. This and the everyday deeds of charity are the new cultus that is pleasing to God (13:15–16; cf. 10:34).

Whether the writer hoped that the community, once it had reaffirmed its commitment to Christ and ventured out in the wider world, would commend the gospel to others we do not know. Confessing the faith (the *homologia*) receives emphasis in the sermon (3:1; 4:14; 10:23), but whether this includes witness to unbelievers is uncertain. William Manson made Hebrews 13:13 pivotal to his interpretation of Hebrews as a call to the Gentile mission, and much as the link he made between Hebrews and Acts 7 proved a suggestive way of approaching Hebrews,[33] his argument has not been generally convincing. The emphasis on holding fast to the confession of faith and the great lengths to which the author goes to deepen the recipients' understanding of and commitment to Jesus Christ rather suggests that he intended his work more as a *praeparatio evangelium* than an actual call to mission. But whether the time before the end was short or long, "Christian existence is a matter of 'going out' in the direction of the *archēgos*."[34]

Summary

The preacher makes his final appeal in chapter 13. He challenges the community to define its identity *vis a vis* Jesus Christ on the one hand and in relation to Judaism on the other hand (13:13). Jesus, by offering his sacrifice independently of the Jewish cultus and "gone out" from it, has shown the church where its future lies. Whatever the psychological and physical securities of their present life, real or imagined, the hearers are urged to renounce these for the life of God's pilgrim people to which the pioneer is summoning them. Such a demanding undertaking suggests that they are not unwilling to respond positively. It is also based upon their reaffirmation of the primacy given to Christ in the early confession (3:1). It implies that the hearers understand that the responding challenge to "go

33. Manson, *Hebrews*, 25–46.
34. Thompson, "Outside the Camp," 148.

out" after the pioneer is made possible by their "going into" the heavenly sanctuary for help. And always they have the sustaining vision of "the city that is to come" (13:14). Thus the preacher concludes by encouraging his hearers to engage in praise to God—and to render assistance to those in need. This is their new cultus (13:15–16).

12

Conclusion

The writer to the Hebrews sets out to help Christians in crisis. It was caused by societal pressures, compounded by an inadequate understanding of the Christian faith, particularly the fact that they had not progressed in their understanding of the core of Christian belief, viz. Jesus Christ. The consequences were painfully obvious. The church's commitment to Christ and its way of life left a lot to be desired. Its relation to Judaism was ill-defined, and its own membership was harmed by disunity. The author's response to the crisis is a remarkable document. It won for itself a signally important place in the canon of scripture and continues to influence the thought and life of Christians to this day. Its great importance lies in its exposition of who Jesus Christ is, what he did on the cross and what he continues to do for those who entrust themselves to him. Directly related to the needs of the community, it is essentially a pastoral response to those needs. Key to its message is Jesus Christ the pioneer and the high priest and the functions attributed to them. These interlocking concepts and what they stand for are a paradigm for Christians today.

The images of the priest and the pioneer form a dual Christology that is integral to the meaning of the sermon. Their binary relationship means that they cannot be treated separately as discrete and unrelated ways of looking at Christ and his saving work but must be taken together. Jesus is not pioneer without also being high priest, and his priesthood is only properly understood through the lens provided by the pioneer figure. The double analogy conveys the meaning of the Christian faith and helps us understand the distinctive character of the homily.

The importance of Christology is indicated right at the outset of the sermon. In an expansive statement Jesus Christ is invested with the greatest possible significance. "He is the reflection of God's glory and the exact imprint of God's very being, and he sustains all things by his powerful word" (1:3). His cosmic role is followed by his redeeming work on behalf of humanity. "When he had made purification for sins, he sat down at the right hand of the Majesty on high" (1:3). As son, Christ is one with God (1:2, 5; 3:6; 5:8; 7:28). His solidarity with God is the *sine qua non* of his saving work in reaching out to rescue the human race. It ensures his priesthood is efficacious, final and enduring. Simultaneously, Christ is one with humanity (2:11). "He had to become like his brothers and sisters in every respect, so that he might be a merciful and faithful high priest in the service of God, to make a sacrifice of atonement for the sins of the people" (2:17). His twin solidarities equip Christ to be mediator. In representing God to us he is merciful and representing us to God he is faithful.

For the author of Hebrews, Christ's solidarity with God and his solidarity with his followers are not two independent christological themes or traditions that somehow came together in the development of the church's understanding of Christ and his work. Their relationship was symbiotic from the start. This had to be. Those who formulated the early Christian confession knew that there was no other way that mortals could ever hope to approach God without someone making access possible, just as there was no other way that Christ could have become mediator of the new covenant. Who Christ is depended entirely upon the union of these two solidarities. This is the matrix in which Hebrews sets its interpretation of Christ as pioneer and priest.

Christ's identification with the human race is total. "Jesus offered up prayers and supplications, with loud cries and tears" and "learned obedience through what he suffered" (5:7, 8). He has no powers available to him that are not also available to his followers. Sharing a common stock (2:11), he and they are equally dependent upon the one source, God. Like his siblings, Jesus perseveres towards perfection. Like them, he lives by faith in God. His humanity is of great consequence for his ongoing ministry. "He had to become like his brothers and sisters in every respect, *so that* he might be a merciful and faithful high priest" (2:17).

In affirming Jesus' humanity, Hebrews rules out any possible suggestion that he is an unrelated patronal figure and makes the greatest effort to portray him as a representative kinsman, integrally belonging to the human family and unreservedly devoted to its well-being. The destiny that God intended for humanity, which it proved itself incapable of achieving, is now exercised by Jesus on its behalf (2:8–9). It was for the express purpose of leading humanity to its intended destiny that God appointed Jesus pioneer (2:10). The contrast is graphic: he who was "for a little while lower than the angels" and endured a shameful death now enjoys glory and honor. Tellingly, the preacher makes his point by stressing that Jesus reached his exalted position not in spite of his suffering and death but because of this. The congregation may not yet see everything in subjection to Jesus (2:8) and struggle with the dissonance between what they believe (*homologia*) and what they experience, but they are assured that their leader, having successfully completed his mission, is now actively engaged in his ministry on their behalf (7:25). Christ's experiences as a human being are thus translated directly into the writer's pastoral intention. Encouragement is thereby given to those who endure suffering and humiliation.

The description of Christ as pioneer (*archēgos*) is a distinctive and intrinsically significant feature of Hebrews (2:10; 12:2). In 2:10 it refers to one who leads others to the desired goal. (In this text it possibly also contains a hint of a hero figure (cf. 2:14c)). In 12:2 it means starter or founder and thus resembles "source" (*aitios*) in 5:9. Close to *archēgos* in meaning is "forerunner"(*prodromos*). This is illustrated in 6:19–20 where the forerunner alias pioneer opens up the holy of holies for his followers. Although the terms pioneer and forerunner are closely connected there is a sliver of difference between them. While both have a relative nuance and imply a sequence this is more pronounced in the case of *prodromos*. The pioneer as scout must on occasion forge ahead of his company; the forerunner as pacesetter must stay close. The pioneer concept in particular is bound up with the strongly eschatological orientation of the sermon, viz. the pioneer's mission to lead his followers to their heavenly destination (2:10). This is confirmed by the perfection language of the homily and its dynamic character. "Let us go on toward perfection (*teleiotēs*)" in 6:1 parallels "making the pioneer perfect (*teleioun*) " in 2:10 and resonates with the sermon's theme of perfecting, thereby indicating that it is not simply mature teaching that is denoted but the pioneer's task in leading his followers to their intended goal (perfection).

Closely linked to the pioneer-priest Christology of Hebrews is the concept of perfection or perfecting. This is dynamically expressed. It has in mind Christ and his followers pursuing their journey to its completion at its eternal destination. The language of perfection used of both Jesus and Christians has the same basic meaning, though with this difference: God perfects Jesus and Jesus perfects his followers. The fact that the word "perfecting" (*teleioun*) is used in both cases is significant. This is possible because of the solidarity of Jesus and his people (2:11b) and because in both cases the word has the same formal meaning of completing an undertaking or achieving a predetermined goal. *Teleioun* has other nuances and these need to be kept in mind, but as often as not they are related to the same basic idea of completion. Basically, perfecting is inherent in the sermon's teleological understanding of salvation. It is as pioneer that Jesus completes the process of salvation and in turn makes its outworking possible for his followers. In fact, perfection acquires its dynamic character to a great extent from its connection with the pioneer. It is a connection that is maintained throughout the entire sermon. Christ "having been made perfect (he) became the source of eternal salvation" (5:9). He is "the pioneer and perfecter of faith" (12:2). It is as the perfected high priest that Christ enters and occupies the heavenly holy of holies (7:26; 9:24; 10:20–21). The orientation of perfecting towards its completion in Christ's entry into the holy of holies explains why Hebrews omits direct mention of the resurrection as an event distinguishable from the ascension. It does not have a place in the author's analogical scheme, but is subsumed under the eternal priesthood of Melchizedek who lives forever (5:6; 6:20; 7:3, 17, 21; cf. 7:24, 28; 13:8).

The same thought of the consummation of perfection in the world to come also applies to the perfecting of Christians. Already perfected by Christ, they are being led by him to "glory" for its completion (2:10). The single, objective offering of Christ that initiates the perfection of believers (10:14a) makes possible its continuing subjective appropriation as they proceed on their way to perfection (10:14b). This tension between what Christ did and does and what has to be worked out in the lives of believers is another example of realized and future eschatology in Hebrews. The future hope of perfection for Christ's people is very effectively conveyed in the final vision of "the righteous made perfect" (12:23c).

The pioneer theology of Hebrews reaches its climax in the declaration that Jesus is "the pioneer and perfecter of faith" (*archēgos kai teleiōtēs*) (12:2). Drawing together earlier nuances, the preacher holds up Jesus not simply as the one who leads the participants in the race of faith to its triumphant finish but also as the one who has the honor of starting the whole enterprise in the first place. In calling Jesus the pioneer and perfecter of faith the writer is working in a quite different semantic field from the apostle Paul, even if on occasion he can use a characteristic Pauline word (*hilastērion*, "mercy seat," NRSV, 9:5). His understanding of faith is distinctive. For him faith is essentially trusting God (2:13; 11:9, etc.) and faithfulness or fidelity in discharging one's duties (3:6). Jesus himself was a faithful believer (2:13; 3:2). He lived by faith. Persevering in the work God entrusted to him through trials, suffering, and experiencing an excruciating death, Jesus is the personification of faithful living and obedience to God and is thus the "perfecter of faith." It is precisely as the actualization of faith that he is the basis (*aitios*) of its perfecting in his people and the example they are encouraged to follow (*prodromos*). In the play on the Greek (*pistis*), where the meaning is faith and faithfulness, what Hebrews says about Jesus' faith is a unique insight into his inner life and is in keeping with the sermon's emphasis on Christ's humanity and solidarity with human beings. Faith as faithfulness resonates well with the pioneering concept throughout Hebrews. It means carrying out his divinely appointed task of leading his followers to glory (2:10), journeying to Canaan (4:2), inheriting God's promise (6:12; 10:36–39) and it is given classical expression in faithful heroes and heroines chapter 11 (e.g., 11a, 8, 27, 33). The expected *parousia* will arrive; and in the meantime "the righteous will live by being faithful" (10:38). But Christ is more than a model of faith. He is savior (*ton archēgon tēs sōtērias*) (2:10). He made "purification for sins" (1:3), "a sacrifice of atonement for the sins of the people" (2:17). He is the "source of salvation" (5:9); his blood has saving effect (9:12–14; 10:19, 29; 12:24; 13:12, 20).

What Hebrews says about the continuing validity and efficacy of Christ's saving death is a major contribution to the Christology of the New Testament. The belief that on the cross Christ died to redeem humankind from sin appears in all the main strands of the New Testament, but it takes the form of a terse statement, such as we find in the early kerygma that "Christ died for our sins" (1 Cor 15:3). Hebrews makes a significant development by setting out to deal with the subject in a comprehensive and systematic way, with the aim of showing that the sacrifice of Christ is effective for all time. "By the power of an indestructible life" (7:16), i.e., by virtue of his resurrection, Christ lives to care for his people (10:21) and to be their advocate and intercessor (7:25). Both roles issue from his offering on the cross. Both are the reason for the confidence believers have in approaching him. Hebrews is not of course the only New Testament writing to testify to the continuing work of Christ on behalf of his people, but its use of the Melchizedek figure and its development of the high priestly work of Christ makes its contribution distinctive and important. What Hebrews says on this subject needs to be emphasized in the church's doctrine and worship: Christian faith depends not only on who Christ was but who he is, not simply what he did but what he is doing now.

The self offering of Christ provides direct access to God. Once closed to all except a single privileged individual, the way into God's presence is now thrown open to all, thanks to the pioneer-priest (10:19; cf. 9:8). The free access they enjoy is due not to any achievement on their part but to what Christ has done. It is Christ who has opened the way. Familiarity with this extraordinary message should not be allowed to blunt its power. In a world that spared no effort to preserve the holiness of the supreme being the invitation to suppliants to enter the divine presence is nothing short of revolutionary. Those who receive such assistance can hope to undertake costly discipleship and will want to offer prayer and worship (13:15–16). Access to God is their sustaining blessing. It would be unwarranted, however, to take access to God to mean that Christians are priests, as is the case in 1 Peter 2:5. What we can say with some confidence is that there is evidence that the author's thought was moving in this direction (10:10,14; cf. 9:19c) for the hearers are exhorted to offer spiritual sacrifices to God through Jesus Christ (13:15–16). If Hebrews is anticipating the priesthood of Christians then we have a fascinating convergence of thought, inasmuch as both Hebrews and 1 Peter are thinking of the priesthood of the Christian community, not that of individual Christians.

The attention devoted to the high priest in Hebrews is unique. It is to be attributed not only to the preacher's attempt to woo his listeners away from Judaism but also to his making clear the significance of Jesus Christ for their present and future discipleship. The perpetuity of Christ's saving work is emphasized under the Melchizedek figure and kept steadily to the fore in the entire central section of the sermon. The author was not the first person to use Psalm 110 messianically, but although it was widely used in the early church its possibilities do not appear to have been exploited. Psalm 110:4 does not actually call Melchizedek a high priest, but extrabiblical sources do, and it is not impossible that our author knew of this. In any event, it is a tribute to his creative genius that he made Psalm 110:4 central to his christological argument. What makes Melchizedek particularly important is his endless life. He is a type of him who surpasses the Levitical priesthood because he is a priest *forever* by virtue of his resurrection and his sacrifice therefore avails for all time (5:6; 6:20; 7:3, 17, 21). Once this point is made Melchizedek fades from the scene; attention is fixed on the ongoing ministry of Christ. In marked contrast to the significant role given to him in the eschatological denouement by Jewish writers, Melchizedek is not present, still less given a role, in the final drama on Mount Zion (12:22–24).

It is ironic that the Levitical system that the author finds to be defective and ineffective should supply him with such a valuable key for explaining what he has to say about Christ. His use of the analogy is singularly effective. It is of course strange to modern readers. It helps however if we see statements like "without the shedding of blood there is no forgiveness of sins" (9:22) as part of the writer's rhetorical aim. He is using Levitical categories to assist the hearers to understand that Christ's sacrifice fulfilled and outclassed all that traditional sacrifices attempted to do. The language of sacrifice remains (but is less of a problem for moderns who know the inescapable place sacrifice has in a life that attempts to acknowledge its familial and societal obligations), notwithstanding the fact that the sacrifice of Christ is a redemptive act for the salvation of the world. And Hebrews is at pains to show that there is all the difference between the voluntary self-offering of one who is both offerer and offering and the sacrifice of dumb animals. This is the essential point of the argument: the priesthood of Christ issues from his self-offering (7:27; 9:26). What Christ does as high priest in the heavenly sanctuary is all of a piece with what he did on the cross.

The "true tent" (otherwise the "greater and more perfect tent") (8:2), enjoys much attention from exegetes, although it is less important than what actually happens inside it, viz. the ministry of the high priest. The importance it has results from the place it occupies in the writer's rhetorical strategy. Christ's ministry acquires special significance from the fact that it takes place in the "true tent." How exactly the "true tent" is to be understood has taxed the minds of exegetes. The subject is, happily, becoming clearer. The work of Barrett has established beyond doubt that Hebrews owes its framework not to Plato's metaphysical dualism but to Jewish eschatology and is to be found in the apocalyptic and rabbinic dualism of this age and the new age to come and its Christian realization. However, it does not follow, as Barrett argued, that the dualism inherent in the linear/vertical cosmology of apocalyptic and rabbinic Judaism rules out the possibility that Hebrews contains any evidence of Platonism (Middle Platonism). But to acknowledge such dependence does not call in question the belief that the author's presuppositions are fundamentally eschatological. What is from one point of view an eternal archetype is from another viewpoint an eschatological credo, with the former serving the latter. But whatever part cosmology played in the preacher's argument, the "true tent" tells us more about the superiority of the new faith than its metaphysical character.

It is the author's Christian presuppositions that are most determinative. The archetypes that Plato so resolutely believed to be immutable are subjected to draconian treatment. In a way unimaginable to Plato this results from a historical event, viz. the death of Christ on the cross. More generally the ancient world would have been repelled and offended by the idea that the holiest place imaginable had been stripped of its protective screens and barriers and stood open to all, who, incredibly, are invited to enter it. At the same time, the world of his day supplied our architect author with materials for his new sanctuary. On the one hand, Judaism provided the conceptual framework in the Day of Atonement analogy. This was ideally suited to the needs of the Jewish audience and the author's aim to show how the sacrifice of Christ outperformed and superseded the Levitical sacrifices. On the other hand, the all-embracing cosmology of Stoicism and Hellenistic Judaism gave the author his ground plan for the "true tent." Hence the forecourt now includes the area where Christ made his priestly offering on the cross. It is the vestibule, so to speak, from which the pioneer-priest proceeds to his heavenly holy of holies. Very conveniently, the cosmology which joined earth and heaven thus enabled the author to depict what Christ did on the cross and what he does in heaven as a single event. But however intriguing the imaginative design and construction of the new temple is it should not be allowed to divert attention from the purpose it serves, that is, from its occupant, what he does in it and how Christians can avail themselves of the help he offers. "Since we have a great priest over the house of God, let us approach with a true heart in full assurance of faith" (10.21–22).

On completing his exposition of Christ and his ministry in the heavenly temple, the author returns to the pilgrimage of faith. That is where his friends are and are likely to be, short of death or the *Parousia*. But they can be confident that God will yet bring them to the inheritance he has promised them. The roll call of the pilgrims who have been on this journey leads very effectively to the "pioneer and perfecter of faith"(12:2) and the summons to follow him "outside the camp"(13:13). Theological exposition funnels into practical application, making Hebrews the outstanding manual of Christian discipleship that it is. The temple of Jerusalem is very likely still standing and covertly serves as a useful foil for the writer's rhetorical strategy, but what it represents is no longer of relevance to those who follow Christ. The future is with Christ. The sermon has relevance today to Christians for whom it is a matter of the greatest importance that they move forward with Christ from where they are to where God wants them to be.

The author evidently believed that he could end in such a way, having shown that all the help that pilgrims need has been gratuitously provided for in and through Jesus Christ. At any stage of the journey they can enter the presence of God, receive help and share in the worship of the heavenly Mount Zion. Indeed, they may hope to experience something of the joy that was Christ's as he pioneered the way for them (12:2). Thus they are expected to give praise to God and share what they have with those in need (13:15—16).

Appendix A

Words, Contexts, and Meanings

Christ is referred to both as "priest" and "high priest." "High priest" is used throughout, while alongside it "priest" is used when the reference is to Psalm 110:4 (5:6; 7:11, 15, 17, 21). There are two exceptions to the latter. In 5:10 and 6:20 "high priest" is used with Psalm 110:4. (See appendix C). Otherwise the use of these terms is straightforward. It is "pioneer" (*archēgos*) and the words closely related to it ("forerunner," *prodromos*) and ("source," *aitios*) that require attention.

Scholars differ on how *archēgos* in 2:10 should be translated. Whilst the companion term *prodromos* in 6:20 has the clearly defined meaning of one who is followed by others, *archēgos* has a wide range of meanings in the Bible and extrabiblical sources. This is reflected in the different ways the word is translated in versions of the Bible. The REB, NRSV, and TNIV all have "pioneer." The NEB has "leader." The NKJV has "captain." "Leader" is the preferred translation for many commentators. In his important study of *archēgos*, Paul-Gerhard Müller demonstrates how the idea of leadership issues from the recurring theme of Israel as a people who are led by God (e.g., Exod 3:8, 17; 6:6–7; 7:4–5, *passim*).[1] He argues that the presentation of Jesus as the new leader of God's people comes out of this tradition.[2] A number of scholars, bearing in mind that in the classical writings *archēgos* is also used for the founder of a city or kingdom, note how *archēgon tēs sōtērias* in 2:10 parallels *aitios sōtērias* in 5:9 and take *archēgos* here in the sense of "founder" or "initiator."[3]

1. Müller, *ΧΡΙΣΤΟΣ ΑΡΧΗΓΟΣ*, 141–48.
2. Müller, *ΧΡΙΣΤΟΣ ΑΡΧΗΓΟΣ*, 141–48, 286–88.
3. Delling, "Archēgos," 487–88; Käsemann, *Wandering People*, 128–30. See

A different line of thought is suggested by those who believe that Hebrews is using the Hellenistic idea of the divine hero.[4] This is vigorously canvassed by Lane, who translates *archēgos* as "champion" and takes it in this sense in both 2:10 and 12:2.[5] This understanding of *archēgos* in 2:10 is attractive for approaching the statement in 2:14 that Christ destroys the one who has the power of death and frees those who live in fear of death. Seneca depicts Hercules achieving glory through suffering (*Oetaeus* 1434–40; 1557–59, 1940–88) and by undergoing death liberates others from the fear of death (*Furens* 889–92). This resonates with Heb 2:14–15 where the author incorporates Christ's victory over the devil into his *archēgos* Christology.[6] The predominant idea conveyed by *archēgos* in 2:10 is that of leader and pioneer. We see this in the immediate context (*agagonta*), in the pilgrimage motif and in the author's repeated use of the Day of Atonement analogy when describing Christ's entry into the heavenly holy of holies and his leading his people there (4:14–16; 6:20; 9:12, 24).

The word *archēgos* appears only in Hebrews (2:10; 12:2) and the Book of Acts (3:15; 5:31). In the LXX and the classical writings the term covers a number of meanings.[7] It is used in the LXX to translate the Hebrew *nasî, sār* and especially *rôš*, and most often means "leader" or "ruler."[8] The prefix *archē* has the same function as *arch* in *archiereus* and connotes primacy. In Greek literature the term describes Athena as the founder of Athens (Plato, *Tim.* 21e) and Zeus as the "founder and begetter of all" (Plato, *Tim.Loc.* 96b). It thus has the sense of "initiator" (Aelius Aristides, *Or.* 43:41; Polybius, *Hist* 1.66.10 [where interestingly it is used with *aitios* ("source"), cf. Heb 5:9]; 1 Macc 9:61; 10:47) or "originator" (Josephus. *Ant.* 7:207; Isocrates 4:61; Diodorus Siculus 5.64.5; 2 Clem 20:5), "pioneer" (Lucius Annaeus Florus, *Epitome* 1.14.3). "Leader" or

O'Brien, *Hebrews*, 106.

4. Knox, "The Divine Hero," 229–49. This meaning is also adopted Manson, *Hebrews*, 102–105; Montefiore, *Hebrews*, 61; Thiselton, "Hebrews," 1458.

5. Lane, *Hebrews 1–8*, 56–57, 61–63.

6. Weiss, *Hebräer*, 203; Lane, *Hebrews 1–8*, 57.

7. Delling, "Archēgos," 487; Müller, *ΧΡΙΣΤΟΣ ΑΡΧΗΓΟΣ*, 72–102; Simpson, "Vocabulary of the Epistle to the Hebrews," 35–38; Scott, "*Archēgos* in the Salvation History," 47–54; Attridge, *Hebrews*, 87–88, 356; Lane, *Hebrews 1–8*, 56–57; Ellingworth, *Hebrews* (1993), 160–61.

8. Hatch and Redpath, *Concordance*, 165. Cf. Johnston, "Christ as Archēgos," 381–85.

"scout" of an army is a common meaning (Euripides, *Tro.* 1267; Polybius, *Hist* 10.34.2) and the sense is close to "forerunner" (*prodromos*) (Heb 6:20). The view that the meaning *archēgos* has in Hebrews is essentially the Hellenistic idea of the divine hero (particularly Hercules)[9] fails to recognize the fact that the other uses of *archēgos* in the Hellenistic church do not refer to a divine hero (Acts 3:15; 5:31) and it does not do justice to the strong communal meaning that the word *archēgos* has in Hebrews. "Leader" is used with some justification by the NEB and the JB.[10] More to be preferred for its use in 2:10 is "pioneer"(so RSV, NRSV, REB, TNIV). This suits both the immediate context (*agagonta*) and, importantly, the futuristic orientation of the whole sermon, depicting Jesus as the one who opens up the way for those with him. If the use of the term in 2:10 contains the sense of "originator" or "founder" (cf. *aitios*) this is secondary to "pioneer" and "leader"(cf. *prodromos*). In 12:2 the use of *archēgos* in conjunction with *teleiōtēs* ("perfecter") gives it very definitely the sense of "founder" or "starter." Here *archēgos* thus approximates in meaning to *aitios*. "Champion" is quite unsuitable as a translation for its use in 12:2.

There is much to be said for Ellingworth's suggestion that the pioneer metaphor in 2:10 may well owe something to Jesus' calling disciples to follow him (Mark 1:16–20; 2:14; cf. John 1:43) and going ahead of them (Mark 10:32; Luke 19:28; cf. Matt 28:19–20).[11]

Hebrews presents the pioneer as the representative of the "many sons" who are on their way to "glory." Strong familial overtones are conveyed in 2:10. As we saw in chapter 3, the motif is connected with the perfecting of Jesus and his followers, understood as the completing of their journey to the heavenly world. See further in the study of *archēgos* in appendix B.

Related to *archēgos* are the terms *prodromos* (6:20) and *aitios* (5:9). The meaning of *prodromos* has been much discussed; there is general agreement that the basic meaning is "going ahead." Hence the REB, NRSV and TNIV render it as "forerunner." The term is rare in the LXX (Wisd 12:8; Isa 28:4). In the classical writings it is used for an advance

9. Knox, "The Divine Hero," 229–49. So also Lane, *Hebrews 1–8*, 56–57, 410; Thiselton, "Hebrews," 1458. For an attempt to interpret Christ as the victorious ruler in political terms based on the Flavian triumph commemorating Titus's destruction of Jerusalem in 70 CE, see Aitken, "Portraying the Temple in Stone and Text," 131–48.

10. Cf. Müller, *ΧΡΙΣΤΟΣ ΑΡΧΗΓΟΣ*, 535–41.

11. Ellingworth, *Hebrews* (1993), 161. For Mark's description of Jesus pioneering discipleship see, e.g., Best, *Following Jesus*, 120–22.

military guard (Herodotus, *Hist* 1. 60; 4.121; 7.203; 9.14; Polybius, *Hist.* 12.20.7; Sophlocles, *Atig* 108; cf. Josephus, *Ant.* 7:345; 12:314, 372), or a runner who outpaces others to win the race, though the latter image is less frequent (Julius Polux, *Onom.* 3.30,148).[12] In the New Testament the word "forerunner" is used by translators for John the Baptist, who is remembered as the one who prepared the way for Jesus (Mark 1:1–8 and *par.* Cf. Isa 40:3–11; Mal 3:1). *Prodromos* conveys strongly relational overtones. The word makes one invariably think of those who follow. To think of John the Baptist is to think of Jesus. Thus in Hebrews 6:19–20 there is no suggestion of a delay between the entry of the forerunner into the holy of holies and those following him (cf. 10:19–21; cf. 12:1–2).

The analogous word *aitios*, "source," is used to describe Jesus in Hebrews 5:9 (*aitios sōtērias*, "source of salvation," REB, NRSV, TNIV). In the books of Maccabees *aitios* has pejorative and positive meanings (2 Macc 4:47; 4 Macc 1:11). A close grammatical parallel to its presence in Hebrews 5:9 is Philo's use of the word in *De Agricultura* 96, where the brazen serpent of Numbers 21:8 is referred to as the "author of salvation" (*aitios sōtērias*) (cf. *Contempl. Life* 86; *Virt.* 202). Josephus has Julius Caesar declare Antipater to be "(the one) responsible for their victory and also for their safety (*kai tēs sōtērias aition*)" (*Ant.*14:136). In the classical writers *aitios* invariably means "source," "cause," or "reason" (Polybius 1.43.2; Diodorus Siculus, 4.18.2; Plato, *Crat.* 401).[13] Plato (*Crat.* 401D) and Polybius (1.67) in fact conjoin *archēgos* and *aitios*. In Acts 19:40, the only other place in the New Testament where the term occurs, the meaning is clearly "cause." *Aitios* connects with the sense in which *archēgos* is used in 12:2, viz. "founder" or "starter." It does not have any connection with *archēgos* in 2:10 as "pioneer" or "leader," and it should not be automatically taken as equivalent to *archēgos*, as is sometimes done.[14]

If one may use athletic imagery one could say that the *aitios* is the one who gets the race organized and started while the *archēgos* is one who participates in the race with others and, as *prodromos*, leads the others to the finishing line.

The Afrikaans word *vortrekker* conveys the main idea of leadership and pioneering in *archēgos*. It took its origin from the Dutch settlers

12 Baurernfeind, "Prodromos," 235; Ellingworth, *Hebrews* (1993), 348; Lane, *Hebrews 1–8*, 154, 410; Koester, *Hebrews*, 330.

13. Simpson, "Vocabulary of the Epistle to the Hebrews," 35–36. Cf. Attridge, *Hebrews*, 153–54.

14. Scott, "*Archēgos* in Salvation History," 51.

in the Cape Colony of South Africa who trekked into the unchartered interior in the mid-nineteenth century in search of a new home. The success of the huge undertaking depended upon the *vortrekkers* who led the way and their continuous and well-organized liaising with those who followed. Colloquially, the word *vortrekker* today calls to mind anyone who sets out on a particular human endeavor and by means of contact and feedback helps those depending upon the outcome of his or her endeavors.

Fundamental to the pioneer motif is the bond between leader and followers. This is made clear from the start, in 2:10. "It was fitting that God, for whom and through whom all things exist, in bringing many children (*huious*) to glory, should make the pioneer of their salvation perfect through sufferings." The NRSV's use of the word "children" for *huioi*, in the interests of inclusive language, fails to convey the sort of relationship one normally thinks of when one has in mind a leader and followers. More satisfactory is "sons and daughters" in the TNIV, though it is somewhat cumbersome. "Siblings" is the word preferred by Scott Mackie.[15] Its inclusivity commends it and it is an appropriate translation as long as one does not overlook that fact that while siblings is a satisfactory translation for *adelphoi* ("brothers") in 2:11 and 2:17 it is not suitable for *huioi* ("sons") in 2:10 (even if Jesus and not God is the subject of 2:10).[16] In favor of "sons" is the solidarity with the "Son" that this conveys. Since solidarity is such an important feature of both 2:10 and the sermon, generally there is something to be said for this rendering of the Greek. In what follows I alternate my use of terms, speaking of "sons and daughters," "siblings," or "sons" as seems appropriate.

As far as *archēgos* itself is concerned, I use the translation "pioneer" wherever possible, without forgetting that its other nuances ("initiator" or "source"). In doing so I am not making a claim for the correct translation of the Greek but attempting to do justice to the conceptual/contextual and semantic nexus in which the key term is found.

15. Mackie, *Eschatology and Exhortation*, 45, 221–22, following Bartchy, "Undermining Ancient Patriarchy," 68–78.

16. On the difficult syntax of 2:10 see more in chapter 3.

Appendix A

Summary

"High priest" is the preferred title for Christ in Hebrews. "Priest" is restricted to references to Psalm 110:4 in all but two instances (5:10; 6:20). The companion word *archēgos* has several nuances but in 2:10 its predominating sense is "pioneer." In the case of 12:2 the juxtaposition of *archēgos* with *teleiōtēs* indicates that the meaning is "founder" or "initiator." It thus closely resembles *aitios*, which unequivocally means "cause" or "source." Much depends on the context and whether in the use of *archēgos* the stress is on the prefix or on the verb. The meaning of *prodromos* is not ambiguous. It has a strong communal referent. Those following are expected to keep close to the forerunner. Jesus did not enter the heavenly sanctuary alone but in company with his "many sons."

Appendix B

Pioneer in the Hebrew Bible and Extrabiblical Sources

The term *archēgos* ("pioneer") is used in the LXX most often of a political or military leader, who may lead the whole people or part of it. Thus the Israelites, disgruntled with Moses and their life in the wilderness, schemed to choose an *archēgos* who would lead them back to Egypt (Num 14:4). In the time of the judges we find leaders often called by the name of *archēgos* (Judg 5:2, 15; 11:6, 11). Jephthah was asked to become *archēgos* by the people of Gilead in order to deliver them from the Ammonites (11:6). He agreed on condition that the post was made permanent. The elders concurred and Jephthah was made *kephalē* and *archēgos* ("head and commander") (11:11). Jephthah then proceeded to lead the people to victory and ruled Israel for six years (12:7). Elsewhere *archēgos* can mean envoy or forerunner (Isa 30:4). The dominant idea in numerous other texts is leadership (Num 10:4; 13:2–3; 1 Chron 5:24; 8:28; 26:26; 2 Chron 23:14; Isa 3:3–6; 1 Macc 9:61; 10:47; Jdt 14:2; cf. Mic 1:13; 1 Clem 14:1; 2 Clem.20:5).[1] The term is used figuratively in five other places (Mic 1:13; Jer 3:4; Lam 2:10; 1 Macc 9:61; 10:17). We have to look to classical sources for the other nuances the term has in the New Testament.

Related to our subject are the stories of venturesome individuals who make the journey to the heavenly temple that are to be found in apocalyptic and rabbinic writings[2] and in literature of the Greco-Roman

---

1. Müller, *ΧΡΙΣΤΟΣ ΑΡΧΗΓΟΣ*, 141–48.

2. Bietenhard, *Himmlische Welt*, 135–42; Alexander, "3 (Hebrew Apocalypse) Enoch," 247–51; Dean-Otting, *Heavenly Journeys*; Himmelfarb, *Ascent to Heaven*; Alexander, *Mystical Texts*, 75–92. Mackie, "Heavenly Sanctuary Mysticism," 88–92.

world generally.[3] Here however a distinction has to be made between those who make the journey for their personal edification, often to return and make further such journeys, and the leader in Hebrews who pioneers a single journey expressly for the benefit of others who are following. The sources in question are generally later than the New Testament, but the visits to heaven mentioned in 2 Corinthians 12:1-5 and Revelation 4 are evidence that such traditions have an ancient ancestry. We have accounts of the journeys made by Enoch (1 *En* 14: 8-23; 39:3-8; 71:1-11; 87:2-3; cf., 2 *En*. 1:1-10; 22:10), Levi (*T Levi* 2:5-12; 5:1-2), Abraham (*Apoc.Ab.* 15:4) and Isaiah (*Asc.Isa.* 7-9). The *Testament of Levi* is close to our sub-ject.[4] It describes how the patriarch, guided by an angel, passes through the different realms and on reaching the "gates of heaven" (5:1) and ap-pearing before God, is invested with priestly and royal offices (5:1-3; 8:1-10). Other accounts of the ascents to heaven report the journey to heaven as a difficult undertaking. In the *Ascension of Isaiah* the traveler is accosted, "How far is he who dwells among aliens to go up" (9:1; cf. 3 *En* 2:2; 4:6-10; 6:1-3). A barrier that protects the heavenly world, akin to the cosmic wall separating earth and heaven in later Gnosticism, is depicted in some texts (1 *En* 14: 9; 3 *Bar*. 2:1, 2 ; *T Levi* 2:7). Those who make the journey return to earth afterwards (*Test.Abr*. 15; 3 *Bar 17*), where, for ex-ample, Baruch "comes to himself," i.e., regains consciousness (3 *Bar 17*).

The Dead Sea Scrolls abound with accounts of mortals worshipping with the heavenly hosts.[5] They "stand before" God (1QH 11:21-22) or "with the holy ones" (19:10-12). They become "united with the sons of your truth and in the lot of your holy ones" (19:11). Along with the angels they form "a holy council" (1QSa II:1-11).What is not clear, however, is whether the worship is actually taking place in heaven and not on earth.[6] However, there are passages which imply that a member of the

The translation of Enoch and Elijah to heaven in Gen 5:24 and 2 Kgs 2:2-12 was not understood as ascent in the apocalyptic tradition.

3. Segal, "Heavenly Ascent," 1333-94; Smith, "Ascent to the Heavens," 403-29. Stories tell of ascents in dreams, visions, or by the soul parting from the body before or after death, or on occasion bodily ascents.

4. Himmelfarb, *Ascent to Heaven*, 30-37. On the question of what exactly the as-cents entailed see Alexander, *Mystical Texts*, 76-77.

5. Frennesson, "*In a Common Rejoicing*," 1999; Fletcher-Louis, *All Glory to Adam*; Brooke, "Men and Women as Angels," 159-77.

6. Rowland, *Open Heaven*, 113-20; Alexander, *Mystical Texts*, 118-19. On the sub-ject of realized eschatology in the Qumran writings see Aune, *Cultic Setting*, 29-44; Alexander, *Mystical Texts*, 108.

community has enjoyed the ultimate experience of standing in the presence of God (1QH 19:10–14; 4Q491:11.I: 13–15). *The Self-Glorification Hymn* is particularly apposite.[7] The anonymous speaker declares that he sat on a throne in the council of the angels and was instructed in the heavenly mysteries (4Q 491:11.I: 11–15). Although this has been taken to mean that the speaker had ascended to heaven to take up residence and was not on a episodic visit, the latter is much more likely to be what is intended as we see from the sequel. Just as the sailor returns home from distant parts, the speaker returns to tell of his adventure (4Q491:11:I. 15). Ascent is followed by descent. In fact, the traveler must return. What he has to tell the community is essential not only to his personal standing and the authority of his teaching but also to the legitimacy of the community. If *The Self-Glorification Hymn* was composed by the Teacher of Righteousness, the founder of the community, as is likely, it is best understood as presenting his ascent and his priestly and prophetic credentials.[8]

Jewish Mysticism

The journey to heaven that features so prominently in Jewish *merkabah* mysticism is believed by some scholars to provide the background to Hebrews.[9] The Jewish mystical writings are later than the New Testament, but evidence of *merkabah* ideas has emerged at Qumran.[10] The journey made by the mystic elites in order to reach the heavenly sanctuary or God's throne and discover secrets about God and the future is described at length.[11]

---

7. Alexander, *Mystical Texts*, 85–90.

8. Alexander says. "He (the ascender) is in some sense a forerunner, or trail blazer" (*Mystical Texts*, 90).

9. Schenke, "Erwägungen zum Rätsel," 421–37, Williamson, "Background to Hebrews," 232–37. Cf. McCullough, "Some Recent Developments," 141–65; Hurst, *Hebrews*, 82–85; Eskola, *Messiah and Throne*, 203–211. On the ways in which the ascent to heaven in the *merkabah* literature differed from that in the apocalyptic literature, see Himmelfarb, *Heavenly Ascent*, 73–100.

10. Strugnell, "Angelic Liturgy at Qumran," 318–45. On the question of the relationship of the mysticism at Qumran and that in the later *Heikhalot* literature, see Alexander, *Mystical Texts*, 5–12.

11. Scholem, *Major Trends in Jewish Mysticism*, 48–62; Alexander, *Textual Sources*, 16–32; Elior, "From Earthly Temple to Heavenly Shrines," 217–67; Schäfer, "Engel und Menschen," 201–25. Cf. generally Rowland, *Open Heaven*, 282–348. Scholem made the mystic's heavenly journey the central feature of Jewish mysticism, but it is now

Those who undertake the journey must be well-versed in the law and well prepared by reciting hymns, purification and ecstasy-inducing prayers.[12] The mystic can expect obstacles and dangers on entering the heavenly world (3 En 2:2; 4:6–10; 6:1–3; b Hag. 11b–16a).[13] Even the great R. Akiba encountered difficulty: angels wanted to stop him (b Hag. 15b).[14] Rabbi Ishmael is highly privileged to be shown the veil that shields the angels from the brilliance of the divine presence and hides the divine mysteries (3 En. 45). He is introduced to Metatron who is the patriarch Enoch (Gen 5:18–24), and who, on ascending to heaven, is transformed into an archangel and high priest (3 En 3–16) and functions as a pioneer figure, leading visitors (represented by R. Ishmael) through the heavenly world (17–48). Notwithstanding the difficulties faced by travelers to the heavenly world, the beatific vision and the mystical transformation that followed it were so greatly desired that ascent to heaven was repeated many times over. As at Qumran, the mystic returns to earth,[15] his return and the recounting of his experiences being an important part of the legitimatizing of the sect.

Scholars working on the epistle to the Hebrews are not generally convinced that the mystic's journey in Jewish mysticism influenced the writer.[16] We have already noted that although the literature in question is much later than Hebrews this is not the problem that it is sometimes thought to be because it has antecedents in earlier times. Nevertheless, the mystic's ascent bears only a formal resemblance to what Hebrews has in mind. There is no suggestion in Hebrews that entrance into the

recognized that it represented only one aspect of the literature. There is no question, however, that the mystic's ascent to heaven was of very great importance (Morray-Jones, "Paradise Revisited," 179). For the view that John's ascent to heaven in Rev 4 is closely paralleled on Jewish ideas, see Rowland, "The Vision of the Risen Christ," 1–11.

12. Scholem, *Major Trends in Jewish Mysticism*, 56–62; Gruenwald, *Apocalyptic and Merkavah Mystics*, 99–109; Rowland, *Open Heaven*, 273–75.

13. Scholem, *Major Trends in Jewish Mysticism*, 50–53; Gruenwald, *Apocalyptic and Merkavah Mystics*, 111, 122.

14. Rowland, *Open Heaven*, 313. The angelic gate-keepers are described in 3 En. 18:1–4; *Hekhalot Rabbati* 15:8; 17:6. Cf. Alexander, *Textual Sources,* 122–3; "3 (Hebrew Apocalypse of) Enoch," 248–49, 240, 296.

15. Alexander, "3 (Hebrew Apocalypse of) Enoch," 238; Morray-Jones, "Transformational Mysticism," 1–31. On the question of the individuals who it would appear were transformed into angels and did not return to earth see Alexander, *Mystical Texts*, 90.

16. McCullough, "Some Recent Developments," 150–51; Williamson, *Philo and Hebrews*, 234–5; Hurst, *Hebrews,* 82–5; Lane, *Hebrews 1–8*, cvi, cix.

presence of God is for the favored few and depends upon preparatory efforts on the part of the mystic.

The worship that is offered in heaven by the angelic hosts and in which they claim to share is also of interest to us. The heavens literally teem with angels who offer spiritual sacrifices and engage in prayer and sacred song. Of particular interest is the combination of earthly and heavenly worship. The sense of deprivation after the fall of the temple of Jerusalem was compensated to some degree by complex ritual bridges that the sages built for the purpose of joining worshippers on earth with those in heaven.[17] Elior says of this prayer, "Shared prayer is the prayer of two corresponding communities—the company of the angels on high and the congregation of human worshippers on earth, which together recite the Kedushah prayer and extol the Creator."[18]

Philo

Philo frequently thinks of life as a journey to the heavenly world.[19] He has God saying, "(I) have laid down the road that leads to heaven and appointed it as a highway for all suppliant souls, that they may not grow weary as they tread it" (*Post.* 31). Sometimes it is God who is guide (*Migr.* 71; *Decal* .81). At other times it is an angel (*Agr.* 51), or the *Logos* (*Deus* 182).

The journey that the souls of the wise undertake is their way back to the heavenly world, their true home.

> When they have stayed awhile in their bodies, and beheld through them all that sense and mortality has to show, they make their way back to the place from which they set out at the first. To them the heavenly region, where their citizenship lies, is their native land; the earthly region in which they became sojourners is a foreign country (*Conf.* 78).[20]

Philo's imagery invariably draws on the journey of Abraham or the Israelites to the promised land (*Migr.* 127–30; *Decal* .81). The pilgrims "tread the true King's way, the way of the one sole almighty King,

17. Elior, "From Earthly Temple to Heavenly Shrines," 230–65.

18. Elior, "From Earthly Temple to Heavenly Shrines," 232.

19. Käsemann, *Wandering People*, 75–8; Williamson, *Philo*, 274–76.

20. "At the heart of Philo's religious philosophy is a concern to portray the pilgrimage of the soul to God" (Hay, "Philo of Alexandria," 364).

swerving and turning aside neither to the right nor the left" (*Gig.* 64; cf. *Spec.* 2.45). In a passage which patently reveals Greek influence, Philo says that souls bound for the heavenly world must divest themselves of bodily passions (*Post.* 31, 101; *Spec.* 2:45–48; *QG.* 2:45).

Here too , the journey is far from easy (*Mos.* 1:192–5). Pilgrims "find their way contested by Edom . . . who threatens to bar them from the road and render it such that none at all shall tread or travel on it" (*Deus* 144). But God helps them (*Mos.* 1:255), and there are other leaders who provide assistance: Moses (*Mos.* I:193), wisdom (*Deus* 142–3), and the *Logos* (*Deus* 182). Philo does not actually use the word *archēgos*, but has a comparable word for the one who heads the pilgrims. "(They) follow in the steps of a guide who could never err . . . a forerunner (*proēgoumenos*)" (*Opif.* 28; *Mos.* I:166; cf. *Post.* 31; Deut 20:9; 1 Esd 5:8–9; 9:12; 2 Macc 11:8; 1 Clem 21:6).

Even a summary examination of Philo shows that his understanding of the journey to heaven is visibly different from Hebrews. While both writers use the story of Israel's pilgrimage as their starting point they develop it in quite different ways. As Barrett says, pilgrimage for Philo is "primarily ethical with a metaphysical twist."[21] Life is a journey in which the minds of the wise labor to escape from the "foul prison-house" of the body (*Migr.* 9). The "mind of the sage" turns away from the earthly sphere of the material and physical to its real home in "the archetypal ideas which, invisible and intelligible there, are the patterns of things visible and sensible here" (*Her.* 280).[22] Such dualism is of no interest to the writer to the Hebrews. He is emphatic that what makes Jesus the leader of the Christian pilgrimage is what he accomplished during his time on earth and by means of his earthly, bodily life (2:17; 5:7; 10:10; 12:2).[23]

Classical Sources

Some scholars believe Hebrews modeled Christ the pioneer on the hero-figure in the classical texts.[24] Attridge cites the striking parallel in Lucius Annaeus Florus.

---

21. Barrett, "Eschatology," 377. Williamson, *Philo*, 489.

22. Williamson, *Philo*, 490.

23. Williamson, *Philo*, 274–76.

24. Knox, "The Divine Hero," 222–49; Simon, *Hercule et le Christianisme*; Tiede, *Charismatic Figure*, 171–200; Lane, following William Manson (*Hebrews*, 102–3), says

While the other consul [i.e., Decius Mus], as though acting upon a warning from heaven, with veiled head devoted himself to the infernal gods in front of the army, in order that, by hurling himself where the enemy's weapons were thickest, he might open up a new path to victory along the track of his own lifeblood (*Epitome* 1.9.14).[25]

Hercules is the model *par excellence* for leadership in the classics. "He stands at the head of humankind, leading all" (Aelius Aristides, *Or.* 40.14). Seneca developed the Hercules myth around the idea of his having broken open a way into the terrifying underworld and then leading out its benighted denizens (*Hercules Furens* 40–60).[26]

The myth was metamorphosed many times, but the hero remains a savior figure and leader throughout. Isocrates presented Hercules as a fitting model for Philip of Macedon to emulate, while Philip's son, Alexander, was pleased to consider himself a direct descendant of Hercules (5.109–110).[27] In the Roman Stoics Hercules became the embodiment of the Stoic virtues of courage, endurance, and wisdom.[28]

It is Seneca's treatment of Hercules that has greater fascination for us. He represents the hero achieving glorification as a result of suffering (*Hercules Oetaeus* 1434–40, 1940–88).[29] His acceptance of death delivers others from the fear of death (*Hercules Furens* 889–92).[30] "When the last day shall bring the final hour, glory will open wide the path to heaven" (*Hercules Oetaeus* 1988).[31]

Since Seneca's development of the hero myth has proved attractive to some students of Hebrews in their study of the pioneer concept in Hebrews 2:10 we shall consider this. For the present we note that while

that Hebrews "drew freely" upon this tradition (*Hebrews*, 1–8, 57). Cf. Aune, "Heracles and Christ," 3–19; Aitken, "The Hero in Hebrews," 179–88. On the subject of heavenly ascent in classical antiquity, see Dean-Otting, *Heavenly Journeys*, 13–20. The "warrior" imagery of 11QMelch has no place in Hebrews (Thiselton, "Hebrews," 1464).

25. Quoted by Attridge, *Hebrews*, 285.

26. On the importance of Hercules' journey to and from the underworld to lead out its captives, see Fitch, *Seneca's Hercules Furens*, 33–35, 134–35; 566–68. Cf. Attridge, " Liberating Death's Captives," 103–15.

27. Galinsky, *The Herakles Theme*, 103.

28. Galinsky, *The Herakles Theme*, 126–52.

29. Tiede, *Charismatic Figure*, 79–90; Aune, "Heracles and Christ," 16; Attridge, *Hebrews*, 80; Lane, *Hebrews 9–13*, 56–57.

30. Tiede, *Charismatic Figure*, 78–80; Attridge, *Hebrews*, 80.

31. Attridge, *Hebrews*, 80.

Hebrews emphasizes the sufferings of Jesus and sees him as the one who leads many to glory (2:10), it eschews any suggestion that he was taken up into glory as a reward for his achievement.[32]

Gnostic Sources

The gnostic myth of the pilgrimage of human souls to their heavenly homeland was used by Käsemann as the background to the pilgrimage and pioneer motifs of Hebrews.[33] For Käsemann, "One possesses the *euangelion* on earth only as *epangelia*. But then it follows *that the form of existence in time appropriate to the recipient of the revelation can only be that of wandering*."[34] He believed the gnostic redeemer who descends to earth to set souls free from their entanglements with the material world and lead them back to heaven is relevant for understanding the pioneer of Hebrews. The cosmic leader has breached the boundary or veil dividing heaven and earth.[35] In words reminiscent of what Hebrews says about Christ being the new and living way (10:20), is the Gospel of Truth: "Jesus Christ shed light upon those . . . travelers. He enlightened them and gave them a way and the way is the truth about which he instructed them" (18:18).[36] He is their guide to the heavenly world (19:17; 22:20). "On my path shall the chosen come; in my steps shall the faithful go."[37] The Hermetic writings frequently describe *gnosis* as the way (4:11; 6:5, 6; 10:15; 11:21).[38] The souls on their journey to the heavenly world can expect to face difficulties,[39] especially the boundary wall (alias the veil of

---

32. Of more general interest is the model which Cynic and Stoic moralists found in Heracles. "Hercules again appears as the great example of the moral athlete toiling for virtue" (Epic *Diss.* III 22,26,31,57; IV.10.10 (Pfitzner, *Paul and the Agon Motif*, 29).

33. Käsemann, *Wandering People*, 17–25, 87–96. So also Bultmann, *Theology of New Testament*, 177; Grässer, *Glaube*, 272–76.

34. Käsemann, *Wandering People*, 19. Italics are the author's.

35. Käsemann, *Wandering People*, 128–31, 209, 223–25. See *Odes of Solomon* 17.8–16 for the bursting of the cosmic barrier. The dividing wall is defined by Käsemann as "nothing else than the ban of the material world which humans cannot break" (225; cf. 229).

36. Bentley Layton, *Gnostic Scriptures*, 254. Cf. *Gos. Thom.* 49; Käsemann, *Wandering People*, 225; Attridge, *Hebrews*, 286.

37. Käsemann, *Wandering People*, 92. Cf. *Acts Thom* 156.

38. Michaelis, "Hodos," 47.

39. Käsemann, *Wandering People*, 93, 225.

the temple),[40] but they have nothing to fear; they will have divine help all the way (*Odes of Solomon* 41.11). Fascinatingly, the eventual entry of the gnostic soul into the state of gnosis is like the entry of the high priest into the holy of holies (Clement of Alexandria, *Excerpta* 27.1).[41]

While many scholars found Käsemann's exposition of the pilgrimage motif opened up the meaning of Hebrews for them, few regarded his use of gnosticism as convincing.[42] The idea of the gnostic redeemer descending from heaven in order to rescue souls (that once lived in the heavenly world) flies in the face of what Hebrews says about Jesus who "had to become like his brothers and sisters in every respect" (2:17; 4:15; 5:7–8). Similarly, where gnosticism cannot think of access to God taking place while one is in this sinful world, Hebrews has no hesitation in speaking of this (4:15–16; 6:19–20; 10:19–22; 12:23).

Summary

The accounts of intrepid individuals who journey to heaven to be found in Jewish and Greco-Roman literature provide us with background of a general kind. However, the attempt of Hofius and others to suggest that Jewish *merkabah* mysticism provides a parallel to Christ's ascent to the heavenly sanctuary is not convincing. The same must be said of parallels that are sought in apocalyptic and Qumran accounts of individuals who make it to heaven. The traveler to the heavenly temple in the *Self-Glorification Hymn* is interesting, but Alexander's description of this individual as a forerunner does not help us greatly with Hebrews' understanding of the *prodromos*, since the latter does not travel alone but in company with others. The hero-figure in the classics, depicted by Seneca as Hercules achieving glory through suffering, bears some resemblance to Christ, but there is no suggestion in Hebrews that Jesus' exaltation is in any sense a reward for what he succeeded in achieving. The gnostic parallel that Käsemann sought is disqualified by the fundamental difference between the world-denying gnostic leader and the Jesus of Hebrews whose humanity is so strongly emphasized.

40. Käsemann, *Wandering People*, 223–25.

41. Daniélou, *Gospel Message*, 452, 461.

42. Hurst, *Hebrews*, 67–75; Ellingworth, *Hebrews* (1993), 42–45; Lincoln, *Hebrews*, 47. In support of finding Gnostic ideas behind Hebrews are Grässer, *Glaube*; Jewett, *Letter to Pilgrims*.

The chief value of the stories of individuals journeying to the heavenly realm found in such a variety of sources is evidence that the cosmological background and the perpetual efforts of individuals to gain access to God independently of established procedures was no aberration of Jewish fringe movements but part of a widely-held tradition. They had their origin in the age-old doctrine of the heavenly world as the counterpart of the earthly.

Appendix C

High Priest in the Hebrew Bible and Extrabiblical Sources

Central to the thought of Hebrews and the pastoral encouragement offered to those listening to the sermon is Christ the high priest and the help he has to give them to undertake the challenges ahead of them.[1] Its presentation in the New Testament is unique and makes Hebrews such a valuable part of the New Testament. The subject is introduced in 2:17 and subsequently expanded at length. Rissi thinks that the brief and somewhat casual way in which it is introduced is evidence that it was familiar to the readers,[2] but this fails to take account of the rhetorical aim

---

1. On the possible antecedents of the high priest figure in Hebrews see Attridge, *Hebrews*, 97–103; Lane, *Hebrews 1–8*, cxl–cxli. Some scholars believe that it is the creativity of the author of Hebrews that we should credit for the high priestly motif, e.g., Windisch, *Hebräerbrief*, 13; Hughes, *Hebrews and Hermeneutics*, 30; Lindars, *Theology*, 22. Moe argues that the high priesthood of Jesus is implicit elsewhere in the New Testament, "Priestertum Christi," 335–38; cf. Montefiore, *Hebrews*, 95–96. Higgins believes that the ultimate source of the Christology of Hebrews is to be found in the teaching of Jesus on the Son of Man as intercessor and advocate on behalf of those who confessed him on earth ("The Priestly Messiah," 211–39). Barker suggests that Jesus understood himself to be Melchizedek according to Luke's account of the baptismal experience (*The Risen Lord*, 86–93). There is much to be said for Longenecker's conclusion. "There are reasons to believe that the high-priestly motif of Hebrews is unique in the New Testament not in the fact of its appearance but in the emphasis it receives" ("Melchizedek Argument," 173). So also Lindars, *Theology*, 45, 126. The popularity of the image of Christ as high priest is shown by the fact that it appears in early Christian writings outside the New Testament, some of which are not dependent upon Hebrews: Ignatius, *Phld.* 9:1; *Mart.Pol* 14:3; Polycarp, *Phil.* 12:2; Tertullian, *Adv. Marc.* 3.7.6; Clement of Alexander, *Prot. 12*; *Paed.* 2:8. Cf. 1 Clem. 61:3; 64:1; *Apos. Const.* 8.12.7. Cf. Attridge, *Hebrews*, 102.

2. Rissi, *Theologie*, 35.

of Hebrews, viz. to introduce the subject with a light touch so that it will more easily win acceptance.

Christ is presented as both priest and high priest. The puzzlement that results is explained by the fact that "priest" is normally used when Psalm 110 is in mind (5:6; 7:11, 15, 17, 21, 24): 5:10 and 6:20 are exceptions.[3] "High priest" is the preferred title (2:17; 3:1; 4:14; 5:5, 10; 6:20; 8:1; 9:11) since the author views Christ's redemptive work as the antitype and the fulfillment of the sacrificial ritual of the Day of Atonement. Melchizedek adds a very significant development to the argument.[4] What the possible source of the high priestly Christology of Hebrews was remains a matter of conjecture. The fact that the writer can embark upon the subject without providing an exposition (3:1; 4:14–16) suggests that it was known in the Hellenistic branch of the church.

As we are to see, an important feature of Hebrews is the way in which the high priest operates not on his own but in unison with the pioneer and this must be kept in mind in determining the meaning of each concept.

Priesthoods were a prominent feature of the ancient world. In the Roman Empire the office of priesthood was a valued form of imperial patronage, which could be held alongside other offices.[5] For example, Tacitus tells us that immediately after his consulate Agricola was made governor of Britain and honored with a priesthood (*Agric.* 9:6).[6] Augustus became high priest (*pontifex maximus*) by popular election, and thereafter the office passed to his successors (Dio 53.17.8).[7] But however familiar the recipients of Hebrews were with the imperial priesthoods it

3. Braun, *Hebräer*, 71–72; Scholer, *Proleptic Priests*, 83. The "great priest" in 10:21 is the equivalent of "high priest" (e.g., 4:14).

4. For the portrayal of Moses as a priest in Philo, Josephus and the rabbis see Lierman, *New Testament Moses*, 120–22. See also the Samaritan text, *Memar Marqah* (IV.6), in Macdonald, *Memar Marqah*, 155. This prompts one to ask whether the reference to Moses as a servant in God's house (*oikos*) in Heb 3:2–5 intends us to see Moses as priest in the temple. Cf. Aalen, "'Reign' and 'House,'" 236–37; D'Angelo, *Moses*, 65–93; 161–74; Koester, *Hebrews*, 244–45. Against this possibility is the use of the word "builder" (*kataskeuzein* in 3:3, 4) and the fact that in the underlying text in Num 12:7 "house" signifies the household of God. Nothing can be inferred from the use of *oikos* in 10:21.

5 Millar, *Emperor in the Roman World*, 355–61. See Koester, *Hebrews*, 79, 187.

6. Millar, *Emperor in Roman World*, 357.

7. Millar, *Emperor in Roman World*, 355. On the use of the term *archierus* for the high priesthood of the emperor see Josephus, *Ant.* 14:192. Cf. Koester, *Hebrews*, 187.

was the Jewish priesthood that was of much more importance to them. Nothing could have been of greater interest to a church that was very largely of Jewish background than the high priest and his part in the Day of Atonement (Yom Kippur) ceremonies. In choosing this subject for presenting the significance of Jesus Christ and his saving work, the writer to the Hebrews could scarcely fail to appeal to his hearers. At the same time he was making a strikingly valuable addition to the early church's kerygma that "Christ died for our sins" (1 Cor 15:3).

What Hebrews says about Christ as high priest should be viewed in the light of the great importance the office acquired over time (Exod 28:1–43; Sir 45:6–13; 50:1–21). By the Hasmonean period it had become a powerful institution, shaped by political and messianic influences as well as religious needs (1 Macc 14:4–15, 35–37, 41–49). Throughout most of the postexilic period the high priest was a figure of towering influence in Judaea. In the Hellenistic era he was supreme. This is reflected in the way in which Ben Sira extols Aaron (45:6–22) more than David (47:2–11), and delivers a lengthy panegyric on Simon the Just, the high priest of the day (50:1–21). The office of high priest continued to be highly regarded, even after it had been seriously harmed by corruption in the Maccabean period. Josephus referred to the title of high priest as the "most honored of venerated names" (*J.W.* 4:164; cf. 4:149), while Philo declares that "the law invests the priests with the dignity and honors of royalty" (*Spec.* 1:142).

With the Roman conquest of Judaea and the Herodian rulers running the country, the high priestly office became a political tool of the administration. It never recovered its earlier importance. And after the destruction of the temple in 70 CE the character of the Day of Atonement changed completely. Sacrifices and priestly rituals were replaced by prayers, worship, and acts of charity. But the ritual formula for the Day of Atonement was recited on the day in question as if the ceremony was being carried out as of old.

Also affecting the high priestly office was the negative effect that was generated by the disputes, compromises and corruption that often engulfed it and the priesthood generally. Examples of the criticism that resulted can be found in Mal 1:6—2:4; 3:3–4; 1 Macc 7:9, 15–16, 25; 2 Macc 4:24–25; Pss Sol 1:8; 2:3–4; 8:10–14; *T Mos* 5:5–6; *T Levi* 14:5–8; CD. 4:17; 5:6–8; 1QpHab. 9:4–5; 11:12–14; 12:8–9. A number of these texts aim not only to subvert the dominant priestly authority but also to set out an alternative. As we shall see, this took the form of hope of an eschatological or angelic priest. This figure, beyond the vagaries of history, was to function as a better high priest.[8]

The High Priest and the Day of Atonement

Of all the privileges and responsibilities of the high priest the most important by far was his right to enter the holy of holies on the Day of Atonement. The greatest of Israel's festivals, it acquired such importance that it was called simply "The Day" or "The Fast" (Acts 27:9). Philo describes it as a fast that was a feast, "the greatest of the feasts" (*Spec.* 2:194; *Mos.* 2:23). Held on the tenth day of the seventh month, Tisri, it required both Israelites and non-Israelite residents to fast and not engage in any form of work. It was to all intents and purposes a Sabbath (Lev 16:31). In time it acquired eschatological significance (11QMelch). The latter is of particular importance for understanding what Hebrews depicts as Christ's Day of Atonement.

The initial preparations for the Day of Atonement were designed to ensure that the high priest was in a state of absolute purity. Jeremias summarizes the high priest's preparations thus.

> In the week before the Day he had to undergo the seven-day purification prescribed in Num. 19, so as to eliminate any possibility of defilement through contact with the dead (*M Par.* iii.1; Philo *Somn.* 1.214) . . . He had to take up his residence in his official room in the Temple on the south side of the priests' forecourt, and to spend three nights there (*M Yoma.* 1.1), so as to exclude all possibility of contracting levitical uncleanness, particularly through his wife (*T Yoma.* 1.1,180) . . . A third precaution against his defilement at this time consisted in keeping him awake on the preceding night (*M Yoma* 1.6–7) to avoid the kind of defilement mentioned at the end of Lev 22.4 .[9]

The prescribed ritual comes from Leviticus 16, though it seems clear that the author of Hebrews was familiar with contemporary practices.[10] The ritual is also described in the Temple Scroll, which reworks and conflates many of the rules in the Pentateuch into a succinct new law written

8. We find a positive view of the Aaronic priesthood in Philo (*Sacr.* 132) and Josephus (*Apion* 2:184–88).

9. Jeremias, *Jerusalem*, 152–54.

10. Horbury, "Aaronic Priesthood," 43–71.

in biblical form (25–27). The Mishnah provides a useful summary, while the tractate *Yoma*, in the Talmudic commentary is the fuller account. The purpose of the Day of Atonement was to make expiation for sins committed unwittingly during the preceding year of which the community was unaware, notwithstanding careful scrutiny. These offerings were intended to deal with Israel's impurities as well as its sins (Lev 16:16).[11] The contrast of the role of the priests in general and that of the high priest in particular could not be greater. They carried out their duties all the year round in the outer court; he only once a year and in the holiest sanctum (Num 28:3; Heb 9:7).

Leviticus 16 would appear to combine what originally were two distinct rituals. As the text now stands, the high priest begins by offering a young bullock at the great bronze altar in the open court at the front of the sanctuary. This was a sacrifice for his own sins and those of the priests (16:6, 11, 14). Divested of his ceremonial garments he was dressed in simple linen vestments (Lev 16:4, 23). In preparation to enter the holy of holies as the people's representative, he carried on his breast-piece the names of the twelve tribes engraved on twelve onyx stones (Exod 28:8–21), called "stones of remembrance for the sons of Israel" (Exod 28:12).[12]

The high priest made his first entry into the holy of holies by proceeding along the corridor formed by the ornate double veil that hung in front of the inner sanctuary (*m Yoma* 5.1). The Mishnah informs us that there was a space of a cubit between the two drops (*Yoma* 5:1; *Mid.* 4:7; cf. *b Yoma.* 54a). The purpose of the double veil was to prevent anyone seeing into the sanctuary were the high priest to enter through an opening in a single veil. [13]

On his first entry into the holy of holies the high priest filled the place with incense, lest he should see God's throne (or God?) and die (Lev 16:12–13; *m Yoma* 5:1). On his second entry he sprinkled blood from the bull on the slab of gold, the so-called "mercy seat" (*kappōret, hilastērion*, propitiatory) that covered the ark of the covenant (Lev 16:13–14; *m Yoma.*

---

11. It should be noted that Hebrews groups together the Day of Atonement sacrifice and other sacrifices (5:1; 7:27; 8:3; 9:13; cf. Ellingworth, *Hebrews* (1993), 395; Koester, *Hebrews*, 368; O'Brien, *Hebrews*, 282). Whilst this serves the writer's aim of emphasizing the repetitive and multitudinous nature of the sacrifices, it obscures the single great propitiatory act of Yom Kippur.

12. Both the Mishnah (*Yoma* 5:1) and Philo (*Legat.* 306) say that the high priest prayed for the people in the sanctuary.

13. For the Talmudic legend of the bleeding curtain see *b.Git.* 56b; Schneider, "Katapetasma," 629.

5:3). Viewed as God's throne (Exod 25:20–22; 2 Kgs 19:15; Ezek 10:1), it was supremely the place where Israel met with her God and atonement was made (Lev 16:13–16).[14] The sense of awe and apprehension caused by the entry of the high priest into the pitch-black and eerie adytum is conveyed by the Mishnah (5:8).

Next in the order of proceedings the high priest vacated the holy of holies and went to slaughter the sacrificial goat. Taking the blood, he made his third entry and performed further sprinkling (Lev 16:15; *m Yoma.* 5:4). Thereupon he left the sanctuary and gave his attention to the remaining goat, the so-called scapegoat. He confessed over it "all the iniquities of the people of Israel" (Lev 16:21), whereupon it was driven out into the wilderness (16:21–22). According to the Mishnah, the high priest made a further entry, the fourth, in order to remove the censer (*m Yoma.* 7:4).[15]

To conclude the ceremony the fat of the bull and the goat from the sacrifices offered earlier was burned on the altar (Lev 16:25) and the remaining parts of the carcasses were destroyed outside the camp, i.e., outside the holy enclosure (16:27).[16, 17] This completed, the high priest removed his turban and exchanged his linen vestments for his ceremonial attire. At the conclusion of the ceremonies the high priest was required not to prolong his prayers "lest he put Israel in terror" (*m Yoma* 5:1; cf. Luke 1:10–12, 21).[18] The effusive account of the appearance of the high priest in Ben Sira 50:1–21 conveys very effectively the sense of relief felt by the worshippers when the high priest emerged from the sanctuary. His reappearance signaled God's acceptance of the offering and thus God's acceptance of the people. One is not surprised that the Mishnah says that when the ceremonies were all completed the high priest held a party with

14. On propitiating the wrath of God see Num 16:46; 25:11, 13; cf. Wis 18:20–25. Hebrews has a strong sense of the threat of God's wrath (3:7—4.13). Cf. Rom 3:24–25.

15. For the numerous entries of the high priest into the holy of holies see Stökl Ben Ezra, *Impact of Yom Kippur,* 30–31.

16. Remains from the carcasses were not eaten (Lev 6:30; 6:23 in the MT), but considered unclean and taken outside the boundaries of holiness staked out by the camp and destroyed there (Lev 9:11; 16:27; Exod 29:14).

17. For a detailed account of the area marked off as "outside the camp" see 4QMMT 30–34 and further in chapter 11.

18. Both Josephus and the Talmud have accounts of the strange experiences of some high priests in the holy of holies (Josephus, *Ant.* 13:282. Cf. 13:300, 322); Cf. *b.Sot.* 33a; *bYoma* 39ab. Cf. Luke 1.21; Jeremias, *Jerusalem,* 149.

his friends to celebrate his having "come forth safely from the sanctuary" (*m Yoma* 7:4).

Features of the Day of Atonement ceremony important for our understanding of Hebrews include:

(a) Entry into the holy of holies was restricted solely to the high priest on pain of death (Lev 16:2). Only one entry a year was permitted (Lev 16:2). Cf. Philo, *Spec.Leg.* 1:72; Josephus, *J.W.* 5:236. Cf. 9:7, 12, 25–26; 10:2, 12). Even when the high priest was inside the holy of holies the place was filled with incense so that the mercy seat (throne of God) was hidden (Lev 16:13; *m Yoma.* 5:1).[19]

(b) During Yom Kippur the high priest entered the holy of holies several times (Lev 16:12,15). Cf. Heb 9:12; cf. 7:27; 10:14.

(c) Sacrifice was offered by the high priest for his own sins and the sins of the people (Lev 16:6, 11). Cf. Heb 1:3c; 9:14, 26.

(d) The high priest took the blood into the sanctum (Lev 16:14). Cf. Heb 7:27; 9:11, 25.

(e) The blood sprinkled on the top of the ark was from an animal (Lev 16:14–15, 18–19). Cf. Heb 9:12–14, 25; 10:4,19.

(f) The high priest bore the names of the tribes of Israel on his breastpiece as their representative, asking God to remember his people (Exod 28:29–30). Prayers were offered by the high priest on behalf of the people (2 Macc 15:12; *m Yoma* 5:9; Josephus, *Ant.* 3:189; Philo, *Spec.Leg.* 1:97; 3:131. Cf. Heb 7:25; 9:24.

(g) The curtains or veils, but more especially the inner one, served to preserve the sanctity of the holy of holies (Exod 26:31–35; 36:35–36). The double inner curtain in the second temple (*m Yoma* 5:1) was to prevent anyone from seeing into the holy of holies. Cf. Heb 6:19; 9:3,8; 10:20.

(h) The "mercy seat" (*kapporēt*) (Lev 16:13; Exod 25:17). Cf. Heb 4:16; 9:5.

(i) Outside the camp was regarded as unholy ground. There the remains of the victims slaughtered were taken and destroyed (Lev 16:26, 28; Exod 29:14). Cf. Heb 13:11–13.

---

19. Philo comments on the great clouds of incense, "when everything all around is enveloped in it, then the sight of men is clouded and prevented from penetrating in, being wholly unable to pierce the cloud" (*Spec.Leg.* 1:72).

(j) The return of the high priest to the expectant people on the completion of his work (Lev 16:18; Sir 50:5). Cf. Heb 9:28.

The author of Hebrews is selective in his use of the Day of Atonement ritual, using only those features that served his purpose and passing over others (as he does for the furniture of the sanctuary in 9:1–5). He makes no mention of the scapegoat ritual (Lev 16:8–10, 20–22), the use of incense (Lev 16:12–13), atonement for the sanctuary, or the altar outside the sanctuary (Lev 16:15–19). On the other hand, he mentions the high priest's atonement for his own sins before he makes atonement for the people's sins (Lev 16:6, 11. Cf. Heb 5:3; 7:27) and there is repeated reference to the "sanctifying" or "purifying" of the people (Lev 16:15–19. Cf. Heb 9:9, 13–14; 10:10,14, 29; 13:12). What we have in the Yom Kippur ritual is a complex series of actions: the death of the victim, the movement of the high priest into the sanctuary, and the sprinkling of the blood. These form an integrated whole. Hebrews, as we shall see, follows this series of actions and makes it fundamental to its argument.

The decision of the author not to use the Day of Atonement as an allegory, but as a "parable" (9:9), in which the attention of the congregation is directed to one basic point, is further evidence of his rhetorical strategy.

The Eschatological Priest[20]

Of specific interest to students of Hebrews is the eschatological priest who makes an appearance in different Jewish writings around the time Christianity arrived on the scene.[21]

The account of the priest in the *Testament of Levi* has interesting parallels with Hebrews. This priest is a definite eschatological figure (18:2–5). The angels rejoice in his presence (18:5). He will deal effectively with sin (18:9), death (18:10), and the devil (18:12). Noteworthy is the fact that his priesthood is "for ever" (18:8, 13). The latter raises the question whether the figure in mind may possibly be Melchizedek.[22] In any event, the importance attributed to Levi as the eschatological priest is

20. Vanhoye traces interest in the eschatological priest back to the prophetic criticisms of the priesthood and the promise of the reform of the priesthood in Mal 3–4 (*Old Testament Priests and the New Priest*, 43–44).

21. Dunn, *Christology in the Making*, 151–59; Rowland, *Open Heaven*, 94–113; Gieschen, *Angelomorphic Christology*, 294–314.

22. Tantlevskij, *Melchizedek Redivivus*, 45–46.

also clear from other *Testaments* (*T Reuben* 6:7; *T Simeon* 7:1–2; *T Judah* 21:1–2).

An eschatological priest appears alongside a prophet and a royal leader in the Qumran writings. The "messiahs of Aaron and Israel" in 1QS 9:11 and the closely related "messiah of Aaron and Israel" in CD 12:23; 14:19; 19:10; 20:1 have puzzled scholars, even though it is obvious that the dual leadership is modeled on the Moses-Aaron and Joshua-Zerubbabel partnerships. Some scholars have attempted to resolve the puzzle by suggesting that in the development of eschatological ideas at Qumran the expectation of two messiahs fused into a single figure.[23] An eschatological priestly being is also in mind in 4Q541:

> He will atone for all the children of his generation, and he will be sent to all the children of his people. His word is like the word of the heavens, and his teaching, according to the will of God. His eternal sun will shine and his fire will burn in all the ends of the earth; above the darkness his sun will shine (9:2–4).

The angelic priest in *The Self Glorification Hymn* (4Q491.11.1), which we shall note presently, is taken by some scholars to be an eschatological priest.

The figure of Melchizedek is of special interest.[24] This mysterious being first appears in Genesis 14:17–20. Strangely, he is introduced as "priest of God Most High": the priesthood had not yet been established in Israel.[25] No less strange is his reappearance in Psalm 110:4. The priestly functions ascribed to him in these texts reflect the functions the king had in Israel, like kings generally in the ancient Near East (e.g., 2 Sam 6:17–18; 1 Kgs 8:14, 54–55). Already in the LXX we have an indication of the great importance attributed to Melchizedek. Psalm 109:3–4 (LXX, 110:5) reads, "I have begotten you from the womb before the morning." If the words are God's (as the context suggests) they mean that Melchizedek

23. Kuhn, "Two Messiahs of Aaron and Israel," 57–58; Vermes, *Dead Sea Scrolls*, 18–20; Schürer, *History of the Jewish People*, 550–54; Collins, *Scepter and Star*, 74–83; Brooke, "The Messiah of Aaron," 215–30. On the twin eschatological figures in 11QMelchizedek, see below.

24. Also see chapter 5. Cf. Demerest, *Interpretation of Hebrews 7.1–10*; Horton, *Melchizedek Tradition*; Kobelski, *Melchizedek and Melchireša*; Anderson, *King-Priest of Psalm 110*, 137–75; Kugel, "Melchizedek," 276–93; Mason, "*You Are a Priest Forever.*"

25. "What Melchizedek *does* is to bless Abram. In fact this may be the central feature of his priestly office in this text; it should be noted that he offers no sacrifice" (Polon, "Leviticus and Hebrews," 223). The italics are the author's.

is God's son, i.e., an angel. In this case, the "son of God," who is at God's right hand, is a very special angel, a kind of angelic "prince of justice."[26]

We see the full flowering of such speculation in 11QMelchizedek. It depicts Melchizedek taking the leading role on the definitive Day of Atonement to be held in the "last days" (ii:4). Citing Isaiah 61:1, the text promises salvation for God's people and vengeance on his enemies (ii:11–14). Alongside Melchizedek in 11Q Melchizedek is another figure, an anointed one, who is also described in eschatological terms from Isa 52:7 and 61:1–2 (ii:19, 23). He is a more irenical being, and may possibly be the Teacher of Righteousness, but it is Melchizedek who remains the chief character (ii:24). Although not actually referred to as a priest the fact that Melchizedek functions on the Day of Atonement (ii:7–8) makes this clear enough.[27]

The similarities and differences between 11QMelchizedek and Hebrews are considered in chapter 5.

Interest in a priesthood exercised in a heavenly sanctuary, which predates the Levitical priesthood in the traditions on Melchizedek, is significant. How it relates to the disenchantment with the terrestrial temple and priesthood which we note elsewhere invites consideration, even if it cannot be pursued here.[28]

26. Kugel, "Melchizedek," 280–81.

27. So, for example, Campbell, *Exegetical Texts*, 56–66.

28. Also on Melchizedek as an eschatological high priest see 2 *Enoch* 71:29, 34; 72:2 (A) and Nag Hammadi *codex IX* 16.2–12. If the restorations to *codex IX* are correct, the story is as follows. Melchizedek begins as a human being and functions as a high priest, offering animal sacrifices (16:2–12). In a vision he is told of the eschatological role he is to play as the new high priest. He offers not blood sacrifices but intercession (8:28). He defeats the powers of evil and is greeted by the heavenly host (26:2–14; cf. 5:24—6.10). The account is reminiscent of the role of the triumphant Melchizedek in the Qumran text (11Q Melch), but reflects the widely documented New Testament story of Jesus doing battle with evil and resurrected to become the triumphant savior and high priest. Josephus elevates Melchizedek by saying that he was the first person to serve as God's priest and first to build the temple, and for this reason its city was named Jerusalem (*Ant.* 1:180–82; *J.W.* 6:438). Philo similarly honors Melchizedek by referring to him as the *Logos* (*Spec.Leg.* 3:79–82) and to the *Logos* in turn as high priest (*Somn.* 1:214–15). At the same time Philo thinks of Melchizedek as an historical figure (*Abr.* 235; *Spec.Leg.* 3:79). The foregoing evidence and the interest taken in Melchizedek by the Hasmonean establishment as well as that shown by their avowed enemies at Qumran is testimony to his widespread popularity. There is further evidence of the interest Melchizedek evoked in the attacks on him by early Christian writers. See at length Horton, *Melchizedek Tradition*, 87–114.

Angelic Priests

Included among the priestly figures, and enjoying an important place in the heavenly temple, are angels.[29] Even before the Qumran writings showed the prominent place given to angels in the heavenly liturgy, this was clear from apocalyptic texts. The *Testament of Levi* is the outstanding example:

> In the uppermost heaven of all dwells the Great Glory in the Holy of Holies superior to all holiness. There with him are the archangels, who serve and offer propitiatory sacrifices to the Lord in behalf of all the sins of ignorance of the righteous ones. They present to the Lord a pleasing odor, a rational and blood-less oblation (*T Levi* 3:4–6).[30]

Resonating with Hebrews is the role of the "new priest" (*T Levi* 18:1) in dealing with sin (18:4, 9, 12) and the declaration that he will be priest forever (18:8) and the righteous will find "rest" in him (18:9).

Angels frequently function as priests and mediators. Most important of these are the archangels who stand in the presence of God (Tob 12:15; *T Levi* 3:4–8; Luke 1:19; Rev 8:2), known as the "angels of the presence" (1 *En* 20:1–7; etc.; Jub 1:27; etc.; 1 QH 14:13; 4Q 400:4–6; 1Q28b IV:25–26; etc.; cf. Jude 9; Rev 12:7; 15:6), most well-known of whom is Michael (Dan 10:13, 21; 12:1; 1 *En.* 50:2; 2 *En.* 22:4–9). Resembling Christ's role in making intercession for his people in Hebrews are the priestly angels who direct the prayers of the righteous to God (Dan 9:20–23; 10:10–14; etc.; Tob 12:12; 1 *En.* 9:1–11; 13:4; 89:76; *T Dan* 6:1–5; cf. Rev 8:2–4). *Metatron* "offers up the souls of the righteous to atone for Israel in the days of the exile" (*NumR* 12:12), while the archangel Michael makes sacrifices on the heavenly altar (*b Hag.* 12b).

Philo's allegorical exposition of the ministrations of the high priest in the tabernacle is relevant.[31] Although Philo does not make the high priest an angel, the priestly status he attributes to the *Logos* and his equation of the *Logos* with Melchizedek are close enough to what is attributed to angels in other traditions to warrant inclusion here. "The great high

29. Strugnell, "Angelic Liturgy," 318–45; Newsom, *Songs of the Sabbath Sacrifice*; Brooke, "Men and Women As Angels," 159–65.

30. On the question of Christian interpolations, see de Jonge, *Testament of the Twelve Patriarchs*.

31. For example, Williamson, *Philo*, 409–34; Schenck. "Philo and the Epistle to the Hebrews," 112–35.

priest," Philo declares, "is the divine word (*logos*)" (*Somn.* 1:214–15; cf. 2:133. Cf. *Fug.* 109; *Migr* 102) and interestingly we find Melchizedek is high priest (*Abr.* 235). The high priest offers prayers (*Mos.* 2:133) and plays the all-important role of mediator between God and the world (*Her.* 205–06). Like Christ in Hebrews, Philo's high priest is sinless (*Spec.* 1:230; *Somn.* 2:249). Although Philo's influence on Hebrews is disputed [32] what he says is important for its evidence that belief in priestly functionaries in heaven was not limited to the traditions we have noted.

The *Songs of the Sabbath Sacrifice* show an absorbing interest in angels and their worship in the heavenly sanctuary (4Q 400:2–6), especially those who serve as priests (400:7–8; 11Q17: iv–v).[33] The prominence given to the individual priest in *The Self-Glorification Hymn* is a particular attraction. The anonymous speaker exults in his exalted position in heaven, where he shares the lot of the angels, "I reside [. . .] in the heavens [. . .] I am counted among the gods and my dwelling is in the holy congregation (holy of holies?)" (4Q491:11.I, 13–14).[34] The speaker, according to Collins,[35] is the eschatological priest expected as the leader of the community in the last days. Alexander finds support for this in 1Q28b,[36] where this messianic figure is promised a place in the holy of holies (4:24–26, 28). Some authorities think the one in question is the archangel Michael,[37] but the suffering he tells us he endured may identify him rather with the Teacher of Righteousness and the treatment the latter underwent at the hands of the Wicked Priest (1QpHab xi).

The importance of priestly angels was considered to be so great that one Qumran text goes so far as to say that God established the heavenly temple "so that for him they can be priests"(4Q400:3).

32. Williamson, *Philo*, 409–34; Loader, *Sohn und Hoherpriester*, 229–31.

33. Strugnell, "Angelic Liturgy," 318–45; especially Newsom, *Songs of the Sabbath Sacrifice*; Alexander, *Mystical Texts*, 12–73. For the contrast drawn between the heavenly and the earthly cult, see 4Q400:6–7.

34. The Hebrew of 4Q491:11.13 (translated here as "I reside") is obscure. It could mean "I have sat down" and refer to the speaker on his throne. If this is the sense , as Alexander points out, "The startling nature of such a claim can scarcely be overemphasized. There was a tradition in early Judaism that only God sits in heaven: he alone has a throne . . . If the speaker was seated in heaven, then his position was exalted indeed, above that of the angels" (*Mystical Texts*, 86).

35. Collins, *Scepter and the Star*, 146–49.

36. Alexander, *Mystical Texts*, 88–89.

37. Eshel, "4Q471b. A Self-Glorification Hymn," 198.

Alexander's defense of the view that Melchizedek in 11QMelchizedek is a priest and an angelic high priest merits quoting.

> The agent of this redemption is here called Melchizedek. The word "Elohim" in Ps. 82.1 is applied to him, and he is unquestionably an angel. He makes atonement for the Sons of Light (11Q13 ii 7–8). Given that Melchizedek is an angel, and that the whole stress in the text is on what is happening in the spirit world, it is natural to assume that the atonement he effects is made in the heavenly sanctuary, and since only the high priest can make atonement on the Day of Atonement, then Melchizedek must be the heavenly high priest. [38]

The *Hekhalot* literature displays enormous interest in angels and the prayers they offer.[39] One finds detailed descriptions of splendid heavenly choirs, their musical instruments, and their unceasing worship. At the head of the angelic hierarchies is *Metatron*, the great Prince of the Divine Presence. [40]

Interest in angelic beings appeared early in Christian circles. The archangel Michael is mentioned in Jude 9 and Revelation 12:7. Passages like Rev 19:9–10 and 22:8–9 may possibly reflect the growing importance angels were generally receiving.[41] In postapostolic writings Christ is frequently referred to as an angel (Justin Martyr, *Dial.* 34:2; 58:3, 10; 59:1; 61:1; 128:1).[42] The "glorious angel" is a characteristic feature of Hermas (*Sim.* 7:5; 8:1; 9:3, 7, 12) and Michael, the "great and glorious angel," is on occasion actually equated with Christ (*Sim.* 8:1, 3). Christ is an angel in the *Apostolic Constitutions* (8:12.7).[43]

In view of the foregoing it is not surprising that Hebrews begins by giving prominence to angels and by making it clear to the listeners that the angels worship Christ (1:6) and are subordinate to him (1:4–14; 2:5). However, they have their place in God's service (1:14). They had the honor of handing down the law to Israel (2:2) and share in worship in the heavenly Zion (12:22). The downgrading of the angels in chapter 1

---

38. Alexander, *Mystical Texts*, 70.

39. Elior, "Earthly Temple to Heavenly Shrines," 235–45.

40. Elior, "Earthly Temple to Heavenly Shrines," 238–40.

41. Bauckham, *Climax of Prophecy*, 133–37.

42. Daniélou, *Jewish Christianity*, 117–34.

43. Tertullian reacted to the place angels had come to have in Christian worship (*Adv. Prax.* 122). Epiphanius attacked the Ebionites for saying that Christ was "created as one of the archangels" (*Pan.* 30.16.4; Daniélou, *Jewish Christianity*, 125–26).

is usually taken to mean that the recipients of the letter were involved in or attracted by worship of angels, similar to what commentators tend to find in Colossians 2:18.[44] Attridge says: "If there is a problem involving worship and angels behind either Colossians or Hebrews, it is more likely that our author was concerned about a worship that was understood to take place *with* angels than a worship that had angels as its object."[45] When Hebrews 1–2 is read in the light of 11Q Melchizedek one cannot but agree with de Jonge and van der Woude in seeing evidence here of what the author of Hebrews may well have been up against.[46]

High Priest and Day of Atonement: A Necessary Medium of Communication

In electing to depict Christ and his saving work by means of the analogy of the high priest and the Day of Atonement ritual the author of Hebrews creates a symbolic world which is foreign to the modern reader.[47] It is not only the imagery that is strange; the reasoning is opaque. The statement that "without the shedding of blood there is no forgiveness of sins" (9:22) makes one ask whether the theology of Leviticus must be taken as the presupposition of the theology of Hebrews. Lincoln believes that it must.[48] Ellingworth asks, "Does the writer really believe that 'without the shedding of blood there is no forgiveness of sins'(9:22), or does he, here and in similar passages (9.13, 23), use his first readers' presuppositions as common ground from which to lead them on to a fuller understanding of the newness of Christianity?"[49] In other words, is sacrificial language intrinsic and essential to his thinking or simply a strategy by which the writer hopes help his recipients to reach a better appreciation of Christ

44. See, for example, Stuckenbruck, *Angel Veneration and Christology*; Hamerton-Kelly, *Pre-Existence, Wisdom and Son of Man*, 245; Attridge, *Hebrews*, 51–52. The service which Hebrews attributes to angels in 1:14 is usually taken by commentators to refer not to cultic roles in the heavenly temple but service on earth.

45. Attridge, *Hebrews*, 51. Author's italics. The reference to angels in 12:22 will be considered later.

46. De Jonge and van der Woude, "11QMelchizedek," 317.

47. On the use of the Day of Atonement analogy in Hebrews see, for example, Young, *Impact of the Jewish Day of Atonement*; Lindars, *Theology*, 84–94; Stökl Ben Ezra, *Impact of Yom Kippur*.

48. Lincoln, *Hebrews*, 82.

49. Ellingworth, *Hebrews* (1993), 69. Cf. Lincoln, *Hebrews*, 82–84, 112–13.

and Christianity? Ellingworth's conclusion should satisfy most students of Hebrews. He writes, "the best solution to the dilemma is perhaps to say that the writer uses sacrificial language *both* as a suitable medium of communication with his readers *and* as a means of communicating a central element of Christian truth."[50]

Summary

The outstanding feature of the conceptual background of Hebrews is the high priest and the Day of Atonement. It plays an integral part in what is the sermon's most important contribution to Christology, depicting both Christ's priesthood and his all-prevailing offering, and it is the key to its meaning. An important dimension is added to the new priesthood by Melchizedek. This makes Christ a priest who owes his appointment directly and solely to God, who invests him with a never ending priesthood. The pioneer proceeding through the heavens (the outer court) to his sanctuary (the holy of holies) pictures the movement of the high priest through the sanctuary courts into the holy of holies. The new priest is the eschatological priest. The eschatological priest who features in *T Levi* and the angelic priests and Melchizedek in the Qumran texts, all show that Hebrews in presenting Christ as the "great high priest" is part of a widely canvassed tradition. The same inference is to be drawn from references to Christ as high priest in early Christian texts outside the New Testament that are not influenced by Hebrews.

---

50. Ellingworth, *Hebrews* (1993), 70. The author's italics.

Appendix D

A Sanctuary Not Made with Hands

The concept of a heavenly temple in different Jewish traditions developed over the centuries from being the guarantor of the earthly temple until it eventually became its rival. It served to answer the problem created for faith and practice by its discredited earthly counterpart and was used in certain circles to validate the substitute created.[1] Access to the temple in heaven became the greatly desired goal of venturesome individuals. See appendix B.

The heavenly archetype paralleled its earthly counterpart and in time its greatness was emphasized to the point where it was believed that it would eventually replace the earthly temple. What if the earthly temple did not come up to expectations (Hab 2:9; Ezra 3:12.13; 1 Esd 5: 63–65; 1 *En.* 89:73; Josephus, *Ant.* 11:80–81)? God had a much better temple. It was a temple not made by human hands, which he would bring down to earth in the promised new age (1 *En.* 90:28–29; 2 *Bar* 4:2–6; 4 *Ezra* 10:44, 48–50; *M Shek.* 6:3; *M Mid.* 2:6; *Tos.Suk.* 3:3; *B Meg.* 17b–18a; *Bet. ha-Midrash* 1.55,23; 3.67,29). This fusion of the heavenly temple and the new temple of eschatological hope is of particular interest to students of Hebrews.

1. The concept of a temple in heaven which was the archetype of the earthly temple was a familiar feature of ancient Near Eastern thought from early times. In Enuma Elish we read, concerning the temple for Marduk, "This Babylon, the place that is your home (is) . . . A likeness on earth of what he has wrought in heaven" (lines 71, 113) (Pritchard, *Ancient Near Eastern Texts*, 68–69). Cf. Clements, *God and Temple*, 2–4, 65–67; Hurowitz, *I Have Built you an Exalted House*, 38–67, 168–70. For the heavenly sanctuary in the Israelite tradition see Exod 25:40; 26:30; Ezek 40–48; Wisd 9:8. Cf. Acts 7:44; Heb 8:5. See chapter 6.

The need for the existing temple on earth to be replaced by the heavenly one is memorably described in 1 *Enoch* 90. First the earth is cleansed of its evil and the defamed temple removed, lock, stock and barrel (90:20–28).

> All the pillars and all the columns were pulled out; and the ornaments of that house were packed and taken out together with them and abandoned in a certain place in the South of the land. I went on seeing until the Lord of the sheep brought about a new house, greater and loftier than the first one, and set it up in the first location which had been covered up—all its pillars were new, the columns new; and the ornaments new as well as greater than those of the first, (that is) the old (house) which was gone (90:28–29).

The advent of the new temple will herald great events. The ancient hostility between Jews and Gentiles will end and both will worship in the temple (90:33). "And I saw," concludes the writer, "that the house was large, wide, and exceedingly full" (90:36).

The *Testament of Levi* tells us that "in the uppermost heaven of all dwells the Great Glory in the Holy of Holies" (3:4).[2]

> The angel opened for me the gates of heaven and I saw the Holy One Most High sitting on the throne. And he said to me, "Levi, to you I have given the blessing of the priesthood until I shall come and dwell in the midst of Israel" (5:1–3).

The replacement of the earthly temple by the heavenly is not actually mentioned in *T Levi* but the fact that it is in the heavenly temple that Levi is consecrated for a priesthood which is to be exercised eventually in the earthly temple (2:10–11) points to the problems surrounding the earthly temple.

We find the same thing in *2 Baruch* and *4 Ezra*. In these writings the heavenly temple is subsumed under the thought of the heavenly Jerusalem that is here revealed (*2 Bar* 4:2–6; *4 Ezra* 10: 44, 48–50). *2 Baruch* could not dissociate the new city from the old one more strongly. The city of the future will be entirely different (4:2–6). The existing city will be destroyed so that the new and better one can be erected (32:2–3). Similarly, *4 Ezra* makes a point of emphasizing the difference of the new city from

---

2. Cody, *Heavenly Sanctuary*, 51–55; Alexander, *Mystical Texts*, 79–80. On the suspected Christian additions to *T Levi* see de Jonge, *Testaments of the Twelve Patriarchs*.

the old.[3] It is to be erected on uncontaminated land, "for no work of man's building could endure in a place where the city of the Most High was to be revealed." (*4 Ezra* 10:54).

The superiority of the heavenly temple is very clearly depicted in the Qumran *Songs of the Sabbath Service*.[4] These texts are in a fragmentary state, but a good deal has been gleaned from them. Curiously, only the inner courts of the temple are mentioned. Possibly the scribe thinks of the heavens at large or the cosmos as the outer courts.[5] The sanctuary is referred to throughout as the tabernacle (*mishkan*, e.g., 4Q403:II.10; 405.14–15). Nothing is said about its being transported to earth; the writer concentrates on describing how great it is. Its excellence is emphasized. It is "the tabernacle of greater height" (403:II.10) and a "wonderful sanctuary" (403: II.22). The same is conveyed by reference to its "walls," "gates," "columns," and "beams" (403: I.1–4, 40–45; 405.23). The latter gives the impression that it is a material construction, but what we find elsewhere would seem to indicate that the description is understood metaphorically. It is certainly complex. We read of a single sanctuary (e.g., 403: II.8) and at other times of seven sanctuaries (403: II.27), in keeping possibly with the scribe's love of the number seven (403:I–II). Alexander makes the intriguing suggestion that the temple in heaven was thought of as a living temple, built up tier upon tier of angelic spirits and their praises.[6]

The heavenly temple is the locale for the final eschatological Day of Atonement in 11QMelchizedek 13 "in which atonement will be made for all the sons of [God] and for the men of the lot of Melchizedek" (ii:7). Melchizedek has the preeminent role; he is surrounded by angels and presented as officiating (ii:7–8). He functions, moreover, as the end-time judge, who finally frees God's people from sin (13:10–14, 24). The eschatological tenor of the whole passage is heightened by the citation of Isaiah 61:2–3 (ii:15–19). Since the great events described take place in the heavenly temple this must mean that the Qumran community regarded the heavenly temple as the true one.[7]

3. The descent of the heavenly city to earth is implied in *4 Ezra* 10:51–54.
4 Newsom, *Songs of the Sabbath Sacrifice*; Alexander, *Mystical Texts*, 52–59.
5. Alexander, *Mystical Texts*, 53.
6. Alexander, *Mystical Texts*, 54.
7. Alexander, *Mystical Texts*, 70.

The superiority of the temple (and city) in heaven receives florid expression in numerous rabbinic texts, [8] and one is not surprised that the rabbis eventually committed themselves to the apocalyptic hope of a descent to earth.[9] This takes us beyond the period marked by the New Testament, but the fact that the Book of Revelation predicts the descent of the New Jerusalem to earth is evidence of its earlier currency. In any event, the New Jerusalem is the true Jerusalem; it is where God is (Rev 21:3).[10]

Summary

The heavenly temple in different Jewish traditions and in Hebrews seeks to deal with the problem of the discredited earthly temple and community's need to validate its alternative. The correspondence of the heavenly and earthly sanctuaries contained within it the possibility, indeed the inevitability, of the relationship turning to the disadvantage of the earthly. Supersessionism features in all of this material. *1 Enoch* describes how the earthly temple of Jerusalem will be torn down and replaced by the magnificent temple brought down from heaven, while *T Levi* rejects the Jerusalem priesthood and temple by having Levi consecrated in the heavenly sanctuary. 11QMelchizedek makes the heavenly temple the true temple by depicting it as the setting for the definitive Day of Atonement and Melchizedek's exaltation. Hebrews, for its part, as we shall see, exploits the heavenly and earthly dualism to elevate the heavenly sanctuary as the true sanctuary and the place for Christ's exaltation and Day of Atonement. The earthly temple is thereby stripped of its *raison d être* without any apparent need to tell us whether it is still standing or not.

---

8. Strack and Billerbeck, *Kommentar,* iii. 848–52.

9. Strack and Billerbeck, *Kommentar,* iii. 796.

10. McKelvey, *New Temple,* 155–78.

Bibliography

Adams, Edward. "The Cosmology of Hebrews." In *The Epistle to the Hebrews and Christian Theology*, edited by R. Bauckham et al., 122–39. Grand Rapids: Eerdmans, 2009.

Aitken, Ellen B. "The Hero in the Epistle to the Hebrews; Jesus as an Ascetic Model." In *Early Christian Voices: In Texts, Traditions, and Symbols*, edited by D. H. Warren et al., 179–88. Leiden: Brill, 2003.

———. "Portraying the Temple in Stone and Text: The Arch of Titus and the Epistle to the Hebrews." In *Hebrews: Contemporary Methods—New Insights*, edited by Gabriella Gelardini, 131–48. Leiden: Brill, 2005.

Alexander, Philip. "3 (Hebrew Apocalypse) Enoch." In *The Old Testament Pseudepigrapha* vol. 1, edited by J. H. Charlesworth, 247–51. London: Darton, Longman and Todd, 1983.

———. *The Mystical Texts: Songs of the Sabbath Sacrifice and Related Texts*. LSTS 61. London: T & T Clark, 2006.

———. *Textual Sources for the Studies of Judaism*. Manchester, UK: Manchester University Press, 1984.

Anderson, David R. *The King-Priest of Psalm 110 in Hebrews*. SBL. New York: Peter Lang, 2001.

Andriessen, Paul. "Das grössere und vollkommenere Zelt (Hebr.9.11)." *BZ* 15 (1971) 76–92.

Armstrong, A. H., ed. *The Cambridge History of Later Greek and Early Mediaeval History*. Cambridge: Cambridge University Press, 1967.

Arndt, William F., et al. *A Greek-English Lexicon of the New Testament and Other Early Christian Literature*. Rev. ed. Chicago: University of Chicago Press, 2000.

Aschim, Anders. "Melchizedek and Jesus: 11QMelchizedek and the Epistle to the Hebrews." In *The Jewish Roots of Christological Monotheism: Papers from the St. Andrews Conference on the Historical Origins of the Worship of Jesus*, edited by C. C. Newman et al., 140–41. *SJSJ* 63. Leiden: Brill, 1999.

Attridge, Harold W. *The Epistle to the Hebrews: A Commentary on the Epistle to the Hebrews*. Edited by H. Koester. Hermeneia 72. Philadelphia: Fortress, 1989.

———. "Hebrews." In *The Oxford Bible Commentary*, edited by J. Muddiman, 1236–54. Oxford: Oxford University Press, 2002.

———. "Liberating Death's Captives." In *Gnosticism and the Early Christian World*, edited by J. E. Goehring et al., 103–15. Sonoma, CA: Polebridge, 1990.

———. "Paraenesis in a Homily (*Logos Paraklēseōs*): The Possible Location of, and Socialization in, the Epistle to the Hebrews." *Sem* 50 (1990) 221–26.

———. "The Uses of Antithesis in Hebrews 8–10." *HTR* 79/1-3 (1986) 1–9.

Aune, David E. *The Cultic Setting of Realized Eschatology in Early Christianity*. Lieden: Brill, 1972.

———."Heracles and Christ: Heracles Imagery in the Christology of Early Christianity." In *Greeks, Romans and Christians: Essays in Honor of Abraham J. Malherbe*, edited by D. L. Balch et al., 3–19. Minneapolis: Fortress, 1991.

———. *Revelation 1–5*. WBC 47A. Dallas: Word, 1997.

Barclay, James M. G. *Jews in the Mediterranean Diaspora*. Edinburgh: T & T Clark, 1996.

Barker, Margaret. *The Risen Lord: The Jesus of History as the Christ of Faith*. SJT: Current Issues in Theology. Edinburgh: T & T Clark, 1996.

Barrett, Charles Kingsley. "The Eschatology of the Epistle to the Hebrews." In *The Background of the New Testament and its Eschatology: C. H. Dodd Festschrift*, edited by W. D. Davies and D. Daube, 363–93. Cambridge: Cambridge University Press, 1956.

———. "New Testament Eschatology." *SJT* 6 (1953) 136–55.

Bartchy, S. Scott. "Undermining Ancient Patriarchy: The Apostle Paul's Vision of a Society of Siblings." BTB 29 (1999) 68–78.

Bauckham, Richard J. *The Climax of Prophecy*. Edinburgh: T & T Clark, 1993.

———. "The Throne of God and the Worship of Jesus." In *The Jewish Roots of Christological Monotheism: Papers from the St. Andrews Conference on the Historical Origins of the Worship of Jesus*, edited by C. C. Newman et al., 43—69. *SJSJ* 63. Leiden: Brill, 1999.

———, et al., eds. *A Cloud of Witnesses: The Theology of Hebrews in its Ancient Context*. Grand Rapids: Eerdmans, 2009.

Bauer, Walter, et al. *A Greek-English Lexicon of the New Testament and Other Early Christian Literature*. 3rd ed. Chicago: University of Chicago Press, 2000.

Bauernfeind, Otto. "Prodromos." *TDNT* 8:235.

Beale, Gregory K. *The Temple and the Church's Mission: A Biblical Theology of the Dwelling Place of God*. Downers Grove, IL: InterVarsity, 2004.

Behm, Johannes. "Egkainizein." *TDNT* 3:453–54.

———. "Haima." *TDNT* 1:172–77.

Becker, Adam H., and Annette Y. Reed. *The Ways that Never Parted: Jews and Christians in Late Antiquity and the Early Middle Ages*. Minneapolis: Fortress, 2007.

Bengel, Johann A. *Gnomon of the New Testament*. Edinburgh: T & T Clark, 1857–88.

Best, Ernest. *Following Jesus: Discipleship in the Gospel of Mark*. JSNTSup.4. Sheffield, UK: JSOT, 1981.

———. "Spiritual Sacrifice: General Priesthood in the New Testament." *Int* 14 (1960) 273–90.

Bietenhard, Hans. *Die himmlische Welt im Urchristentum und Spätjudentum*. WUNT 2. Tübingen: Mohr-Siebeck, 1951.

Blomberg, Craig L. "'But We See Jesus': The Relationship Between the Son of Man in Hebrews 2.6 and 2.9 and the Implications for English Translations." In *A Cloud of Witnesses*, edited by Richard Bauckham et al., 88–99. Grand Rapids: Eerdmans, 2009.

Bourke, Myles M. "The Epistle to the Hebrews." In *The New Jerome Biblical Commentary*, edited by R. E. Brown et al., 381–403. Englewood Cliffs, NJ: Prentice-Hall, 1968.

Bowen, J. "Did the Qumran Sect Burn the Red Heifer?" *RevQ* 1 (1958–59) 73–87.

Bowker, John. *The Targums and Rabbinic Literature*. Cambridge: Cambridge University Press, 1969.

Braun, Herbert. *An die Hebräer*. HNT 14. Tübingen: Mohr, 1984.

Brooke, George J. *Exegesis at Qumran: 4Florilegium in its Jewish Context*. JSOTS 29. Sheffield, UK: Sheffield Academic Press, 1985.

———. "Melchizedek (11QMelch)." *ABD* 4 (1992) 678–88.

———. "Men and Women As Angels in *Joseph and Aseneth*." *JSP* 14 (2005) 159–65.

———. "The Messiah of Aaron in the Damascus Document." *RevQ* 15 (1991) 215–30.

Brooks, Walter E. "The Perpetuity of Christ's Sacrifice in the Epistle to the Hebrews." *JBL* 89 (1970) 305–14.

Brown, Raymond E., and John P. Meier. *Antioch and Rome*. Mahwah, NJ: Paulist, 1983.

Bruce, Frederick F. *The Epistle to the Hebrews*. Rev. ed. NICNT. Grand Rapids: Eerdmans, 1990.

Buchanan, George W. *To the Hebrews, Translation, Comment and Conclusions*. AB 36. Garden City, NY: Doubleday, 1972.

Bultmann, Rudolf. *The Theology of the New Testament*. London: SCM, 1952.

Calvin, John. *Commentary on the Epistle to the Hebrews*. Translated by Wm. B. Johnston. Edinburgh: Oliver & Boyd, 1963.

Caird, George B. "The Exegetical Method of the Epistle to the Hebrews." *CJT* 5 (1959) 44–51.

Campbell, Jonathan G. *The Exegetical Texts*. London: T & T Clark, 2004.

Carlston, Charles E. "The Vocabulary of Perfection in Philo and Hebrews." In *Unity and Diversity in New Testament Theology*, edited by R. A.Guelich, 133–60. Grand Rapids: Eerdmans, 1978.

Charlesworth, James H., ed. *The Old Testament Pseudepigrapha*. 2 vols. London: Darton, Longman and Todd, 1983.

Charlesworth, James H., and C. A. Newsom, eds. *The Dead Sea Scrolls, Hebrew, Aramaic and Greek Texts with English Translations, Vol. 4B, Angelic Liturgy: Songs of the Sabbath Sacrifice*. Tübingen: Mohr, 1999.

Clements, Ronald E. *God and Temple*. Oxford: Blackwell, 1965.

Cockerill, Gareth L. *The Melchizedek Christology in Heb. 7.1–28*. Ann Arbor, MI: University Microfilms International, 1979.

———. "Melchizedek: or 'King of Righteousness.'" *EvQ* 63 (1991) 305–12.

———. "Melchizedek Without Speculation: Hebrews 7.1–12 and Genesis 14.17–24." In *A Cloud of Witnesses*, edited by Richard Bauckham et al., 128–44. Grand Rapids: Eerdmans, 2009.

Cody, Aelred. *Heavenly Sanctuary and Liturgy in the Epistle to the Hebrews: The Achievement of Salvation in the Epistle's Perspective*. St. Meinrad, IN: Grail, 1960.

Collins, John J. *The Scepter and the Star: The Messiahs of the Dead Sea Scrolls and Other Ancient Literature*. New York: Doubleday, 1995.

Congar, Yves M. J. *The Mystery of the Temple*. Translated by Reginald F. Trevett. London: Burns & Oates, 1958.

Coppens, Joseph. "Les affinités qumrâniennes de l'Épître aux Hébreux." *NRT* 84 (1962) 128–41.

Bibliography

Cosby, Michael R. *The Rhetorical Composition and Function of Hebrews 11: In the Light of Antiquity*. Macon, GA: Mercer, 1988.

Croy, N. Clayton. *Endurance in Suffering: Hebrews 12:1–13 in its Rhetorical, Religious, and Philosophical Context*. SNTSMS 98. Cambridge: Cambridge University Press, 1998.

Cullmann, Oscar. *The Christology of the New Testament*. London: SCM, 1959.

D'Angelo, Mary Rose. *Moses in the Letter to the Hebrews*. SBLDS 42. Missoula, MT: Scholars, 1979.

Dahl, N. A. "A New and Living Way: The Approach to God According to Hebrews 10.19–25." *Int* 5 (1950) 401–12.

Daly, Robert J. *Christian Sacrifice: The Judaeo-Christian Background before Origen*. Washington, DC: Catholic University of America, 1978.

Daniélou, Jean. *Gospel Message and Hellenistic Culture*. London: Darton, Longman and Todd, 1973.

———. *The Theology of Jewish Christianity*. London: Darton, Longman and Todd, 1964.

Davies, Philip R. "The Ideology of the Temple in the Damascus Document." *JSS* 33 (1982) 287–301.

Dean-Otting, Mary. *Heavenly Journeys: A Study of the Motif in Hellenistic Jewish Literature*. New York: Peter Lang, 1984.

Delcor, M. "Melchizedek from Genesis to the Qumran Texts and the Epistle to the Hebrews." *JSJ* 2 (1971) 115–35.

Delling, Gerhard. "Archēgos." *TDNT* 1:487–90.

———. "Teleioun." *TDNT* 8:79–87.

Demarest, Bruce. "A History Interpretation of Hebrews 7.1–10 from the Reformation to the Present." PhD diss., University of Manchester, 1973.

DeSilva, David. "Despising Shame: A Cultural-Anthropological Investigation of the Epistle to the Hebrews." *JBL* 113 (1994) 439–61.

———. *Despising Shame: A Cultural-Anthropological Investigation of the Epistle to the Hebrews*. SBLDS 152. Atlanta: Scholars, 1995.

———. *Perseverance in Gratitude: A Socio-Rhetorical Commentary on the Epistle to the Hebrews*. Grand Rapids: Eerdmans, 2000.

Dillon, John. *The Middle Platonists: A Study of Platonism 80 BC to AD 220*. London: Duckworth, 1977.

Dodd, Charles H. *According to the Scriptures: The Substructure of New Testament Theology*. London: Nisbet, 1952.

Dodds, E. R. *Pagan and Christian in an Age of Anxiety*. Cambridge: Cambridge University Press, 1965.

Dumbrell, W. J. "The Spirits of Just Men Made Perfect." *EvQ* 48 (1976) 154–59.

Dunn, James D. G. *Christology in the Making: An Enquiry into the Origins of the Doctrine of the Incarnation*. London: SCM, 1980.

———. *The Parting of the Ways: Between Christianity and Judaism and their Significance for the Character of Christianity*. Philadelphia: Trinity, 1991.

———. *Romans 1–8*. WBC 38A. Dallas: Word, 1988.

Dunnill, John. *Covenant and Sacrifice in the Letter to the Hebrews*. SNTSMS 75. Cambridge: Cambridge University Press, 1992.

Dunning, B. "The Interaction of Alien Status and Cultic Discourse in the Epistle to the Hebrews." In *Hebrews: Contemporary Methods—New Insights*, edited by Gabriella Gelardini, 177–98. Leiden: Brill, 2005.

Du Plessis, P. J. *ΤΕΛΕΙΟΣ: The Idea of Perfection in the New Testament*. Kampen: J. H. Kok, 1959.

Eberhart, Christian A. "Characteristics of Sacrificial Metaphors in Hebrews." In *Hebrews: Contemporary Methods—New Insights*, edited by Gabriella Gelardini, 37–64. Leiden: Brill, 2005.

Ego, Beate, et al. *Gemeinde ohne Tempel—Community without Temple*. WUNT 118. Tübingen: Mohr Siebeck, 1999.

Eisenbaum, Pamela M. *The Jewish Heroes of Christian History: Hebrews 11 in Literary Context*. SBLDS 156. Atlanta: Scholars, 1997.

———. "Locating Hebrews within the Literary Landscape of Christian Origins." In *Hebrews: Contemporary Methods—New Insights*, edited by Gabriella Gelardini, 213–37. Leiden: Brill, 2005.

Elior, Rachel. "From Earthly Temple to Heavenly Shrines: Prayer and Sacred Song in the Hekhalot Literature and Its Relation to Temple Traditions." *JSQ* 4 (1997) 217–67.

Ellingworth, Paul. *The Epistle to the Hebrews*. London: Epworth, 1991.

———. *The Epistle to the Hebrews: A Commentary on the Greek Text*. NIGTC. Grand Rapids: Eerdmans, 1993.

———. "Jesus and the Universe in Hebrews." *EvQ* 58 (1986) 337–50.

———. "The Unshakeable Priesthood: Hebrews 7.24." *JSNT* 23 (1985) 125–26.

Elliott, John H. *A Home for the Homeless: A Sociological Exegesis of 1 Peter, Its Situation and Strategy*. Philadelphia: Fortress, 1981.

Eskola, Timo. *Messiah and Throne: Jewish Merkabah Mysticism and Early Christian Discourse*. WUNT 2/142. Tübingen: Mohr Siebeck, 2001.

Eshel, Esther. "4Q471b. A Self-Glorification Hymn." *RevQ* 17/65–68 (1996) 175–203.

Farrow, Douglas. *Ascension and Ecclesia*. Edinburgh: T & T Clark, 1999.

Filson, Floyd V. *"Yesterday": A Study of Hebrews in the Light of Chapter 13*. London: SCM, 1967.

Fitch, John G. *Seneca's Hercules Furens*. Ithaca, NY: Cornell University Press, 1987.

Fitzmyer, Joseph A. "Further Light on Melchizedek from Qumran Cave 11." *JBL* 86 (1967) 25–41.

Fletcher-Louis, Crispin H. T. *All the Glory of Adam: Liturgical Anthropology in the Dead Sea Scrolls*. Leiden: Brill, 2002.

Floor, L. "The General Priesthood of Believers in the Epistle to the Hebrews." *Neot* 5 (1971) 72–82.

Frennesson, Bjorn. *In a Common Rejoicing: Liturgical Communion with Angels in Qumran*. Studia Semitica Upsaliensia 14. Uppsala: Uppsala University, 1999.

Gäbel, Georg. *Die Kulttheologie des Hebräerbriefs: Eine exegetisch-religionsgeschichtliche Studie*. WUNT 2/212. Tübingen: Mohr Siebeck, 2006.

Gager, John G. *The Origins of Anti-Semitism: Attitudes Towards Judaism in Pagan and Christian Antiquity*. New York: Oxford University Press, 1983.

Galinsky, G. Karl. *The Herakles Theme*. Oxford: Blackwell, 1992.

Gardiner, E. Norman. *Athletics of the Ancient World*. Oxford: Clarendon, 1930.

Gärtner, Bertil. *The Temple and the Community in Qumran and the New Testament*. Cambridge: Cambridge University Press, 1965.

Gelardini, Gabriella, ed. *Hebrews: Contemporary Methods—New Insights*. Leiden: Brill, 2005.

Gieschen, Charles A. *Angelomorphic Christology: Antecedents and Early Evidence*. AGJU 42. Leiden: Brill, 1998.

Gleason, Randell C. "The Eschatology of the Warning in Hebrews 10.26–31." *Tyn Bul* 53 (2002) 97–120.

Goodenough, Erwin R. *By Light, Light: The Mystic Gospel of Hellenistic Judaism*. New Haven, CT: Yale University Press, 1935.

Gordon, Robert P. *Hebrews*. Sheffield, UK: Sheffield Academic Press, 2000.

———. *Hebrews*. 2nd ed. Sheffield,UK: Sheffield Phoenix, 2008.

Grässer, Erich. *Der Glaube im Hebräerbrief*. Marburg: Elwert, 1965.

Grogan, Geoffrey W. "Christ and His People; An Exegetical and Theological Study of Hebrews 2.5–18." *VoxEv* 6 (1969) 54–71.

Gruenwald, Ithamar. *Apocalyptic and Merkavah Mystic*. Leiden: Brill, 1980.

Grundmann, Walter. "Dexios." *TDNT* 2:37–40.

Guthrie, George H. *Hebrews*. Grand Rapids: Zondervan, 1998.

———. *The Structure of Hebrews: A Text-Linguistic Analysis*. NovTSup 73. Leiden: Brill, 1994.

Hahm, David. *The Origins of Stoic Cosmology*. Columbus: Ohio State University, 1977.

Hamerton-Kelly, Robert G. *Pre-Existence, Wisdom and the Son of Man: A Study of the Idea of Pre-Existence in the New Testament*. Cambridge: Cambridge University Press, 1973.

———. "The Temple and the Origins of Jewish Apocalyptic." *VT* 20 (1970) 1–15.

Hanson, Anthony T., *The Image of the Invisible God*. London: SCM, 1982.

———. *Jesus Christ in the Old Testament*. London: SPCK, 1965.

Harris, Harold A. *Greek Athletics and the Jews*. Cardiff: University of Wales, 1976.

Hatch, Edwin, and H. A. Redpath. *A Concordance to the Septuagint and the Other Greek Versions of the Old Testament*. Oxford: Clarendon, 1892–1906.

Hay, David M. *Glory at the Right Hand: Psalm 110 in Early Christianity*. SBLMS 18. Nashville: Abingdon, 1973.

———. "Philo of Alexandria." In *Justification and Variegated Nomism: The Complexities of Second Temple Judaism*, edited by D. A. Carson et al., 357–78. Grand Rapids: Baker, 2001.

Hays, Richard B. "'Here We Have No Lasting City': New Covenantalism in the Epistle to the Hebrews." In *Hebrews and Christian Theology*, edited by Richard Bauckham et al., 151–73. Grand Rapids: Eerdmans, 2009.

Hayward, C. T. Robert. *The Jewish Temple: A Non-Biblical Source Book*. London: Routledge, 1996.

Heil, John P. "Jesus as the Unique High Priest in the Gospel of John." *CBQ* 57 (1995) 729–45.

Hengel, Martin. *Crucifixion in the Ancient World and the Folly of the Message of the Cross*. Translated by John Bowden. London: SCM, 1977.

———. *Judaism and Hellenism: Studies in their Encounter in Palestine in the Early Hellenistic Period*. 2 vols. Translated by John Bowden. London: SCM, 1973 & 1974.

———. *Studies in Early Christology*. Edinburgh: T & T Clark, 1995.

Herbert, A. G. *Intercommunion*. Edited by D. Baillie and J. Marsh. New York: Harper, 1952.

Héring, Jean. *The Epistle to the Hebrews*. Translated by A. W. Heathcote and P. J. Allcock. London: Epworth, 1970.

Higgins, A. J. B. "The Priestly Messiah." *NTS* 13 (1967) 211–39.

Himmelfarb, Martha. *Ascent to Heaven in Jewish and Christian Apocalypse*. Oxford: Oxford University Press, 1993.

Hofius, Otfried. "Das 'erste' und das 'zweite' Zelt: Ein Beitrag zur Auslegung von Hbr 9.1–10." *ZNW* 61 (1970) 271–77.

———. "Inkarnation und Opfertod Jesu nach Hebr 10.19f." In *Der Ruf Jesu und die Antwort der Gemeinde. Exegetische Untersuchungen für J. Jeremias*, edited by C. Burchard and B. Schaller, 132–41. Göttingen: Vandenhoeck & Ruprecht, 1970.

———. *Katapausis: Die Verstellung vom endzeitlichen Ruheort im Hebräerbrief*. WUNT 11. Tübingen: Mohr Siebeck, 1970.

———. "Melchisedek." In *Das Grosse Bibellexikon*, edited by H. Burkhardt et al., 951–52. Wuppertal: Brockhaus, 1988.

———. *Der Vorhang vor dem Thron Gottes. Eine exegetisch-religionsgechichtliche Untersuchung zu Hebräer 6.19f und 10.19f*. WUNT 14. Tübingen: Mohr Siebeck, 1972.

Hooker, Morna D. "Christ, the 'End' of the Cult." In *The Epistle to the Hebrews and Christian Theology*, edited by R. Bauckham et al., 189–212. Grand Rapids: Eerdmans, 2009.

Horbury, William R. "The Aaronic Priesthood in the Epistle to the Hebrews." *JSNT* 19 (1983) 43–71.

Horton, Fred L. *The Melchizedek Tradition: A Critical Examination of the Sources to the Fifth Century*. Cambridge: Cambridge University Press, 1976.

Hughes, Graham. *Hebrews and Hermeneutics: The Epistle to the Hebrews as a New Testament Example of Biblical Interpretation*. SNTSMS 36. Cambridge: Cambridge University Press, 1979.

Hughes, P. E. *A Commentary on the Epistle to the Hebrews*. Grand Rapids: Eerdmans, 1977.

Hurowitz, Victor. *I Have Built you an Exalted House: Temple Building in the Bible in the Light of Mesopotamian and Northwest Semitic Writings*. Sheffield, UK: Sheffield Academic Press, 1992.

Hurst, Lincoln D. *The Epistle to the Hebrews: Its Background of Thought*. SNTSMS 65. Cambridge: Cambridge University Press, 1990.

———. "Eschatology and 'Platonism' in the Epistle to the Hebrews." *SBL Seminar Papers* 23 (1984) 41–74.

———. "How 'Platonic' are Heb. 8:5 and 9:23f ?" *JTS* 34 (1983), 156–68.

Isaacs, Marie E. "Hebrews 13.9–16 Revisited." *NTS* 43 (1997) 268–84.

———. "Priesthood and the Epistle to the Hebrews." *HeyJ* 38 (1997) 51–62.

———. *Reading Hebrews and James: A Literary and Theological Commentary*. Macon, GA: Smyth & Helwys, 2002.

———. *Sacred Space: An Approach to the Theology of the Epistle to the Hebrews*. JSNTSup.17. Sheffield, UK: Sheffield Academic Press, 1992.

Jeremias, Joachim. *Jerusalem in the Time of Jesus. An Investigation into the Economic and Social Conditions during the New Testament Period*. Translated by F. H. Cave and C. H. Cave. London: SCM, 1969.

Jewett, Robert. *Letter to Pilgrims: A Commentary on the Epistle to the Hebrews*. New York: Pilgrim, 1981.

Bibliography

Jonge, Marinus de. *The Testament of the Twelve Patriarchs: A Study of their Text, Composition, and Origin.* Leiden: Brill, 1953.

Jonge, Marinus de, and Adam S. van der Woude. "11Q Melchizedek and the New Testament." *NTS* 12 (1965–66) 301–26.

Johnsson, William G. "The Cultus of Hebrews in Twentieth-Century Scholarship." *ExpTim* 89 (1978) 104–8.

———. "Issues in the Interpretation of Hebrews." *AUSS* 15 (1977) 169–87.

———. "The Pilgrimage Motif in the Book of Hebrews." *JBL* 97 (1978) 239–51.

Johnston, G. "Christ as Archēgos." *NTS* 27 (1981) 381–85.

Kaiser, Walter C. "The Promise Theme and the Theology of Rest." *BibSac* (1973) 135–50.

Käsemann, Ernst. *The Wandering People of God: An Investigation of the Letter to the Hebrews.* Translated by Roy A. Harrisville and Irving L. Sandberg. Minneapolis: Augsburg, 1984.

Kim, Lloyd. *Polemic in the Book of Hebrews: Anti-Judaism, Anti-Semitism, Supersessionism.* PTMS 64. Eugene, OR: Pickwick, 2006.

Klappert, Berthold. *Die Eschatologie des Hebräerbriefs.* TEH 156. Munich: Kaiser, 1969.

Klinzing, G. *Die Umdeutung des Kultus in der Qumrangemeinde und im Neuen Testament.* SUNT 7. Göttingen: Vandenhoeck & Ruprecht, 1971.

Knox, Wilfred L. "The Divine Hero Christology in the New Testament." *HTR* 41 (1948) 229–49.

Kobelski, Paul J. *Melchizedek and Melchireša.* CBQMS 10. Washington DC: Catholic Biblical Association, 1981.

Koester, Craig R. *The Dwelling of God: The Tabernacle in the Old Testament, Intertestamental Jewish Literature and the New Testament.* CBQMS 22. Washington DC: Catholic Biblical Association of America, 1989.

———. "The Epistle to the Hebrews in Recent Study." *Currents in Research: Biblical Studies* 2 (1994) 123–45.

———. *Hebrews: A New Translation with Introduction and Commentary.* AB 36. New York: Doubleday, 2001.

———. "Hebrews, Rhetoric, and the Future of Humanity." *CBQ* 64 (2002) 103–23.

Koester, Helmut. "'Outside the Camp': Hebrews 13.9–14." *HTR* 55 (1962) 299–315.

Kögel, Julius. *Der Sohn und die Söhne: Eine exegetische Studie zu Hebräer 2.5–18.* Gütersloh: Bertelsmann, 1904.

Kosmala, Hans. *Hebräer-Essener-Christen.* Leiden: Brill, 1959.

Kugel, James L. "Melchizedek." In *Traditions of the Bible: A Guide to the Bible as It was at the Start of the Common Era.* Cambridge, MA: Harvard University Press, 1998.

Kurianal, James. *Jesus Our High Priest: Ps. 110.4 as the Substructure of Heb 5.1–7,28.* European University Studies 693. Frankfurt: Lang, 2000.

Laansma, Jon. *"I Will Give You Rest": The Rest Motif in the New Testament with Special reference to Matthew 11 and Hebrews 3–4.* WUNT 2/98. Tübingen: Mohr Siebeck, 1997.

Lane, William L. *Hebrews 1–8.* WBC 47A. Dallas: Word, 1991.

———. *Hebrews 9–13.* WBC 47B. Dallas: Word, 1991.

———. "Standing Before the Moral Claim of God: Discipleship in Hebrews." In *Patterns of Discipleship in the New Testament*, edited by Richard N. Longenecker, 203–24. Grand Rapids: Eerdmans, 1996.

Laub, Franz. *Bekenntnis und Auslegung: die paränetische Funktion der Christologie im Hebräerbrief.* BU 15. Regensburg: Pustet, 1980.

Layton, Bentley. *The Gnostic Scriptures*. London: SCM, 1987.

Lehne, Susanne. *The New Covenant in Hebrews*. JSNTSS 44. Sheffield, UK: JSOT, 1990.

Lewis, N., and M. Reinnhold. *Roman Civilization: Volume 2: The Roman Empire*. New York: Columbia University Press, 1955.

Lierman, John. *The New Testament Moses: Christian Perceptions of Moses in the Setting of Jewish Religion*. WUNT 2/173. Tübingen: Mohr Siebeck, 2004.

Lieu, Judith M. "'The Parting of the Ways': Theological Construct or Historical Reality?" *JSNT* 56 (1994) 101–19.

Lincoln, Andrew T. *Hebrews: A Guide*. London: T & T Clark, 2006.

———. "Sabbath, Rest, and Eschatology in the New Testament." In *From Sabbath to Lord's Day*, edited by D. A. Carson, 197–220. Grand Rapids: Zondervan, 1982.

Lindars, Barnabas. "Hebrews and the Second Temple." In *Templum Amicitiae: Essays on the Second Temple Presented to Ernst Bammel*, edited by W. Horbury, 410–33. JSNTSS 48. Sheffield, UK: JSOT, 1991.

———. "The Rhetorical Structure of Hebrews." *NTS* 35 (1989) 382–406.

———. *The Theology of the Letter to the Hebrews*. Cambridge: Cambridge University Press, 1991.

Lindeskog, Gösta. "The Veil of the Temple." *CN* 11 (1947) 132–37.

Loader, William R. G. "Christ at the Right Hand: Ps. 110.1 in the New Testament." *NTS* 24 (1977–78) 199–217.

———. *Sohn und Hoherpriester: Eine traditionsgeschichtliche Untersuchung zur Christologie des Hebräerbriefes*. WMANT 53. Neukirchen: Neukirchener, 1981.

Longenecker, Richard. "The Melchizedek Argument of Hebrews: A Study in the Development and Circumstantial Expression of New Testament Thought." In *Unity and Diversity in New Testament Theology*, edited by R. A. Guelich, 160–83. Grand Rapids: Eerdmans, 1978.

Luck, Ulrich. "Himmlisches und irdisches Geschehen im Hebräerbrief: Ein Beitrag zum Problem des historischen Jesus im Urchristentum." *NovT* 6 (1963) 192–215.

Macdonald, John. *Memar Marqah: The Teaching of Marqah*. BZAW 84. Berlin: Alfred Töpelmann, 1962.

Mackie, Scott D. *Eschatology and Exhortation in the Epistle to the Hebrews*. WUNT 2/223. Tübingen: Mohr Siebeck, 2007.

———. "Heavenly Sanctuary Mysticism in the Epistle to the Hebrews." *JTSns* 62 (2011) 77–117.

MacRae, George W. "Heavenly Temple and Eschatology in the Letter to the Hebrews." *Semeia* 12 (1978) 179–99.

Manson, William. *The Epistle to the Hebrews*. London: Hodder & Stoughton, 1951.

Martínez, Florentino García. *The Dead Sea Scrolls Translated: The Qumran Texts in English*. 2nd ed. Translated by Wilfred G. E. Watson. Leiden: Brill, 1992.

———. "Priestly Functions in a Community without a Temple." In *Gemeinde ohne Tempel—Community without Temple*, edited by Beate Ego et al., 304–19. Tübingen: Mohr Siebeck, 1999.

Mason, Eric F. *"You Are a Priest Forever": Second Temple Jewish Messianism and the Priestly Christology of the Epistle to the Hebrews*. STDJ 74. Leiden: Brill, 2008.

Matera, Frank J. "Moral Exhortation: The Relation between Moral Exhortation and Doctrinal Exposition in the Letter to the Hebrews." *TJT* 10 (1994) 169–82.

Mauchline, John. "Jesus Christ as Intercessor." *ExpTim* 64 (1952–53) 355–60.

Maurer, Christian. "Phosphatos." *TDNT* 6:766–67.

McCullough, J. Cecil. "Melchizedek's Varied Role in Early Exegetical Tradition." *ThRev* 1 (1979) 52–66.

———. "Some Recent Developments in Research on the Epistle to the Hebrews." *IBS* 2 (1980–81) 141–65.

McEleney, N. J. "Conversion, Circumcision and Law." *NTS* 20 (1974) 316–41.

McKelvey, Robert J. "Jews in the Book of Revelation." *IBS* 25 (2003) 175–94.

———. *The Millennium and the Book of Revelation.* Cambridge: Lutterworth, 1999.

———. *The New Temple: The Church in the New Testament.* Oxford: Oxford University Press, 1969.

McNamara, Martin. *Targum Neofiti: Genesis.* Aramaic Bible A1. Edinburgh: T & T Clark, 1992.

Meier, John P. "Structure and Theology in Heb. 1.1–14." *Bib.*66 (1985) 168–89.

Merean, P. "Greek Philosophy from Plato and Plotinus." In *The Cambridge History of Later Greek and Early Mediaeval History,* edited by A. H. Armstrong, 14–136. Cambridge: Cambridge University Press, 1967.

Michaelis, Wilhelm. "Hodos." *TDNT* 5:42–114.

———. "Skēnē." *TDNT* 8:368–94.

Michel, Otto. *Der Brief an die Hebräer.* 6th ed. Meyer K 13. Göttingen: Vandenhoek & Ruprecht, 1966.

———. "Oikos." *TDNT* 5:125–31.

Millar, F. *The Emperor in the Roman World.* London: Duckworth, 1992.

Moe, Olaf. "Der Gedanke des allgemeinen Priestertums im Hebräerbrief." *TZ* 5 (1949) 161–69.

———. "Das Priestertum Christi im Neuen Testament ausserhalb des Hebräerbrief." *TLZ* 72 (1947) 335–58.

Moffatt, James. *A Critical and Exegetical Commentary on the Epistle to the Hebrews.* ICC. Edinburgh: T & T Clark, 1924.

Moffitt, David. M. "'If Another High Priest Arises': Jesus' Resurrection and the High Priestly Christology of Hebrews." In A *Cloud of Witnesses,* edited by Richard Bauckham et al., 68–79. Grand Rapids: Eerdmans, 2009.

Montefiore, Hugh W. *A Commentary on the Epistle to the Hebrews.* BNTC. London: A & C Black, 1964.

Moore, G. F. *Judaism in the First Centuries of the Christian Era.* 3 vols. Cambridge, MA: Harvard University Press, 1927–30.

Morray-Jones, C. R. A. "Paradise Revisited (2 Cor.12.1–12): The Jewish Mystical Background of Paul's Apostolate. Part 1: The Jewish Sources." *HTR* (1993) 203–15.

———. "Transformational Mysticism in the Apocalyptic-*Merkabah* Tradition." *JJS* 43 (1992) 1–31.

Motyer, Steve. *Discovering Hebrews.* Leicester: Crossway, 2005.

———. "The Temple in Hebrews: Is it There?" In *Heaven on Earth: The Temple in Biblical Theology,* edited by T. D. Alexander and S. Gathercole, 175–89. Carlisle, UK: Paternoster, 2004.

Moule, Charles, F. D. *An Idiom-Book of New Testament Greek.* 2nd ed. Cambridge: Cambridge University Press, 1960.

———. "Sanctuary and Sacrifice in the Church of the New Testament." *JTS* ns 1 (1950) 29–41.

Moulton, J. H., and G. Milligan. *The Vocabulary of the Greek Testament Illustrated from the Papyri and Other Non-Literary Sources.* Grand Rapids: Eerdmans, 1949.

Müller, Paul-Gerhard. *ΧΡΙΣΤΟΣ ΑΡΧΗΓΟΣ, Der religionsgeschictliche und theologische Hintergrund einer neutestamentlichen Christusprädikation.* Frankfurt: Lang, 1973.

Murray, John. "The Heavenly, Priestly Activity of Christ." In *Collected Writings of John Murray,* edited by I. Murray, 44–58. Edinburgh: Banner of Truth, 1982.

Nairne, Alexander. *The Epistle of Priesthood: Studies in the Epistle to the Hebrews.* Edinburgh: T & T Clark, 1913.

Nelson, Richard D. "He Offered Himself: Sacrifice in Hebrews." *Int* 57 (2003) 251–65.

———. *Raising Up a Faithful Priest: Community and Priesthood in a Biblical Theology.* Louisville: Westminster John Knox, 1933.

Newsom, Carol A., and James H. Charlesworth, eds. *The Dead Sea Scrolls: Hebrew, Aramaic and Greek Texts with English Translations. Vol. 4B, Angelic Liturgy: Songs of the Sabbath Sacrifice.* Tübingen: Mohr Siebeck, 1999.

———. *The Songs of the Sabbath Sacrifice: A Critical Edition.* HSS 27. Atlanta: Scholars, 1985.

O'Brien, Peter T. *The Letter to the Hebrews.* Grand Rapids: Eerdmans, 2010.

Pearson, B. A. *Nag Hammadi Codices IX and X.* Leiden: Brill, 1981.

Pelser, Gerhardus M. M. "A Translation Problem: Heb. 10.19–25." *Neot* 8 (1974) 43–53.

Peterson, David. "An Examination of the Concept of 'Perfection' in the Epistle to the Hebrews." PhD diss., University of Manchester, 1978.

———. *Hebrews and Perfection: An Examination of the Concept of Perfection in the Epistle to the Hebrews.* SNTSMS 47. Cambridge: Cambridge University Press, 1982.

Peuch, E. "Notes sur le manuscrit de XIQMelchîsédeq." *RevQ* 12 (1987) 484–513.

Pfitzner, Victor C. *Hebrews.* ANTC. Nashville: Abingdon, 1997.

———. *Paul and the Agon Motif: Traditional Athletic Imagery in the Pauline Literature.* NovTSup 18. Leiden: Brill, 1967.

Polon, Nehemia. "Leviticus and Hebrews and . . . Leviticus." In *The Epistle to the Hebrews and Christian Theology,* edited by Richard Bauckham et al., 213–25. Grand Rapids: Eerdmans, 2009.

Porter, S. E., ed. *Handbook of Classical Rhetoric in the Hellenistic Period 330 B.C.—A.D. 400.* Leiden: Brill, 1997.

Pritchard, James B., ed. *Ancient Near Eastern Texts Relating to the Old Testament.* Princeton: Princeton University Press, 1955.

Procksch, Otto. "Hagios." *TDNT* 1:89–97.

Pursiful, Darrell J. *The Cultic Motif in the Spirituality of the Book of Hebrews.* Lewiston, NY: Mellen Biblical, 1993.

Radcliffe, Timothy. "Christ in Hebrews." *NB* 68 (1987) 490–504.

Rengstorf, K. H. "Manthanein." *TDNT* 4:410–12.

Richardson, Christopher. "The Passion: Reconsidering Hebrews 5.7–8." In *A Cloud of Witnesses,* edited by Richard Bauckham et al., 51–67. Grand Rapids: Eerdmans, 2009.

Riggenbach, Eduard. "Der Begriff der teleiōsis im Hebräerbrief. Ein Beitrag zur Frage nach der Einwirkung der Mysterienreligion auf Sprache und Gedankenwelt des Neuen Testaments." *NKZ* 34 (1923) 184–95.

———. *Der Brief an die Hebräer.* NKZ 14 Leipzig: Deichert, 1913.

Rissi, Mathis. *Die Theologie des Hebräerbriefs: Ihre Verankerung in der Situation des Verfassers und seiner Leser.* WUNT 41. Tübingen: Mohr Siebeck, 1987.

Robinson, John A. T. *Twelve New Testament Studies.* London: SCM, 1962.

Rooke, Deborah W. "Jesus as Royal Priest: Reflections on the Interpretation of the Melchizedek Tradition in Hebrews 7." *Bib* 81 (2000) 81–94.

———. *Zadok's Heirs: The Role and Development of the High Priesthood in Ancient Israel.* Oxford: Oxford University Press, 2000.

Rowland, Christopher. *The Open Heaven: A Study of Apocalyptic in Judaism and Early Christianity.* London: SPCK, 1982.

———. "The Vision of the Risen Christ in Rev. i. 13ff.: The Debt of an Early Christology to an Aspect of Jewish Angelogy." *JTS* ns 31 (1986) 1–11.

Salevao, Lutisone. *Legitimation in the Epistle to the Hebrews: The Construction and Maintenance of a Symbolic Universe.* JSNTSS 219. Sheffield, UK: Sheffield Academic Press, 2002.

Schäfer, Peter. "Engel und Menschen in der Hekhalot-Literatur." *Kairos* 22 (1980) 201–25.

Schenck, Kenneth L. *A Brief Guide to Philo.* Louisville: Westminster John Knox, 2005.

———. "A Celebration of the Enthroned Son: The Catena of Hebrews 1." *JBL* 120 (2001) 469–85.

———. *Cosmology and Eschatology in Hebrews: The Settings of the Sacrifice.* SNTSMS 143. Cambridge: Cambridge University Press, 2007.

———. "Philo and the Epistle to the Hebrews: Ronald Williamson's Study After Thirty Years." In *The Studia Philonica Annual: Studies in Hellenistic Judaism,* edited by D. T. Runia and G. E. Stirling, 112–35. Atlanta: Scholars, 2002.

———. *Understanding the Book of Hebrews: The Story Behind the Sermon.* Louisville: Westminster John Knox, 2003.

Schenke, Hans-Martin. "Erwägungen zum Rätsel des Hebräerbriefes." In *Neues Testament und christliche Existenz,* edited by H. D. Betz and L. Schottroff, 421–37. Tübingen: Mohr Siebeck, 1973.

Schierse, F. J. *Verheissung und Heilsvollendung: Zur theologischen Grundfrage des Hebräerbriefs.* Munich: Karl Zink, 1955.

Schille, G. "Erwägungen zur Hohenpriesterlehre des Hebräerbriefes." *ZNW* 46 (1955) 90–91.

Schlier, Heinrich. "Parrēsia." *TDNT* 5:871–86.

Schneider, Carl. "Katapetasma." *TDNT* 3:628–30.

———. "Kathairein." *TDNT* 3:411–13.

———. "Proserchomai." *TDNT* 2:683–84.

Scholem, Gershom G. *Major Trends in Jewish Mysticism.* 3rd ed. New York: Schocken, 1955.

Scholer, John M. *Proleptic Priests: Priesthood in the Epistle to the Hebrews.* JSNTSS 15. Sheffield, UK: JSOT, 1991.

Schrenk, Gottlob. "Archiereus." *TDNT* 3:274–82.

Schürer, Emil, *The History of the Jewish People in the Age of Jesus Christ.* Vol. 2. Revised and edited by Geza Vermes et al. Edinburgh: T & T. Clark, 1979.

Scott, J. Julius. "*Archēgos* in the Salvation History of the Epistle to the Hebrews." *JETS* 29 (1986) 47–54.

Segal, Alan F. "Heavenly Ascent in Hellenistic Judaism, Early Christianity, and their Environment." *Aufstieg und Niedergang der römischen Welt* 2:23/2 (1980) 1333–94.

Silva, Moises. "Perfection and Eschatology in Hebrews." *WJT* 39 (1976) 60–71.

Simon, Marcel. *Hercule et le Christianisme.* Publications de la Faculté des lettres de l'Université de Strasbourg 19/2. Paris: Les Belles Lettres, 1955.

———. "Saint Stephen and the Jerusalem Temple." *JEH* 2 (1951) 127–42.

Simpson, E. K. "The Vocabulary of the Epistle to the Hebrews." *EvQ* 18 (1946) 35–38.

Sims, Colin, "Rethinking Hebrews 12.1." *IBS* 27 (2008) 54–88.

Smith, Jerome. *A Priest Forever: A Study of Typology and Eschatology in Hebrews.* London: Sheed & Ward, 1969.

Smith, M. "Ascent to the Heavens and the Beginning of Christianity." *Eranos* 50 (1981) 403–29.

Son, Kiwoong. *Zion Symbolism: Hebrews 12.18–24 as a Hermeneutical Key to the Epistle.* Milton Keynes, UK: Paternoster, 2005.

Sowers, Sidney. *The Hermeneutics of Philo and Hebrews.* Richmond, VA: John Knox, 1965.

Spicq, Ceslas. *L'Épître aux Hébreux.* 2 vols. Paris: Gabalda, 1952–53.

———. "La Panégyrie de Hébr. XII. 22." *ST* 6 (1952) 30–38.

Stadelmann, Luist J. *The Hebrew Concept of the World.* Rome: Pontifical Biblical Institute, 1970.

Sterling, Geoffrey E. "Ontology Versus Eschatology: Tensions between Author and Community in Hebrews." *SPhA* 13 (2001) 190–211.

Still, Todd D. "*Christos* as *Pistos*: The Faith(fulness) of Jesus in the Epistle to the Hebrews." *CBQ* 69 (2007) 746–55.

Stökl Ben Ezra, Daniel. *The Impact of Yom Kippur on Early Christianity: The Day of Atonement from Second Temple Judaism to the Fifth Century.* WUNT 163. Tubingen: Mohr Siebeck, 2003.

———. "Yom Kippur in the Jewish Apocalyptic *Imaginaire* and the Roots of Jesus' High Priesthood. Yom Kippur in Zechariah 3, 1 Enoch 10, 11QMelchizedek, Hebrews and the Apocalypse of Abraham 13." In *Transformations of the Inner Self in Ancient Religions*, edited by J. Assmann and G. G. Stroumsa, 349–66. Leiden: Brill, 1999.

Strack, Herman L., and Paul Billerbeck. *Kommentar zum Neuen Testament aus Talmud und Midrasch.* 6 vols. Munich: Beck, 1922–61.

Strathmann, Hermann. "Martus." *TDNT* 4:474–514.

Strugnell, John. "The Angelic Liturgy at Qumran—4Q Serek šîrôt *'ôlat haššabat.*" VTSup to vol.7 (1960) 318–45.

Stuckenbruck, Loren T. *Angel Veneration and Christology: A Study in Early Judaism and in the Christology of the Apocalypse.* WUNT 2/70. Tübingen: Mohr Siebeck, 1995.

Swetnam, James. "Christology and the Eucharist in the Epistle to the Hebrews." *Bib* 70 (1989) 74–95.

———. "Form and Content in Hebrews 1–6." *Bib* 53 (1972) 368–85.

———. "Form and Content in Hebrews 7–13." *Bib* 55 (1974) 333–48.

———. "The Greater and More Perfect Tent: A Contribution to the Discussion of Heb. 9:11." *Bib* 47 (1966) 91–106.

Synge, Francis C. *Hebrews and the Scriptures.* London: SPCK, 1959.

Tantlevskij, Igor R. *Melchizedek Redivivus in Qumran: Some Peculiarities of Messianic Ideas and Elements of Mysticism in the Dead Sea Scrolls.* Krakow: Enigma, 2004.

Thiselton, Anthony C. "Hebrews." In *Eerdmans Commentary on the Bible*, edited by James D. G. Dunn and John W. Rogerson, 1451–82. Grand Rapids: Eerdmans, 2003.

Thompson, James W. *The Beginnings of Christian Philosophy: The Epistle to the Hebrews.* CBQMS 13. Washington DC: Catholic Biblical Association of America, 1982.

————. *Hebrews*. Paideia: Commentaries on the New Testament. Grand Rapids: Baker, 2008.

————. "Outside the Camp: A Study of Hebrews 13.9–14." *CBQ* 40 (1978) 53–63.

————. "'That Which Cannot Be Shaken': Some Metaphysical Assumptions in Heb. 12:27." *JBL* 94 (1975) 580.

Thurén, Jukka. *Das Lobopfer der Hebräer: Studien zum Aufbau und Anliegen von Hebräerbrief 13*. Turku, Fin.: Abo Akademi, 1973.

Tiede, David L. *The Charismatic Figure as Miracle Worker*. SBLDS 1. Missoula, MT: Scholars, 1972.

Tomes, Roger. "Educating Gentiles: Explanations of Torah in the New Testament, Philo and Josephus." In *Torah in the New Testament*, edited by Michael Tait and Peter Oakes, 208–17. London: T & T Clark, 2009.

————. "Heroism in 1 and 2 Maccabees." *BI* 15 (2007) 171–99.

Toussaint, Stanley D. "The Eschatology of the Warning Passages in the Book of Hebrews." *GTJ* 3 (1982) 67–80.

Traub, Helmut. "Ouranos." *TDNT* 5:497–543.

Trebilco, Paul R. *Jewish Communities in Asia Minor*. SNTSMS 69. Cambridge: Cambridge University Press, 1991.

Trudinger, L. Paul. "The Gospel Meaning of the Secular: Reflections of Hebrews 13.10–13." *EvQ* 54 (1982) 235–37.

Übelacker, Walter G. *Der Hebräerbrief als Appell: Untersuchungen zu Exordium, Narratio und Postscriptum (Hebr 1–2 und 13.22–25)*. Stockholm: Aklmqvist & Wiksell, 1989.

Vanhoye, Albert. *Old Testament Priests and the New Priest According to the New Testament*. Petersham, MA: St. Bede's, 1986.

————. "La Structure centrale de l'' Épître aux Hébreux (Héb. 8/1–9/28)." *RSR* 47 (1949) 44–46.

————. *La structure littéraire de l'Épître aux Hébreux*. 2nd ed. Paris: Desclee de Brouwer, 1976.

————. *Structure and Message of the Epistle to the Hebrews*. Rome: Editrice Pontificio Instituto Biblico, 1989.

————. "La '*teleiosis*' du Christ: Point capital de la christologie sacerdotale d'Hébreux." *NTS* 42 (1996) 321–38.

————. "Par la tente plus grande et plus parfaite . . . Hebr. 9.11)." *Bib* 46 (1965) 1–28.

VanderKam, J. C. *From Joshua to Caiaphas: High Priests after the Exile*. Minneapolis: Fortress, 2004.

Vermes, Geza. *The Dead Sea Scrolls in English*. London: Penguin, 1962.

Vorster, W. S. "The Meaning of PARRHESIA in the Epistle to the Hebrews." *Neot* 5 (1971) 51–59.

Walker, Peter W. L. *Jesus and the Holy City: New Testament Perspectives on Jerusalem*. Grand Rapids: Eerdmans, 1996.

Wedderburn, A. J. M. "The 'Letter' to the Hebrews and Its Thirteenth Chapter." *NTS* 50 (2004) 390–405.

————. "Sawing Off the Branches: Theologizing Dangerously Ad Hebraeos." *JTS* 56 (2005) 393–414.

Weiss, Hans-Friedrich. *Der Brief an die Hebräer: Übersetzt und Erklärt*. KEK 13. Göttingen: Vandenhoeck & Ruprecht, 1991.

Westcott, Brooke F. *The Epistle to the Hebrews*. London: Macmillan, 1889.

Westfall, Cynthia L. *A Discourse Analysis of the Letter to the Hebrews: The Relationship between Form and Meaning.* LNTS 297. London: T & T Clark, 2005.

Wikgren, Allen. "Patterns of Perfection in the Epistle to the Hebrews." *NTS* 6 (1959–60) 159–67.

Williamson, Clark M. "Anti-Judaism in Hebrews?" *Int* 57 (2003) 266–79.

Williamson, Ronald. "The Background to the Epistle to the Hebrews." *ExpTim* 87 (1976) 232–37.

———. "The Eucharist and the Epistle to the Hebrews." *NTS* 21 (1975) 300–312.

———. "Hebrews 4.15 and the Sinlessness of Jesus." *ExpTim* 86 (1974–75) 4–8.

———. *Philo and the Epistle to the Hebrews.* Leiden: Brill, 1970.

———. "Platonism and Hebrews." *SJT* 16 (1963) 415–24.

Willi-Plein, Ina. "Some Remarks on Hebrews from the Viewpoint of Old Testament Exegesis." In *Hebrews: Contemporary Methods—New Insights*, edited by Gabriella Gelardini, 25–31. Leiden: Brill, 2005.

Wills, Laurence. "The Form of the Sermon in Hellenistic Judaism and Early Christianity." *HTR* 77 (1984) 277–99.

Wilson, Robert McLachlan. *Hebrews.* NCB Commentary, Grand Rapids: Eerdmans, 1987.

Windisch, Hans. *Der Hebräerbrief.* 2nd ed. HNT 14. Tübingen: Mohr Siebeck, 1931.

Wolfson, Harry A. *Philo: Foundations of Religious Philosophy in Judaism, Christianity and Islam.* Cambridge, MA: Harvard University Press, 1963.

Wray, J. H. *Rest as a Theological Metaphor in the Epistle to the Hebrews and the Gospel of Truth.* SBLDS 166. Atlanta: Scholars, 1998.

Yadin, Yigael. "A Note on Melchizedek and Qumran." *IEJ* 15 (1965) 152–54.

Young, Norman H. "'Bearing His Reproach' (Heb 13.9–14)." *NTS* 48 (2002) 243–61.

———. "The Gospel According to Hebrews 9." *NTS* 27 (1981) 198–210.

———. "The Impact of the Day of Atonement on the New Testament." PhD diss., University of Manchester, 1973.

———. "'Tout' estin tēs sarkos autou (Heb.x.20)': Apposition, Dependent or Explicative?" *NTS* 20 (1973–74) 100–114.

Zerwick, Max, and Mary Grosvenor. *A Grammatical Analysis of the Greek New Testament* 2. Rome: Biblical Institute Press, 1979.

Ancient Document Index

GRECO-ROMAN WRITINGS

Aelius Aristides

Aristotle

EARLY CHRISTIAN WRITINGS

Index of Authors

Subject Index

Abraham, 53, 54, 62, 67, 68, 143, 144, 159, 178, 181
Access to God. *See* God
Aitios. See Source
Altar, 4, 14, 36, 37, 84, 106, 118, 152, 153, 158, 159, 191, 192, 194, 197
Angels,
    In Hebrews, 2, 9, 24, 64, 141, 144, 146, 147, 150, 164
    In Qumran literature, 49, 66, 68, 85, 93, 101, 119, 148, 178, 179, 198, 199, 204, 209, 211
    In apocalyptic and rabbinic literature, 65, 68, 104, 117, 180, 181, 194, 197, 199, 204, 209
Apocalyptic, 15, 16, 23, 27, 42, 43, 47, 48, 50, 61, 68, 79, 82, 83, 84, 85, 86, 87, 95, 102, 114, 115, 117, 119, 126, 142, 143, 147, 148, 168, 177, 178, 185, 197, 205
Archēgos, See Pioneer
Ascents, 38, 47, 48, 83, 114, 177–95. *See* Travellers
Athletic metaphor, xx, 130–34
Atonement, 34, 38, 73, 84, 138, 152, 158, 163, 166, 184, 192, 194, 199, 204. *See* Day of Atonement

Camp, ix, 152–61, 192
Chiasms, 92, 97, 111
Christ
    Advocate, 102–3
    Ascension, 46, 48. *See* Exaltation

Continuity of earthly and heavenly offering, 35–36, 37, 46, 49, 105–6, 168, 168
Cross, 6, 35, 36, 37, 39, 49, 60, 82, 93, 106, 134, 135, 136, 137–38, 140, 152, 153, 160, 166, 168, 169
Death, 14, 21, 23, 24, 25, 26, 33, 34, 36, 38, 46, 49, 52, 69, 94, 104, 105, 108, 126, 127, 128, 135, 136, 138, 152, 153, 154, 158, 159, 164, 166, 169
Endurance, 130, 134, 139
Enters the heavenly sanctuary, 21, 27, 35, 36, 37, 43, 48, 49, 86, 89, 90, 91, 92, 94, 96, 100, 105, 108, 121, 124, 149, 165, 185, 205
Enthronement. *See* Exaltation
Exaltation, 23, , 25, 26, 27, 33, 35, 46, 48, 101, 108, 164
Faith and Faithfulness, 26, 50–56, 129, 136, 137
Forerunner, xxiii, xxiv, 19, 22, 41, 43, 49–50, 120, 121, 122, 139, 166, 173
High Priest, xxiii, xxiv, 4, 13, 19, 32, 34–39, 101, 115–16, 121, 162, 171, 176.*See* Levitical priesthood.
Humanity, 25, 35, 38, 60, 66, 105, 106, 107, 112, 127, 163, 166, 182
Incarnation, 35, 38, 105, 127, 210
Indivisibility of earthly and heavenly minister, 35, 36, 37, 39, 46, 49, 105–6
Intercession, 60, 99–113, 105 *See* prayer. *See* Prayer